The
New Elite

INSIDE THE MINDS OF THE TRULY WEALTHY

JIM TAYLOR, DOUG HARRISON, & STEPHEN KRAUS

American Management Association

NEW YORK • ATLANTA • BRUSSELS • CHICAGO • MEXICO CITY •

SAN FRANCISCO • SHANGHAI • TOKYO • TORONTO • WASHINGTON, D.C.

Special discounts on bulk quantities of AMACOM books are
available to corporations, professional associations, and other
organizations. For details, contact Special Sales Department,
AMACOM, a division of American Management Association,
1601 Broadway, New York, NY 10019.
Tel: 212-903-8316. Fax: 212-903-8083.
E-mail: specialsls@amanet.org
Website: www.amacombooks.org/go/specialsales
To view all AMACOM titles go to: www.amacombooks.org

This publication is designed to provide accurate and authoritative
information in regard to the subject matter covered. It is sold with the
understanding that the publisher is not engaged in rendering legal,
accounting, or other professional service. If legal advice or other expert
assistance is required, the services of a competent professional person
should be sought.

Various names used by companies to distinguish their software and
other products can be claimed as trade and service marks. AMACOM
uses such names throughout this book for editorial purposes only, with
no intention of trademark violation. All such software or product
names are in initial capital letters or ALL CAPITAL letters. A list of
trade and service marks in this book can be found on pages ix and x.
Individual companies should be contacted for complete information
regarding trademarks and registration.

Library of Congress Cataloging-in-Publication Data

Taylor, Jim, 1947–
    The new elite : inside the minds of the truly wealthy / Jim Taylor, Doug Harrison,
and Stephen Kraus.
        p.   cm.
    Includes index.
    ISBN-13: 978-0-8144-0048-7 (hbk.)
    ISBN-10: 0-8144-0048-5 (hbk.)
    1. Wealth—United States.   2. Rich people—United States.   I. Harrison, Doug,
1965–   II. Kraus, Stephen.   III. Title.

    HC110.W4.T39   2009
    332.024'010973—dc22   2008021605

Printing number

10 9 8 7 6 5 4

This book is dedicated . . .

*From Jim, with love, to my dear wife Ellie and my lovely daughters
Kate, Lana, and Yulia*

*From Doug to my loving wife Kim, father-in-law Ben, and parents
Robert and Elsie*

*From Steve to Simone Madan and Ethan Kraus,
with love and appreciation*

Contents

Acknowledgments

Every book is a story in the making as well as the telling—in this book, perhaps more so than most. First, we owe a debt of gratitude to the 6,000 people who allowed us to talk with them about their families, their dreams, and the lives they lead. Second, the book began with the support of Lyle Anderson, Bill Curtis, Dan Merchant, Andrew Sacks, and the many people and clients in the luxury industry who encouraged this project with money, time, and advice. Chief among these have been our colleagues at American Express Publishing, particularly Cara David, Senior Vice President, Strategic Insights, Marketing & Sales, Ed Kelly, President and CEO, and the many people who work with them. You have contributed greatly to this project, and we thank you all.

A number of other people also lent their minds and their time to the project—without whom we would not have been successful—including Isabel Aguerre at Balenciaga, Rollie Vincent and Sylvain Lévesque at FlexJet, Mark Miller at Team One, Jeff Senior at Fair-

mont, Barbara Talbot and Susan Helstab at Four Seasons, Chris Glo-
wacki and Tom Scott at Plum TV, Brenda Ng, and Steve Elliott.

The book would not have happened without twelve wonderful
women, especially Christine Kemper and Susan Wright, who scat-
tered to the four corners of America to conduct our earliest interviews. Along the way, we were guided by the thoughts of Frank
Boster and Bill Schmidt at Michigan State, Burr Brown at Harrison
Group, and Andrea Trachtenberg who works on Wall Street. The
members of our editing team, Ellen Coleman, Adrienne Hickey, and
particularly Christina Parisi, were both delightful and patient. Associate Editor Erika Spelman polished our drafts and smoothed their
rough edges. And we owe a special note to our friend John Butman
who worked on our original proposal and lent us enormous support
and advice.

We'd also like to thank the whole team at Harrison Group, especially Paul Lundquist, Don Winter, Julie Wallace, Chris Cox, Kevin
Sturmer, Kristen Conover, and Heather Whitehead for their hours,
intelligence, support, and dedication. This has been a four-year journey in which we have been joined by some of the most wonderful
companies in the world, and we appreciate the support their marketing teams in particular have shown. Finally, of course, we owe a
special thanks to our families for their encouragement, understanding, and patience.

Jim Taylor
Doug Harrison
Stephen Kraus

May, 2008

Trade and Service Marks in *The New Elite*

1-800-FLOWERS
Abercrombie & Fitch
Acura
Adobe
Aèropostale
Alcoa
Alexander McQueen
Amazon.com
America Online
American Eagle
American Express
American Express
  Publishing
American Honda
American Motors
  Corporation
American Outfitters
Ameriprise
Apple
Aston Martin
Audi
Avedis Zildjian
Banana Republic
Bang & Olufsen
Bank of America
Barbour
Barnes & Noble
Baume & Marcier
Beneteau Rodriguez
  Group
Bentley
Beretta
Bergdorf-Goodman
Berkshire Hathaway
Best Buy
Bloomberg, L.P.
Bloomingdale's
BMW
Boeing
Bombardier Flexjet
Borders
Breitling
Bugatti
Bulgari

Burberry
Cadbury Schweppes
  PLC
Cadillac
Cartier
Chanel
Chevrolet
Chevy
Christian Dior
Christies
Chrysler
Citicorp
Citigroup
Clorox
CNBC
CNN
Coca-Cola
Costco
Cristal
Curtco Media
CVS
DeBeers
Dell
Dior
Dom Pérignon
Donald Duck
Donna Karan
Dow Jones
Dow Jones Industrial
  Average
DreamWorks
eBay
Eclipse Aviation
Emilio Pucci
Ernst & Young
Escada
ExxonMobil
Fairmont Hotels and
  Resorts
Fendi
Ferragamo
FlexJet
Forbes
Ford

Ford Explorer
Four Seasons Hotels
Frank Russell
  Company
Gap
Gateway Computer
Genentech
General Electric
General Mills
General Motors
Giorgio Armani
Givenchy
Goldman Sachs
Google
GTECH Corporation
Gucci
Gulfstream
Helga Wagner
Hennessy
Hermès
Honda
Humana
IBM
IKEA
Iomega Corporation
iPhone
iPod
J. Crew
J. McLaughlin
J.C. Penney
Jacadi
James Bond
Julius Baer and
  Vontobel
Kmart
Kuoni
La Perla
Lamborghini
Land Rover
Le Cirque
Leading Real Estate
  Companies of the
  World
Lehman Brothers

Lexus
Lifestyles of the Rich
  and Famous
Lilly Pulitzer
Lincoln
Louis Vuitton
LVMH Moët Hennessy
Lyle Anderson
  Company
MAC Cosmetics
Macy's
Marc Jacobs
Marlboro
McDonald's
McKinsey
Mercedes
Mercedes-Benz
Microsoft
Minnesota Vikings
Moët & Chandon
Mont Blanc
MTV
MySpace
Nantucket Nectars
Nash
National Football
  League
National Pubic Radio
Neiman Marcus
New York Yankees
Nokia
Nordstrom
Northwestern Mutual
  Life
Ocean Spray
Old Navy
Oliver Peoples

Oracle
Osco
Pantene
Piaget
Plum TV
Polo Ralph Lauren
Porsche
Prada
Procter & Gamble
Progressive Insurance
Ralph Lauren
Range Rover
Royal Delft
Russell 200 Index
Safeway
Saks Fifth Avenue
Saloman Brothers
Salvation Army
Sam's Club
Sara Lee Corporation
Seaman Schepps
Sears
Sephora
Shell Oil
Sirius Satellite Radio
Slate 60
Sony
Sotheby's
Sports Authority
St. John's
Staples
Starbucks
Stella McCartney
Stubbs and Wootten
Superquartz
Tag Heuer

Target
Team One
The Clinic at Wal-Mart
Tiffany
TiVO
TMZ.com
Tod's
Toll Brothers
Toyota
U.S. Steel
U.S. Trust
Union Bank of
  California
Van Cleef & Arpels
Venetian Las Vegas
Virgin
Vogue
Volvo
Wachovia
Walgreens
Wall Street Journal
Wal-Mart
Walt Disney
WAMU
Whole Foods
Wolf
Wolfgang Puck
World Wrestling
  Entertainment
Wurlitzer
XM
Yahoo!
Yankelovich Partners
YouTube
Yves Saint Laurent
Zara

CHAPTER ONE

Today's Wealth Explosion

The Supernova and the
Gravitational Pull of Money

PROVE IT.

In 2004, those two words started our odyssey of crisscrossing the country to meet with some of the wealthiest individuals in America and to hear the stories of their success. Along the way, we have peered into the heart of one of the biggest explosions of wealth in history.

Those two words—*prove it*—have been uttered to us many times, but in this particular case, they came from Lyle Anderson. For over twenty-five years, Lyle's company has built some of the most spectacular and expensive luxury-housing developments in the world, often centered around award-winning Jack Nicklaus–designed golf courses. In 2004, Lyle was contemplating a new development with properties targeted as second or third homes for families of substantial means, and we were consulting for him on a variety of brand issues. During one of our meetings, Lyle turned to us and asked: "What will be the amenity of the future that will differentiate

1

a property—one that hasn't been already done?" By this, Lyle meant an amenity that went beyond beaches and golf courses and club houses and innovations of architectural design. We thought about Lyle's question: The world was already awash in gated beach/golf communities. We looked at the age of the people for whom the property was targeted, the remote location, and the growing needs for health, and responded: "Put a hospital and healthcare facility on the property for the use of the residents. The hospital can provide immediate life-saving treatment if anyone has a heart attack (during the so-called "golden hour"), offer residential treatment for chronic disease, and even provide cosmetic surgeries. It can make its money on executive family physicals. It could even support emerging therapeutic DNA and homeopathic services. The hospital would not only be an attractive amenity in and of itself, particularly in a world of aging baby boomers, but also it would lessen any anxiety that some might feel about buying a home in a beautiful but slightly remote location."

After Lyle indicated that he thought the idea had some merit, we began our due diligence and examined the potential of putting such a hospital within a property. We concluded that it would cost $50 million in construction costs and another $25 million for staff housing, infrastructure equipment, and supplies. On top of that, another $10 million would be needed for an evacuation helicopter and a landing base. Given the $85 million price tag, Lyle was curious as to whether these costs could be absorbed in the price of the property lots—and whether residents would want to pay proportionately to keep the facility in the black. He considered our top-of-the-mind advice that this could be the amenity of the future, turned to us, and simply said, "Prove it."

Thus began our inquiry into the nature of wealth in America, and the beginning of a series of groundbreaking research studies. We sought not only to answer Lyle's specific question about the willingness of wealthy people to pay for amenities A, B, and C the next time they purchase a multimillion dollar home; we also sought to understand who the wealthy are—at fundamental social and psychological levels: their mind-set and lifestyles; their attitudes and values; their aspirations for themselves, their children, and the world in general.

We sought to understand how they came by their money, and how, if at all, it has changed them; whether money can buy happiness, or if it just brings a new set of challenges; whether they live loudly or quietly; whether the typical wealthy person is more like Donald Trump, Oprah Winfrey, Paris Hilton, or none of the above; indeed, whether or not there is such a thing as a "typical" wealthy person. As market researchers, we were, of course, particularly interested in how they save, invest, and spend their money. In where they shop, what brands they like, and what luxury means to them. And whether conspicuous consumption—a term coined by economist Thorstein Veblen over 100 years ago—is a fair characterization of how they buy and live today, or if it is an unfair generalization based on media stories about an unrepresentative few.

We were, like many people, inherently curious about people who have achieved tremendous financial success, and we found their stories to be not only fascinating but also inspirational—and personally informative, as well. For example, we found that the vast majority of wealthy people today created their own wealth in their lifetimes; and we have at times used the principles that guided their success to shape our own life choices and business growth strategies. At the broadest level, this book is for anyone who shares this interest in stories of success and the desire for financial growth. This is (we hope) just about everyone, as stories of success and achievement have always captured the human imagination, from the heroic epics of the *Iliad* and the *Odyssey*, to Horatio Alger's rags-to-riches novels of the nineteenth century, to Napoleon Hill's *Think and Grow Rich*, to today's multibillion-dollar industries of biographies, financial how-to manuals, and self-help books.

We are also marketing professionals, and this book should hold special interest for anyone who does business (or aspires to do business) with people of considerable financial means. As the following chapters will reveal, the wealthy today are poorly understood, not only by the media and the average American but also by the professional marketer of luxury and high-end products. We'll give a number of examples highlighting how accurately understanding today's wealth dynamics is crucial for success in fields as diverse as marketing, sales, product development, branding, and advertising.

Finally, this book is for anyone interested in understanding the past, present, and future of wealth in our society and the world at large. The past quarter-century has seen a truly dramatic, and in many ways silent, shift in money throughout the world, impacting everything from everyday lifestyles and economics to business and politics. These changes have been so profound that astronomical phenomena seem to provide the only apt metaphors.

The Wealth Explosion: The Supernova and the Gravitational Pull of Money

Supernova: the explosion of a star so violent that it often outshines entire galaxies

Gravitational pull: the fundamental force by which all objects with mass attract one another

History has rarely seen an era in which so much money has been made by so few people in such a short amount of time. We'll explore later whether the poor have gotten poorer, but for now we can show that the rich have gotten much, much richer. We think of it as a supernova of wealth.

The Multimillionaire Next Door

Thomas Stanley published his groundbreaking *The Millionaire Next Door* in 1996, and his profile of the typical millionaire as a hardworking, frugal small-business owner still resonates. The issue today is that the population of millionaires is growing so rapidly that soon everyone may literally have a millionaire living next door to him or her. From 1983 to 2004, the population of the United States grew by about 33 percent. During that same time, after controlling for inflation, the population of millionaires grew 168 percent, those with $5 million in net worth grew 353 percent, and hecamillionaires ($10+ million) grew over 400 percent (see Figure 1-1). The explosion of wealth has been so dramatic that, although a net worth of $1 million is certainly something to which many people still aspire, it

Figure 1-1 Growth in millionaire households, 1983–2004.*

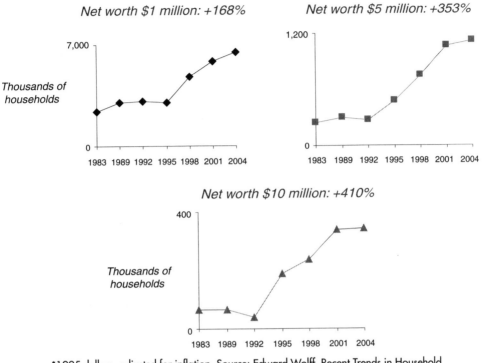

*1995 dollars, adjusted for inflation. Source: Edward Wolff, Recent Trends in Household Wealth in the United States: Rising Debt and the Middle Class Squeeze. http://www.levy.org/pubs/wp_502.pdf

hardly qualifies as true "wealth" anymore, particularly if it includes nonliquid assets, such as one's primary residence. Some have even suggested that net worth is an outdated and irrelevant definition of the term *millionaire*, and if it is still to be used as descriptive of *wealth* it should be defined as someone having an annual *income* of at least $1 million.

The Growing Concentration of Wealth

Another framework for understanding wealth in society is to consider the percentage of all assets in America that are held by a select few. Though the mid-1700s, the wealthiest 1 percent of Americans likely held 10 to 20 percent of the total net worth of the country[1]—a low figure by historical standards, representing a relatively even distribution of wealth and a modest gap between the rich and the poor. The concentration of wealth grew throughout the 1800s, accelerating as the Industrial Revolution took hold, climaxing by the turn of the century, when the wealthiest 1 percent held roughly half of the assets.[2] The twentieth-century high came in 1929, at 44 percent, before the stock market crash and Great Depression led to a half-century decline, bottoming out at around 20 percent in the early 1970s.[3] Since then, the wealth owned by the top 1 percent has grown steadily; it currently stands at 34 percent, down slightly from the dot-com era high of 38 percent, but higher than at any other point since 1929.[4]

If we expand our definition of the financial elite slightly, from the top 1 percent to the top 5 percent, we get an even more dramatic picture of wealth concentration. Five percent of Americans—approximately 6 million households—own roughly 60 percent of the assets.[5] In other words, the top 5 percent own more than the other 95 percent combined.

The *Forbes* 400 Is Now a Billionaires-Only Club

Let's look at an even smaller microcosm of wealth: the *Forbes* list of the 400 richest Americans. Four hundred people is a miniscule 0.0001 percent of the population in a nation of 300 million, but the growth in wealth and influence among this truly elite group is staggering. *Forbes* began publishing the list regularly in 1982, just as the wealth crescendo was emerging, and on that initial list there were just thirteen billionaires; $75 million was enough to make the list. In 2007, a mere $1 billion didn't even get you on the list; it took $1.3 billion just to squeeze into the precarious position of number 400. In 1982, the combined net worth of all 400 people was less than 3 percent of America's gross domestic product; today, it is nearly 10 percent. In the last dozen years alone, the total net worth of this group more than tripled, from less than half a trillion to $1.54 trillion. Today, Bill Gates and Warren Buffett generally trade the title of "richest American" back and forth, with their fortunes fluctuating between $55 and $65 billion, depending on the stock prices of Microsoft and Berkshire Hathaway respectively. Either alone has a net worth greater than the gross domestic product of more than half the countries in the world.[6] As we'll detail in Chapter 9, the changing dynamics of who is on this list, and how they made their money, is just as revealing about the nature of wealth as how much they have.

The Gravitational Pull of Money

Po Bronson titled his novel of dot-com-era corporate intrigue *The First 20 Million Is Always the Hardest*, and that sentiment neatly sums up the gravitational pull of money. Money attracts more money, and once you've got a few million (more later on how people typically achieve that rare feat), getting subsequent millions becomes relatively easier. The old adage "it takes money to make money" is somewhat misleading, because most wealthy people today are self-made, but it is certainly fair to say that "it becomes easier to make money when you've got money." Part of the gravitational pull has simply been the tremendous performance of the stock market over the past twenty years. Let's take a long-term view and set aside the day-to-day fluctuations that dominate the headlines of the business press. The Dow Jones Industrial Average was started in 1896. It didn't reach 1000 until 1972, and it took another eleven years for it to gain a mere 100 points and close above 1100. But 1983 was the start of the biggest and longest bull market in history. It took just four years for the Dow to close above 2000, another four years for it to close above 3000, and four more years to hit 4000. (Alan Greenspan's famous comment about the irrational exuberance of the stock market came on December 5, 1996; the Dow Jones closed that day at 6437).[7] For the final half decade of the 1990s, the Dow added about 1000 points a year, sometimes in much less than a year, rising from 4000 in early 1995 to over 11,700 in early 2000. It took six years for the Dow to recover from the dot-com implosion, but it pushed past 12,000 in October 2006, and past 14,000 less than a year later. Figure 1-2 shows the gradual and then explosive growth of the Dow Jones Industrial Average.

Obviously the bull market helped everyone "in the market," which is approximately half the U.S. population (up from less than

Figure 1-2 History of the Dow Jones Industrial Average.*

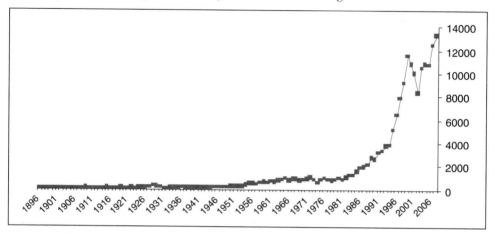

*As shown, the closing price at the end of each year. Broader indices (such as the S&P 500) show similar trends, but can't be tracked back as far. SOURCE: Dow Jones.

20 percent in 1983).[8] Much has been made, and rightfully so, about the growing democratization of stock ownership in America, particularly since the advent and growing popularity of mutual funds. But the average American "in the market" has about $65,000 invested in equities,[9] and most of that is tied up in retirement accounts that can't be accessed easily for many years, so the bull market has minimal impact on the bottom line of most Americans.

The fact is that stock ownership is like net worth—heavily concentrated at the top—and so too are the benefits of the bull market. The top 1 percent of Americans own over one-third of all the stock wealth, and the top 5 percent own two-thirds of all the stock wealth.[10] The wealthy benefit not only from having more money to invest but also from having access to better advice and better investment options that yield higher returns. Once someone has millions to invest, rather than thousands, a whole new class of investment options open up, including access to private banks, hedge funds, and in particular, the ability to invest in high-risk but ultra-high-reward start-up companies, either through their own angel investments or through private equity funds. It is compound interest on steroids.

It isn't just money that attracts money; the people who have accumulated money also come to have a greater "pull" on money. They have learned how to start businesses, fund them, and cash out—a process with a steep learning curve the first time around but one that is more easily repeated. Their social networks have grown, bringing them in more frequent contact with starts-ups they can invest in and others who can fund their own new ventures. Their experience has made them savvier about discerning wise investments from poor ones. Given all these factors, it is not surprising that the longer a person has been wealthy, the more wealth he or she tends to have. Among the top 1 percent, those who have been wealthy more than fifteen years have an average net worth of about $75 million, whereas those who have been wealthy five years or less have an average net worth of less than $10 million. In short, this is the gravitational pull: Over time, large pools of money, and the people who have created them, have a strong magnetic or gravitational pull on money at large. The sun pulls planets into increasingly closer orbits; similarly, money pulls more money and moneymaking opportunities into the orbits of the wealthy.

Who Is "Wealthy," Anyway?

There is no question that the past three decades have seen a remarkable explosion in the quantity of wealthy people, as well as a greater concentration of wealth, regardless of what metrics are used to define wealth. But as we started our investigation into the nature of wealth, we faced the challenge of finding relevant operational definitions for terms like *wealth* and *affluence* in our rapidly changing financial markets. Our primary goal was to study people of truly substantial means, whose options in life and the marketplace were, for all intents and purposes, not limited by financial constraints or necessity. This, of course, left out the traditional definition of wealth as $1 million in net worth. These days, $1 million might get you a 5000+ square-foot spread with five or six bedrooms in Dallas or Minneapolis, but in New York City or San Francisco, you'd be lucky to get a one-bedroom condo in a nice neighborhood or a two-bedroom condo in an iffier area.

Instead, we decided to focus on much more stringent definitions, designed to ensure that we were studying truly wealthy members of the financial elite. We describe the methodology of our main studies on wealth in more detail in the Appendix; unless otherwise noted, all data cited in this book are from our research. For now, when we refer to the *wealthy*, we mean people in the top 1 percent or half of 1 percent of the American economic spectrum: These people typically have at least $5 million in liquid assets (i.e., not including their primary residence) or have at least $500,000 in annual discretionary income. When we refer to the *affluent,* we are referring to approximately the top 5 percent of the economic ladder, which is roughly at least $1 million in liquid assets or $125,000 in annual discretionary income.

It is these elite groups that we have spent the last half-decade studying, using every methodology available, from one-on-one interviews to focus groups to quantitative surveys. To date, we've collected data from over 6,000 members of today's financial elite. When we tell people about our scientific odyssey, we are consistently met with three responses. First, everyone wants to know how the wealthy accumulated their riches, so that they can do the same. Fair enough. The desire to accumulate great gobs of money is as old as money itself, and although this isn't a financial how-to book, the stories of the wealthy certainly provide some insights into how financial success is typically achieved today. Second, business people, such as our clients in marketing and advertising, want to know who the wealthy are psychologically, so that they can more effectively conduct business with them. Again, fair enough; we'll address that in detail as well.

But the third response is particularly telling. After the initial, self-motivated enthusiasm dies down, skepticism settles in. People ask *why* the wealthy would spend hours of their time answering questions for our research. It is in answering this question that we reach one of the most profound insights about the wealthy to be found in our research.

Notes

1. Kevin Phillips, *Wealth and Democracy: A Political History of the American Rich* (New York: Broadway Books, 2002), p. 11.

2. Ibid., p. 43.
3. Edward Wolff, *Top Heavy* (New York: New Press, 2002), pp. 82–83.
4. Edward Wolff, "Recent Trends in Household Wealth in the United States: Rising Debt and the Middle-Class Squeeze" (June 2007; available at http://www.levy.org/pubs/wp_502.pdf, retrieved April 7, 2008).
5. Ibid.
6. GDP data from the World Bank, retrieved on April 7, 2008, from http://siteresources.worldbank.org/DATASTATISTICS/Resources/GDP.pdf
7. Greenspan's speech can be found at http://www.federalreserve.gov/boarddocs/speeches/1996/19961205.htm. Dow closing price from Dow Jones, retrieved on February 28, 2008, from http://averages.dowjones.com/mdsidx/index.cfm?event = showavgIndexData
8. Tracking study conducted by Investment Company Institute and the Securities Industry Association: *Equity Ownership in America, 2005.* http://www.ici.org/statements/res/rpt_05_equity_owners.pdf (accessed April 7, 2008).
9. The $65,000 figure comes from *Equity Ownership in America, 2005.*
10. Wolff, 2007.

CHAPTER TWO

Debunking Paris Hilton

Why the Wealthy Told Us Their Stories

"OF ALL THE CLASSES, THE WEALTHY ARE THE MOST
NOTICED AND THE LEAST STUDIED."

—John Kenneth Galbraith

WE, THE THREE authors of this book, are market researchers by profession. The fact is that most market research today is conducted with methods that fail miserably at collecting meaningful, in-depth data from the wealthiest 1 percent of Americans. Most market research today is conducted online, offering people a few dollars for a few minutes of their time taking Internet surveys about the topic at hand. Even research on physicians conducted by pharmaceutical companies rarely offers an incentive of more than a couple hundred dollars, and that's far from enough to motivate those with millions of dollars in liquid assets. So how did we do it? Why did the wealthy—individuals with substantial assets, businesses to run, and full social calendars—take hours to tell us their stories?

As is so often the case, in market research and in life, there are practical, logistical answers to that question that scratch the surface yet reveal a more profound dynamic underneath. On a practical level we began by building relationships, working with our partners who

already had relationships with wealthy individuals. At first we partnered with Curtco Media, publishers of affluent-targeted publications such as *Worth* magazine and the *Robb Report*. As we expanded
our research, we partnered with American Express Publishing,
whose magazine titles include *Travel + Leisure, Food & Wine, Departures, Travel + Leisure Golf,* and *Executive Travel.* Additional
partners are listed in the Appendix to this book.

As we worked to network toward the wealthy, we appealed to
their intellectual curiosity. We promised to ask intriguing questions,
and we delivered on that promise. The fact is, hardly anyone can
resist a good question, regardless of his or her socioeconomic standing. As one of our respondents said, "You know, people don't ever
ask me questions unless they already know the answer. I like getting
to talk about myself without having to wonder what the other guy is
up to."

Our approach to interviewing began with wide-ranging questions
that let people reflect on their successes and failures without worry-
ing that they would be judged. We asked how people achieved success, what barriers and challenges they overcame, and how they felt
about their success in the battles they have fought. We asked about
their childhood and about their children. We asked what they liked
and disliked. We asked what companies they admired, which marketing techniques enticed them, and what kinds of advertisements
actually cut through the clutter of their busy lives to engage their
attention. And, fortunately for us, most people so enjoyed the questions that they volunteered to extend the amount of time we spent
with them.

Suffice it to say that the process was fascinating for us and engaging for our respondents—so engaging, in fact, that many respondents nominated their friends for subsequent interviews. We further
captivated their intellectual curiosity by offering respondents an
early, close-up look at the results of our work. For any respondent
who wanted it, we provided a coded identification number that enabled the individual to examine the results and reports for personal
reasons. In some cases, we even let them examine their own data in
comparison to others in the financial elite. For a generation of business men and women who believe in measurement, and who grew

up with IQ tests, SAT scores, and other performance metrics, this quantitative capability was an often irresistible source of pleasure. This was particularly true because the individuals had been on a special journey, one their upbringings had left them largely unprepared for, and so understanding the journeys of others was a means for understanding their own trips and themselves.

But there is a deeper, more telling reason the wealthy volunteered hours of their time for us. Simply put, *we promised to tell the world the truth about them.* These days, the wealthy get a bad rap. They know it, and they don't like it. The desire to set the record straight is a powerful motivator. This book is part of our promise to tell the truth as we uncovered it.

Images of Wealth and Excess

The wealthy have always been viewed with a mixture of admiration and resentment. Americans cheer their triumphs, but just as quickly herald their downfalls and embarrassments. Millions watched Martha Stewart's television shows, read her books, and were proud to reflect her sense of style in their own lives (psychologists refer to this kind of mental boost as "basking in reflected glory"). But many just as quickly took joy in her shame and prison term, believing it a just comeuppance for arrogance and greed. This vacillation between basking in reflected glory and *schadenfreude*—taking joy in the misfortune of others—is no longer balanced. As tabloid culture has gone mainstream, it is clear that *schadenfreude* sells, and it is more popular than ever. One of our respondents put it this way: "the media like to exploit celebrity and wealth and affluence. And to get more people to read, the philosophy isn't 'misery loves company,' it's 'misery loves voyeurism.'"

In decades past, the decadence sometimes associated with wealth had something of a romance, almost an elegance to it. For example, think of F. Scott Fitzgerald's *The Great Gatsby,* with Jay Gatsby at play on Long Island; or the ornate parlor cars of railroad magnates such as Cornelius Vanderbilt; or the rich collections of Andrew Carnegie; or John F. Kennedy and his family holding court in the White House. The resentment that some felt toward these wealthy lifestyles was often coupled with a paradoxical respect and admiration for the refinement this wealth engendered. No more. Today, the excesses of wealth are decidedly less classy—they are "celebrated" not in fine novels but in overly candid video clips shot on cell phone cameras and uploaded to YouTube and TMZ.com.

Indeed, mention of wealth today typically brings to mind Paris Hilton, perceived widely as empty-headed, irresponsible, and to many, undeservedly and unfairly wealthy. Certainly there are exceptions to this modern negative view of wealth, as with articulate humanitarians such as U2's Bono, Virgin's Richard Branson, and many others. But unless a person owns the medium (we're talking Oprah here), it's hard to control the message, and even harder to portray a consistently positive image of wealth.

Fictional characters also often perpetuate negative stereotypes of the affluent, a phenomenon we sometimes call "the Mr. Burns syndrome" in honor (or lack thereof) of the character from television's *The Simpsons*. In a nod to Dickens's *Great Expectations*, Charles Montgomery Burns was sent from his family at a young age to live with a cruel billionaire (whom he later discovered was his grandfather). As an adult, he wields his tremendous power and wealth capriciously, running his nuclear power plant with no concern for the environment or his employees. From his gated mansion at the corner of Croesus and Mammon Streets (both historical references to vast, soulless wealth), he cuts deals with Satan and often orders his sycophantic-yet-adoring assistant Smithers to "unleash the hounds" on anyone who gets in his way. His archaic references and often-outdated language reinforce the implication, and the stereotype, of Gilded Age wealth and disdain for those who lack it.

The same archetype of selfish wealth formed the basis of Mr. Burns's forerunner Scrooge McDuck, Donald Duck's miserly uncle who first appeared in 1947 and today is the "first nonmammal to rank as fiction's richest character" on *Forbes*'s tongue-in-cheek Fictional 15 list. Less ironic and only slightly less one-dimensionally evil than Mr. Burns, Scrooge is another obvious caricature of Gilded Era wealth, as highlighted by the only ducks who rivaled him in wealth, Flintheart Glomgold and John D. Rockerduck.

How the Wealthy Are Viewed Today

In January 2006, we conducted our "American Attitudes Toward the Wealthy" study to dig deeply into how the wealthy are viewed by average Americans. The picture is not pretty. As Table 2-1 shows, the wealthy are viewed as lucky, arrogant, excessive, irresponsible, indolent, and self-indulgent.

Of course, the picture isn't entirely negative. When we asked people how they think the wealthy accumulated their wealth (see Table 2-2), some positive attributes are mentioned, including hard work, expertise, creativity, and risk-taking. Still, many people attribute financial success largely to luck, and nearly two-thirds of those surveyed believe that sacrificing moral integrity plays a key role.

Of course, the wealthy have a very different perspective, and you can easily see why they would be motivated to talk with us to share their side of this story. Our research, and our personal experiences with the wealthy, suggest that the perceptions held by the general public are largely unfair at best, and quite often completely wrong. But perhaps it is easy to see why so many Americans are wrong. Only

Table 2-1 **How Americans describe the wealthy***

Description	% of Those Surveyed
Live lavishly	80
Come from families with money	79
Are in the right place at the right time	75
Are somewhat arrogant	72
Are self-indulgent	71
Don't understand how it is for those who don't have money	70
Don't pay enough taxes	66
Are snobs	62
Are self-serving	60
Are lucky (don't earn it)	55
Have sacrificed their principles for money	51

*From Harrison Group's "American Attitudes Toward the Wealthy" study. This nationally representative study of 873 adult Americans was conducted via a thirty-minute Internet survey in January 2006.

Table 2-2 **Americans' beliefs about sources of wealth**

Attributed Source of Wealth	% of Those Surveyed
Coming from money	85
Hard work/determination	85
Having strong social networks	83
Good business background	82
Skill/expertise in one's field	82
Being inventive	81
Having a good education	81
Being willing to take chances and risk it all	81
Good luck	79
Being willing to sacrifice principles	62

19 percent of the general population personally know someone of considerable financial means; 81 percent, on the other hand, have their perceptions shaped by the media or other means.

Luxury Marketers Also Miss the Mark

When it comes to understanding why today's wealthy feel so misunderstood, perhaps even more telling are the attitudes and opinions that luxury marketers have toward them. These are people whose careers are devoted to understanding the wealthy, yet at times their perceptions are just as inaccurate as those of the average person. In 2005, we sought to better understand these dynamics by partnering with AgencySacks, a premier luxury advertising firm, to conduct a study of 130 senior luxury marketing executives, including many CEOs and Chief Marketing Officers. The executives spanned a range of industries, including financial services, jewelry, cars, and travel. Yet these marketing executives were, quite often, off the mark when asked to describe today's wealthy individuals.

Table 2-3 shows just how they missed the mark on demographics—for example, overestimating how many of the wealthy are divorced. These marketers also greatly overestimated the enthusiasm for home entertaining and conspicuous consumption, while underes-

Table 2-3 **Marketers' perceptions of the wealthy vs. self-perceptions***

	Marketers' Guesses %	Wealthy Realities %
Demographics and Attitudes		
Are married	52	83
Are optimistic about the future of America	45	60
Would describe themselves as very happy	75	95
Conspicuous Consumption		
Feel that luxury items like expensive watches, jewelry, and cars are a waste of money	18	48
Want people to know they are wealthy	55	11
Values		
Would describe themselves as middle class at heart	68	81
Have compromised their values to make money	65	9
Friends and Family		
Believe people want to be friends with them because they know they are wealthy	73	12
Entertain others in their home a few times a month or more often	76	53
Are concerned about their children's work ethic because they have always had money	95	50

*This table compares results from interviews with 130 senior luxury executives to results from interviews with 503 wealthy individuals in the *Worth*-Harrison Taylor "Study on the Status of Wealth in America" (described fully in the appendix).

timating how happy and optimistic the wealthy are. They didn't understand the values and family concerns of the wealthy, either. And the list goes on.

Certainly one could argue that the wealthy are merely portraying themselves in a positive light, particularly in terms of the 91 percent who state that they have not compromised their principles for financial success. But it is our experience and belief that the statements by the wealthy about themselves are reasonably accurate. This is not to say that the wealthy are pure as the driven snow or that they see themselves as puritans. But it does mean that most wealthy individuals have a core set of values that guide their business efforts, their family lives, and their interactions with everyone from employees to customers to financial backers. As one of our respondents put it, "We succeeded because of our principles, not our plan." Depictions of these principled, value-driven individuals are often absent from media portrayals. In short, the wealthy feel misunderstood for a reason: they are, in fact, misunderstood by the layperson, the media, and the professional marketer.

The Biggest Misconception About the Wealthy

Perhaps the single biggest misconception about the wealthy concerns the source of their wealth. Most people believe that the wealthy inherited their wealth; as we saw in Table 2-2, 85 percent of Americans believe that the wealthy "come from money." Again, the media play a key role in maintaining this perception. And again, it is radically, dramatically wrong. In fact, over 90 percent of the wealthy created their own wealth, and fewer than 10 percent inherited it.

Recognizing the source of this misperception, and the genesis of wealth today, are keys to understanding the wealthy and to building meaningful connections with them. The myth and the reality of wealth creation requires a historical look at how wealth has, and has not, been created in America. This is the subject of our next chapter.

CHAPTER THREE

The Wealth of the Nation

Four Waves of American Wealth

"SO YOU THINK THAT MONEY IS THE ROOT OF ALL EVIL. . . .
HAVE YOU EVER ASKED WHAT IS THE ROOT OF ALL MONEY?"

—Ayn Rand, *Atlas Shrugged*

IN EVERY ERA, money takes on the flavor of the cultural and economic Zeitgeist. Money, along with the origins of wealth, comes to reflect technological advances, social changes, upheavals (good and bad) in financial markets, and even something as mundane as changes in the tax code. Our focus here is primarily wealth in America, where, as shown in Figure 3-1, there have been four great epochs of wealth

Figure 3-1 Four epochs of wealth formation.

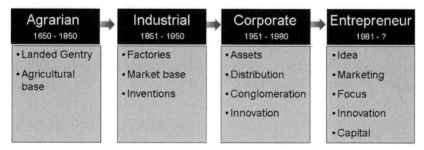

Agrarian 1650 - 1850	Industrial 1851 - 1950	Corporate 1951 - 1980	Entrepreneur 1981 - ?
• Landed Gentry • Agricultural base	• Factories • Market base • Inventions	• Assets • Distribution • Conglomeration • Innovation	• Idea • Marketing • Focus • Innovation • Capital

21

formation: agrarian (1650–1850), industrial (1851–1950), corporate (1951–1980), and entrepreneurial (1981–present). As it turns out, the misperceptions of today's wealthy have their roots in the origins (and mythology) of the wealth creation of previous waves. Decades-old stereotypes about the wealthy die hard, and many still reverberate today.

Agrarian Wealth (1650–1850)

The first era of American wealth accumulation arose with the creation of the United States, and colonial wealth grew largely out of agricultural pursuits. Large tracts of land were given by the British Crown to spur development, reward friends, and encourage western expansion. The landed gentry of Virginia and the farming culture of the middle Atlantic colonies-turned-states resulted in the creation of very large properties whose owners formed most of the original American wealth aristocracy. During this era, when wealth in America was characterized by the ownership of land, George Washington was one of the richest men in America by the time he became president. His wealth came from several sources, including the $25,000 a year he earned as president—which in today's terms is over $500,000 a year—and the fact that he married well.

But in most respects, Washington's accumulation of wealth was fairly typical of the financial elite during his time, and even had a bit of an entrepreneurial flair. Washington came to own huge tracts of land in Virginia and the Ohio Valley, in part by taking property in trade for his services as a surveyor. Like most landowners, he leveraged his agrarian resources with slave labor, which reduced the costs of production of tobacco, cotton, and livestock to levels that gave price advantages to farmers in the colonies even after offsetting the costs of shipping finished products to English markets, the only real market available to the colonists.

On the whole, the life of the wealthy planter was quite comfortable, provided one had no guilt about the gross human inequality and suffering that life was typically built on. Labor—even plantation management—was handled by "employees"—indentured, in slavery, and under salary. The role of the planter was to hunt, engage in social affairs, and participate in the public events of the colonies. As land was accumulated, power was proportionate to the size of the estate. While very large estates generated relatively small amounts of cash, the land produced food, wine, horses, and the necessary underpinnings of the aristocratic good life.

One of the problems with considering land as a basis of wealth, however, is that it cannot always easily be converted into cash. Farmers and landholders loathed to sell land, for a variety of reasons; and perhaps with an asking price of a few cents per acre, it is understandable why. But if they mortgaged the land to gain cash, they had to increase the agricultural yields in order to both pay the bank and fund their operating and living expenses. Given the rudimentary farming methods of the time, this put ownership and the accompanying long-term value of property ownership at risk. Wealth in the form of land-ownership had, in many cases therefore, the potential of cash but not the reality of cash. As a result, wealth did not move easily or quickly in this agrarian society, and certainly in cash terms, colonial fortunes paled in comparison to those of wealthy Europeans. Certainly there were merchants and other successful entrepreneurs who were able to create their own wealth, but land was the coin of the realm, and landed fortunes tended to be relatively modest in size and stayed in families for generations. Borrowing the European inheritance traditions of primogeniture and entail, colonial wealth was typically passed to male heirs.

As the 1800s moved toward their midpoint, land remained a key driver of wealth in America, even as the largely agricultural society of early America gained an increasingly large urban population. The populations of Boston, Philadelphia, and New York had essentially been doubling every twenty years since 1780, and real estate values in those cities grew considerably as a result. High urban real estate values, along with proximity to government connections and banking centers, resulted in a greater concentration of wealth along this northeastern urban corridor. New wealth generation was modest relative to inheritance, with over 90 percent of the wealthy in those three cities having "rich or eminent parents."[1]

What is particularly remarkable about American wealth in the early 1800s is that, although most wealth was inherited, the highest-profile public icons of wealth were more likely to be self-made. Stephen Girard, for example, was widely considered to be the wealthiest man in America when he passed away in 1831, leaving an estate of approximately $6.5 million. For a colonial American success story, he had a lot against him: French-born, an atheist, short, and with a deformed and sightless right eye that sometimes left him socially isolated. He came to the United States as a sailor with little money, and worked his way up to captain. He went on to invest in ships, and opened a highly profitable business selling supplies to soldiers during the American Revolution. He later expanded into real estate and banking, and almost single-handedly helped finance the government's efforts to fight the War of 1812.

John Jacob Astor had a similar rags-to-riches story. The son of a German butcher, Astor came to the United States in 1784, where he began trading with (some say exploiting) Native Americans for furs, which he then sold in his New York City store. He later expanded into shipping, but his greatest engine of wealth creation was Manhattan real estate. He eventually sunk virtually all of his assets into buying parcels that he subdivided and leased, earning him the nickname "Landlord of New York."

Both Girard and Astor were immigrants and entrepreneurs. Both were known for being a bit uncouth, and they were uncomfortable outsiders to the world of country clubs and elegant dinners that were less well known to the average American, but that were springing up in the realm of inherited wealth. It should be pointed out that the famous "Mrs. Astor's 400" list of socially prominent New Yorkers was the 1892 creation of Caroline Webster Schermerhorn Astor, an aristocrat who married John Jacob Astor's third son in 1854. John Jacob Astor, the wealth-creating entrepreneur who beat fur pelts with his own hands, had passed away in 1848 with a then-astounding $20 million. During that same year, a political revolution shook France once again, but a very different kind of revolution was about to reshape America.

Industrial Wealth (1851–1950)

Does this sound familiar? Sweeping technological changes radically reshape the business world in just a few years. Entirely new categories of business emerge, while others are virtually wiped out. Previously unthinkable communications technologies allow people to converse almost instantly across great distances at relatively low costs. The world seems to shrink. Productivity enhancements allow one person to do the work that previously required ten persons. Sound like the Internet boom? It describes the changes of the Industrial Revolution just as well.

Railroads. Steamships and steam locomotives. The telegraph and the telephone. The internal combustion engine. Electrical power generation and all it enabled, from the lightbulb to air-conditioning. Mechanization and mass production. More obscure technological advances in less glamorous fields, such as metallurgy, chemistry, and textiles, had far-reaching implications as well. The list goes on. Technology fundamentally changed how people lived their lives, and not surprisingly, it also fundamentally changed how wealth was accumulated and distributed. So began the era of the wealthy industrialist or, less charitably, the robber baron.

Wealth and Democracy author Kevin Phillips convincingly argues that explosions of wealth in democratic societies tend to occur when three key factors coincide: technological innovations, financial vehicles facilitating investment (or at least more mobility of money), and wealth-friendly governmental regulation. All three were in abundance as the era of industrial wealth took hold.

The technological advances we have already seen. How about the financial innovation? Obviously it ended badly with the stock market crash of 1929, coming after decades of largely unregulated financial speculation, but this was an era with some lasting financial innovations (such as the IPO), which made investing and entrepreneurship easier. Wealth-friendly government regulation? Let's just say it was the golden era of wealth-friendly government regulation. Or, perhaps more accurately, there was a complete absence of wealth-unfriendly regulation.

Indeed, the first half century of the industrial era might best be thought of as the Wild West of big business. Monopolies emerged in oil, steel, and other important industries, as virtually any kind of oligopolistic, and even predatory, business strategy was allowed; indeed, monopolies were legal until the passage of the Sherman Anti-

Trust Act in 1890. Railroads and other aspects of America's transportation infrastructure were unregulated until the passage of the Hepburn Act in 1906. Telephone and telegraph businesses were unregulated until the passage of the Mann-Elkins Act in 1910. The Federal Reserve Board didn't exist to regulate banking until 1913. The Federal Trade Commission didn't exist to prevent unfair business practices until 1914.

Want to create and sell potentially poisonous pharmaceuticals? No problem, as long as you did it before the passage of the Pure Food and Drug Act of 1906. Want to make a quick profit selling bad meat? It was easy before the Meat Inspection Act of 1906. Want to save on manufacturing costs by working children long hours? Go ahead—the Supreme Court repeatedly struck down child labor laws as unconstitutional in the early 1900s, and they didn't make a significant comeback until the 1930s. The government's extreme attitude of laissez-faire not only made it easier for big businesses to get bigger and snuff out the competition, it also made it easier for those who ran these monopolies to keep their money. Income tax? The Supreme Court ruled it unconstitutional in 1895, and it didn't become a permanent part of the U.S. tax code until the Constitution was amended in 1913.

The result of these three influences—technology, finance, regulation—led to an unprecedented shift in American wealth. The transition from the agrarian era to the industrial era had led to a shift in wealth from the agrarian South to the industrial North, fueling the tensions that drove the Civil War. On an individual level, money shifted to an entirely new breed of wealthy individual, and by the end of the nineteenth century, the largest fortunes were in the range of $200–300 million—ten times what Astor had accumulated in his lifetime just a half century earlier. The names of this new elite are still familiar today: Andrew Carnegie. Henry Ford. J. P. Morgan. Thomas Edison. Indeed, in the minds of many, these names are synonymous with wealth today, particularly two of the wealthiest: John Rockefeller and Cornelius Vanderbilt.

Vanderbilt was from a middle-class family, and he dropped out of school to start working when he was just eleven years old, later saying: "If I had learned education, I would not have had time to learn anything else." By sixteen, he had started his own ferry service between Staten Island and Manhattan, and over time he expanded to other routes with a fleet of more than a hundred ships. Anticipating shifts in technology and consumer behavior, Vanderbilt began pulling money out of his shipping business, and he bought a series of railroads, merging them into a transportation empire of increasing scale (his statue still stands in front of New York's Grand Central Station). He was known for being ruthless in business, and was hardly a pushover with his family, either. On his death in 1887, he left 95 percent of his approximately $100 million fortune to his son William, who later became known for responding "The public be damned" to a reporter's question about whether unprofitable but socially important railroad lines should be kept open. The elder Vanderbilt's will effectively disowned his other sons (who sued to contest the will and lost), and spread the remaining 5 percent around to his wife, his eight daughters, and a few charities.

John D. Rockefeller rose from modest means to become America's first billionaire, and he was equally ruthless in his business decision making, using his massive wealth and 90 percent market share in the oil industry to give competitors the choice of being bought out or being crushed. After two decades of government pursuit of Rockefeller's company, the Supreme Court concluded in 1911 that Standard Oil was an illegal monopoly, and ordered it broken up into thirty-four separate companies (including companies that later remerged into what we know today as ExxonMobil), with Rockefeller maintaining equity in all of them. Though Rockefeller was widely hated for many years, his legacy was quite different. By the time of his death in 1937, his net worth had "dwindled" to less than $30 million, after he had donated hundreds of millions of dollars to charities.

In 1918, an upstart financial publication known as *Forbes* published a list of the thirty richest Americans, which they would turn into an annual tradition over sixty years later. Then, Rockefeller was the sole billionaire. Steel magnate Henry Clay Frick was a distant second with $225 million, followed closely by Andrew Carnegie and a host of others who had made their money primarily in oil, railroads, steel, or banking. William Vanderbilt logged in at number ten, having barely been able to add $5 million to the $95 million his father had left him (Vincent Astor was number thirteen, with $75 million).

In broad terms, Vanderbilt was the richest man of the last half of the nineteenth century, and Rockefeller was the richest man of the first half of the twentieth century. It is hard to overstate the impact of their wealth. Simply adjusting their fortunes for inflation would place them in the $10–15 billion range today—far below the fortunes of Bill Gates and Warren Buffett. But if their wealth is calculated as a percentage of the gross domestic product at the time, and projected to today, then Rockefeller's wealth peaked at $305 billion and Vanderbilt's at $168 billion. (Andrew Carnegie actually would have placed second by this measure, peaking at $281 billion.) Buffett, a rich man living in a rich country, comes in a distant fourth by this metric.[2]

Perhaps even more important, Vanderbilt, Rockefeller, and the "lesser" names of the industrial era aristocrats served as the first "market models" of the wealthy personality. This is the bedrock basis for most Americans' attitudes and expectations of the wealthy. Fashion, tobacco, films, and the emergence of the gossip column in the Roaring Twenties created a stereotype of a well-educated, well-cultivated, highly sophisticated wealthy family of dubious morals, descended from a man of tremendous wealth, with a ruthless business ethic and sometimes a passion for philanthropy. This image would become the icon for any portrayal of people of means, presenting an almost un-American image of Victorian manners and noblesse oblige. Wealth "ghost towns," like Newport, Rhode Island, stand as mute testimony to the power and grandeur of those heady, aristocratic days.

They were not only rich, they were powerful. The wealthy owned the mines, the lumber, and the other sources of raw material. They owned the factories and the means of production. They owned the inventions and the patents and the intellectual property. They owned the railroads, the steamships, and other means of distribution. They set the prices. They owned the public stock, the private bonds, and had strong relationships with the merchant bankers who financed it all. Today we'd call it being "vertically integrated." Back then it was less of an admired business strategy and more a source of populist resentment—a resentment which still lingers today.

What happened to these name-brand fortunes? They were passed on to the heirs of these familiar names and distributed through the many high-profile charitable ventures that also bear their names. Little wonder that most people today still know these names and assume that most wealthy people inherited their riches.

As the industrial era wound down and the Great Depression took hold in the 1930s, attitudes toward the wealthy changed dramatically, and the government finally had the mandate and political will to begin reshaping the distribution of money in society. Certainly a change in attitude had been brewing for decades. Starting in 1876, third-party candidates such as William Jennings Bryan launched a series of increasingly strong runs for the presidency, largely on platforms of addressing income inequality and protecting the interests of the urban and rural poor.

These third-party efforts might have helped the poor if they had succeeded, but their failures had unintended consequences; throughout the late 1800s, most presidential victors failed to claim a majority of the popular vote, and the lack of a mandate weakened the presidency. The Senate came to have relatively greater influence, but senators at the time were appointed, not elected, and they used the power vacuum to protect the business interests of the wealthy industrialists who had an inordinate impact on their getting appointed in the first place.

Real political change didn't occur until Theodore Roosevelt assumed the presidency after the assassination of William McKinley in 1901. Buoyed by muckrakers and other journalists who exposed the excesses of the era, Roosevelt aggressively challenged the business interests of the wealthy industrialists, and he spearheaded the progressive legislation highlighted earlier in this section that protected consumers and workers in many respects. But despite these social changes, legislation that truly addressed income equality didn't get passed until Franklin D. Roosevelt's administration.

The Roaring Twenties saw big tax cuts for the wealthy and economic policies (such as corporate dividends paid in stock being non-taxable) that led to an IPO boom the likes of which would not be seen again until the 1990s. The rich got richer. Like today, much of the middle class aspired to live like the rich, and people took on debt to start living certain aspects of an upscale lifestyle. And the poor got poorer; as always, there were different flavors of poverty, from the inner-city poor, to Dust Bowl farmers, to southern sharecroppers, to those living in boom-gone-bust railroad towns.

There simply wasn't the political will to change how money moved in America until the Great Depression. Franklin Roosevelt's rhetoric of redistributing wealth foreshadowed his economic policies:

> For ten years we expanded far beyond our natural and normal growth. . . . Corporate profit was enormous. . . . The consumer was forgotten . . . the worker was forgotten . . . the stockholder was forgotten. . . . Throughout the nation men and women, forgotten in the political philosophy of the Government, look to us here for guidance and for more equitable opportunity to share in the distribution of national wealth. . . . I pledge myself to a new deal for the American people. This is more than a political campaign. It is a call to arms.[3]

In the early 1920s, the top marginal income tax rate had been lowered from 73 percent to 25 percent, where it remained until Franklin Roosevelt took office. The rate then increased to 63 percent in 1932, 79 percent in 1936, and 88 percent in 1942.[4] Fundamental changes in economic policies and social attitudes were under way, and they would radically reshape the nature of wealth in America, even though the largest effects weren't seen until after World War II.

Corporate Wealth (1951–1980)

The period of 1951 through 1980, which we have labeled the era of corporate wealth, is first and foremost remarkable for its lack of tremendous individual wealth creation. Many of Franklin Roosevelt's wealth-equalizing New Deal economic policies continued, with the top tax rate peaking at 91 percent throughout the 1950s, and remaining at 70 percent throughout most of the 1970s. In the meantime, lower- and middle-class workers benefited from a variety of economic changes. With World War II came full employment, abundant overtime, and, at least temporarily, a growing number of women in the workforce. Union membership surged, wages went up, and blue-collar prosperity took hold, but wartime rationing meant that there was relatively little to buy, so savings rates reached historical highs. The middle class swelled while the gap between the rich and poor narrowed, a pattern that economists Claudia Golden and Robert Margo called "the great compression."[5]

Ironically, it was the growing middle class that laid the groundwork for the new wave of wealth. But this new wave was not concentrated in a few individuals; instead, it flowed to the companies that were able to capitalize on the large, stable, relatively homogeneous middle class. As Robert Reich points out in his book *Supercapitalism*, the dynamics of wealth in this era were characterized by an implicit cooperation between corporations and employees. Businesses were highly motivated to ensure that large numbers of Americans could afford to buy their products; indeed, business success in the 1950s and 1960s was often predicated on market scale, being able to invest in technology to mass-produce products and drive the cost-per-item as low as possible.

Instead of offering the lowest possible wages to maximize short-term profits, corporations benefited by offering higher wages, which in turn allowed large numbers of Americans to spend heartily. Corporations and unions increasingly made peace, as both recognized that labor stoppages threatened this unique balance. Marx's ideology of exploitation and class conflict, which seemed at least in part a somewhat accurate description of the excesses of the industrial era, could never have envisioned this kind of symbiotic partnership. When the Senate was in the process of confirming General Motors president Charles Wilson as secretary of defense in 1953, he famously said that there could be no conflict of interest because "what was good for our country was good for General Motors, and vice versa." He said it in all earnestness; as the biggest employer in the nation, GM had a dual interest in maintaining good employee relations and supporting a robust, financially comfortable middle class who could buy GM cars.

To some extent, the counterbalancing effect of large consumer markets against the unilateral power of the industrialists had started to emerge several decades earlier, but had been derailed by the Great Depression. Henry Ford was number eight on *Forbes*'s 1918 list with a fortune of $100 million, and his innovations in mass production are well known. His company produced just over 10,000 cars in 1909, but over 248,000 cars just five years later. Less well known, but equally important, were his innovations in creating demand and consumer markets, doing everything from educating consumers about how these newfangled horseless carriages worked to enabling easy car loans. Similarly, large consumer markets had started to emerge for cameras, radios, sewing machines, telephones, and retail outlets such as Sears. After World War II, these markets exploded.

In the corporate era, bigness ruled. The phrase "big business" came into the lexicon, with largely positive connotations, in 1953 with the publication of the book *Big Business: A New Era* by former New Deal administrator David Lilienthal. Although we call this period the era of corporate wealth, it could in fact equally be considered the era of the "big idea"—an era in which big ideas conspired with advertising and distribution to create the contemporary American economy.

In those halcyon days of innovation, dominated by huge corporate megaliths like Boeing, IBM, U.S. Steel, and General Motors, bringing a product to market was a huge affair. Entrepreneurial intuition was deemphasized, and market scale had to be proven in volume before a product could be developed. Indeed, capital investing was often focused on projects of such massive scale that size alone created barriers to competition, as in computing, aircraft, nuclear weapons, pharmaceutical sciences, agribusiness, machine tools, automobiles, trucking, and a host of other growth categories during this era.

And perhaps most of all, markets had to be big. This era was characterized by the expansion of nearly every category of human consumption, from laundry detergent to radar systems. The companies that were successful were those with marketers who learned how to create demand where there had been none, and how to channel demand from one marketplace option to another. In a very real sense, the new technologies that defined business success in the 1950s and 1960s were not just physics and chemistry, but also psychology and the study of human behavior. It was the heyday of Madison Avenue, illustrated in today's popular television show *Mad Men*, where advertisers shape behavior with their understanding of consumer needs and insecurities. Some considered it overly manipulative, as highlighted in popular books such as Vance Packard's *The Hidden Persuaders*.

Equally psychological was the growing focus on branding, and the recognition that brand choices were often not the perfectly rational decisions posited by economists. In consumer packaged goods, for example, companies like General Mills, Procter & Gamble, and Clorox created new categories, created demand, created brands that have been household names for decades, and managed it all with a scientific precision overseen by seasoned corporate managers. IBM leveraged the same powerful combination. A pioneer of systematic corporate management, its most powerful innovations—the iconic salesman in the blue suit and the implicit message that "Nobody ever got fired for buying IBM"—were more about shaping psychological perceptions than technological offerings.

As wealth shifted to corporations, new wealth among individuals fell largely to those running the corporations. Although the personal fortunes of the wealthy industrialists passed to their families, in many cases their businesses did not. Their corporations, and others that grew to ascendancy during the mid-twentieth century, came to be guided by a new class of professional corporate management, whose wealth derived in part from stock options. As capital gains were taxed at 25 percent, compared to individual income tax rates that topped out at 91 percent, corporations held back their wealth, making stock options a more attractive form of compensation.

A new meritocracy emerged, as corporations began placing substantially greater emphasis on loyalty and ability rather than bloodlines. To be sure, the Watson family was building IBM into a powerhouse in the computer industry, but the key decisions in marketing, product development, and management were being made by the new "hired guns" from America's premier law schools and business colleges. New skills came to be valued: analytic savvy, extreme forms of business literacy, a capacity for teamwork, the ability to "manage up," and a special facility for sales.

Still, the meritocracy had limits. The postwar availability of a college education, thanks to Uncle Sam's G.I. Bill, opened up opportunities for many, but selection for a fast-track executive career often still depended in part on where you were from and whom you knew—and of course, the assumption that you were a white male. Wealth acquisition in the corporate environment of gray flannel suits depended on a no-nonsense loyalty to a corporate game plan, a willingness to invest personal ambitions in the success of the whole business, and a philosophy of working the system to one's advantage. Although first published in 1937, the business success manual of the era was Dale Carnegie's *How to Win Friends and Influence People.* When a colleague once told Dale Carnegie that the secret to success was hard work, Carnegie's retort was, "You've got to be kidding."

As these businesses grew large, a wealthy "trickle-down" aristocracy also took form. Professional corporate managers drove deals, business design, profits, and success. Essentially untethered from the industrial families that created American monolithic corporations, the new management class expected exceptional returns from their service providers such as bankers, lawyers, accountants, and business managers. Suburban new-echelon wealth communities grew up in nearly every city in America. These suburbs, the focus of hip criticism in the 1960s, provided a comfortable spawning ground for another aristocracy, one heavily indebted to values of loyalty, education, relationships, and business competence.

While corporate executives and the new management class that served them were the individual beneficiaries of growing corporate wealth, the magnitude of the wealth they accumulated paled in comparison to that of the industrial era. The richest Americans of the mid-twentieth century were not the new corporate titans but, rather, the inheritors of industrial wealth. This remained true even throughout the 1970s and into the 1980s. When *Forbes* introduced their list of the 400 wealthiest Americans as an annual feature in 1982, the list contained twenty-four Du Pont heirs, fourteen Rockefellers, and six Mellons. There were some new names, but they were largely variations on familiar themes. New oil fields created wealth for the likes of H. L. Hunt and J. Paul Getty, who would in turn create new lines of family wealth.

But the list was about to undergo a seismic change. Within twenty-five years, there would be one Rockefeller, one Mellon, and no Du Ponts on the list. In 1982, twelve "old money" families accounted for over 20 percent of the list's total net worth. In 2006, they accounted for less than 2 percent.[6] Don't feel too bad for them—they aren't poor, and the net worth of each family is still in the billions. But their wealth has been dispersed through five or six generations, and even strong investment returns aren't able to keep up with expanding family trees. The story is often told of one Rockefeller heir who turned twenty-one and was disappointed to learn that his inheritance was only $2 million. But even taking these families as a whole, their collective worth has been far surpassed by that of the entrepreneurial wealthy.

As with the industrial era, the wealth dynamics of the corporate era have left their marks on today's public psyche. Set aside, for the moment, the public perception that most wealth is inherited. What do most people think about the "rest" of the wealthy? They think of white male corporate executives and professionals. They think of slow accumulation of wealth over the course of a career, of Ivy League educations, of elitist attitudes. They think of working the system. It's about "who you know." Connections, country clubs, and deals sealed on the golf course. Perhaps a bit manipulative, and more concerned about what they can get people to do, rather than what people actually need. These are all part of the modern stereotype of today's wealthy, and they are all dramatically wrong. These perceptions stem from the industrial and corporate eras—and today's wealthy emerged during the entrepreneurial era.

Entrepreneurial Wealth (1981–present)

While big companies got bigger, and their senior managers got wealthier, a variety of factors conspired to reshape the economy, and the nature of wealth itself. The corporate appetite for scale left a lot of good ideas on the table—ideas that could be developed to meet niche markets at low cost and with high dividends for the developer.

In addition, globalism and multinational corporations emerged as potent business forces, rattling the symbiotic relationship between companies and employees.

The 1950s and 1960s were largely a time of American companies making products for American consumers. But as the 1970s dawned, foreign companies had finally rebounded from World War II, and they broke forcefully into American markets, while at the same time American companies began looking abroad for more growth opportunities. American automotive companies were shaken by more efficient and innovative imports from Japan, and the federal government increasingly had to intervene to save struggling American companies such as Chrysler.

Union memberships declined, layoffs were widespread, and the notion of lifelong employment with one company gave way to a period of American workers feeling threatened and disempowered. (Two decades later, a new symbiotic paradigm of the "free agent workplace" would emerge, offering workers an occasionally stressful balance of less security for more opportunity.) This transitional period of the 1970s was a difficult one in America, with questions about American economic supremacy and viability, culminating in President Jimmy Carter's reluctant admission that we were living in a "malaise." But as always, there was opportunity in chaos, and a new economic paradigm was about to emerge. With it would come the supernova of wealth we see today.

Again, trends in technology, finances, and regulation tell the tale. The technology elements are well known: the Internet has changed everything, leveling playing fields, lowering the cost of entry, and opening up global opportunities for start-ups and corporate behemoths, alike. Massive government investment in basic research during the Cold War and space race paid dividends with innovations in computer science, wireless phones, pharmaceuticals, biotechnology, and other fields, reshaping entire industries and minting new multi-millionaires.

Less well known, but with almost an equal impact, have been changes in the financial markets and government regulation. Set aside your political preconceptions: Much of it started with the "Reagan Revolution." On August 23, 1981, the Reagan administration changed the American tax code in a way that fostered capital markets. Essentially, the top tax rate for unearned income (passive income from investments) was reduced from a little over 70 percent to either the top tax rate for earned income if the investor is a "partner" in a company, or to the top tax rate for capital gains if the investor is "passive"—that is, plays no management role in a company.

These changes, seemingly obscure, shifted the risks of investing. Losses were now completely deductible and could be carried forward to a more advantageous tax year. Since the losses were deductible, the government paid a significant portion of the risk while reducing the tax burden of the gains. For the savvy investor, this was quite a deal. Return on investments became as personally profitable as the return on the energy it takes to go to work. Meanwhile, capital gains taxes were further reduced to 19 percent, making it possible for an investor to gain a substantial tax break from the sale of assets while the investments remained fully deductible from income. These two tweaks made it possible for capitalists to invest in untested ideas. *The entrepreneurial revolution was on.*

The scope and magnitude of the revolution spawned by the investment in entrepreneurship are unimaginably broad. Reduced risk led to the formation of a gigantic venture capital pool. It inspired the creation of entirely new categories of technology, software, real estate investment, health care, pharmaceuticals, biotechnology, entertainment, communication, retail, and public information. It made it possible to take a great idea and build a business on an extension of that idea. It created jobs, communities, and a new generation of wealth in America. And it provided the potential to revolutionize the lives of the children of the postwar middle class through expanded entrepreneurial opportunities. Consider the numbers. In 1976, the total pool of venture capital—that is, capital put at risk for an idea with no historically reliable history of success—was approximately $49 million.[7] In 2007, venture funds pumped $30 *billion* into the conversion of new ideas into wealth, and the vast majority of new wealth has been created in this "idea rush."[8]

The business world, and the economy in general, have been turned upside down. Since 1980, the economy (in real terms) has doubled in size. Per worker productivity has also doubled. The total wealth in America has tripled. And 70 percent of the 1980 Fortune 500 has disappeared (in 1980, Microsoft was tiny and U.S. Steel was king). We saw earlier the explosion of the individual wealth this new era has created. The fact is that 90 percent of the wealth in America today has been generated since 1980, and more than 70 percent has been generated since 1995.

By the early 1990s, the *Forbes* 400 list began to change appreciably. Yes, names like Rockefeller, Du Pont, and Mellon remained in the top ten. But Wal-Mart founder Sam Walton and his heirs took over the top spot at $25 billion, compared to the $10 billion it took for the Du Pont family to top the list just ten years earlier. Meanwhile, Bill Gates and Warren Buffett climbed into the top ten with relatively "modest" fortunes in the $4–6 billion range. Gates would take over the top spot in 1996, and he remained there until 2008, when Buffett surpassed him.

Since 1980, virtually every category of human endeavor has been transformed, and power has passed from the bankers and the cadres of the corporate executives to the people who conceived and executed on the ideas. Wealth is now just as likely to come from big ideas, and *extensions* of big ideas, crafted in an environment driven by individuals, divorced from the bluster, staffing, and immense cost structure of corporate existence. Whether it was Steve Jobs building small computers in his parents' garage or Bill Gates writing an operating system on punched tape, innovative young people began to create enterprises from scratch. From the early 1980s, the rise of the new entrepreneur, associated venture capital markets, and novel distribution channels remade the industrial and business landscape of America. And the age of entrepreneurial wealth was on.

Consider the story of two young engineers, a story that transformed the nation's view of innovation, personal risk, and capital formation. David Packard and William Hewlett garnered a contract from Disney to build the sound oscillators needed to create sound effects for Disney cartoons and films. They were so clever at creating innovation on demand that their expertise in innovation as a process soon became their point of business distinction. Instead of being rewarded for stability, these two entrepreneurs were rewarded for "nonstandards" of production. Their business grew because of its capacity to respond, adapt, and tailor new solutions to old problems.

Simultaneously, Shockley Labs and the engineers at Stanford University invented the transistor and began to spin out devices that put it to use. Stanford began converting the property it owned to become incubator buildings, and innovators found an invention-friendly environment. This emerging radical business movement found an alternative corporate model that gave birth to the realization that a great idea (given marketing, manufacturing, and unique intellectual property) could readily receive funding from start-up promoters and business.

Examine the list of successful, relatively new companies with similar stories: Google, Dell, Genentech, World Wrestling Entertainment, Whole Foods, Eclipse Aviation, eBay, Microsoft, Yahoo, the University of Phoenix, Humana, Progressive Insurance, WAMU, Adobe, Space Ventures, Aman Hotels, Calloway Golf, DreamWorks, and hundreds of other successful ventures have followed this model. And at the core of every idea, of every successful venture—of every failure, too—lies a single individual with the guts to project him or herself onto risky turf, and to inspire the confidence of people, customers, and investors before the idea had succeeded in the marketplace.

They are the new elite: entrepreneurs with middle-class backgrounds who worked hard for years before achieving sudden wealth, often via initial public offerings (IPOs) or selling their companies. These self-made men and women have little in common with the wealthy from previous eras, and little in common with the stereotypes born of those eras. It is to understanding the new elite that we now turn.

Notes

1. Jeffrey G. Williamson and Peter H. Lindert, *American Inequality* (New York: Academic Press, 1980), p. 286.
2. "Money, Power and Influence," *Forbes Presents: Lives of the Very Wealthy* (2007), p. 6.
3. See "The Roosevelt Week," *Time*, at http://www.time.com/time/

magazine/article/0,9171,743953,00.html   (accessed   April   16,
2008).

4. See http://www.taxfoundation.org/files/federalindividualratehistory
-20080107.xls

5. Claudia Goldin and Robert A. Margo, "The Great Compression:
The U.S. Wage Structure at Mid-Century," *Quarterly Journal of
Economics* 107 (February 1992): 1–34. See http://ideas.repec.org/
p/nbr/nberwo/3817.html (accessed April 16, 2008).

6. Paul Berger, "Heirs, Heirs and More Heirs," *Forbes Presents: Lives
of the Very Wealthy* (2007), p. 79.

7. Jeffery E. Sohl, "The U.S. Angel and Venture Capital Markets:
Recent Trends and Developments," *Journal of Private Equity* 6,
no. 2 (2003): 7–17.

8. "The MoneyTree Report," by PricewaterhouseCoopers and the
Nation Venture Capital Association, based on data from Thomson
Financial.   Available   at   http://www.nvca.org/pdf/07Q4MTRel
EmbargoFINAL.pdf (accessed April 10, 2008).

CHAPTER FOUR

There's a New Sheriff in Town

The Triumph of the Middle Class

"Though i am grateful for the blessings of wealth, it hasn't changed who i am. my feet are still on the ground. I'm just wearing better shoes."

—Oprah Winfrey

CONTRARY TO POPULAR belief, most of the wealthy in America today did not inherit their wealth. In fact, they are undeniable proof that the American dream of unrestricted social mobility in a single lifetime is alive and well. Indeed, we called this epoch the "entrepreneurial era" for good reason. When we asked the wealthy to describe the sources of their wealth, approximately one-third comes from businesses they personally started (see Table 4-1). Another one-third of the money came from having worked on the "front lines" of someone else's business. Typically this means they were there from day one, taking little or no salary in exchange for sweat equity in the company, or joining the company while it was still in an early stage.

Obviously, founding the company is more financially rewarding (assuming, of course, that the business takes off). Among the wealthiest segment—those with over $500,000 in annual discretionary income—35 percent of their money is attributable to companies they founded. Among the "minimally wealthy"—those with $125,000 to

Table 4-1 **Today's sources of wealth (% of assets from each source)**

Sources of wealth	Total	Discretionary income		
		$125K–$249K	$250K–$499K	$500K +
Own business	29	19	**31**	**35**
Someone else's business	36	**50**	33	28
Financial investments	16	14	18	17
Real estate	13	13	13	13
Inheritance	4	3	4	4
Other	2	2	2	2

$249,000—fully half of their money came from working in a business that someone else founded.

Of course, there are other sources of wealth as well. The wealthy attribute over one-fourth of their assets to savvy investing, either in financial markets or in real estate. But for the most part, these types of investments help grow existing wealth rather than create it. Only 3 percent say that over half of their assets came from real estate investments, and a similar number point to financial investments as the majority source of their wealth. And despite the preconceptions of most people, fewer than 5 percent inherited their wealth. The 2 percent who created their wealth by "other" means includes additional high-profile but low-incidence groups that disproportionately shape public opinion about the wealthy, including lottery winners and celebrities who created their wealth from movies, television, and music.

The bottom line is that savings and frugality are great strategies for the average person wishing to achieve financial comfort. But true wealth in today's society almost always comes from entrepreneurial pursuits. One of our respondents summed it up well:

> I think the only way to build wealth is to build equity in something you have part of. I don't think you can work in corporate jobs—the average person will have a great deal of difficulty ever working for a salary and accumulating any wealth. You can do that by investing, investing, and invest-

ing—in yourself and your own projects, building your equity, and then ultimately getting liquidity from that by either selling it or gaining liquidity from your assets.

Just as the entrepreneurship element of the American Dream is thriving, so too is the notion that anyone can achieve wealth regardless of his or her starting point in the social hierarchy, as shown in Figure 4-1. Among today's wealthy, only 1 percent grew up in a gated community, and fewer than 10 percent describe their parents as being affluent or wealthy. Instead, nearly half had a typical suburban upbringing, and significant numbers hailed from big cities and from rural areas. Almost 90 percent grew up in middle-class households, and nearly one in ten had personal stories of rising from poverty to true riches.

In our interviews, some fondly recalled growing up in homes where the front door was never locked, and where kids could safely play in the neighborhood without parental supervision. A typical story goes, "I lived on Elm Street, USA. . . . [Years later] I went back

Figure 4-1 Humble beginnings of the wealthy (% of those surveyed).

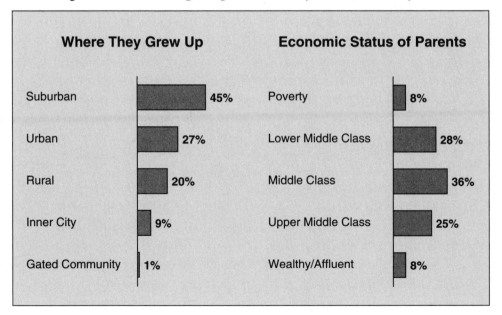

Where They Grew Up		Economic Status of Parents	
Suburban	45%	Poverty	8%
Urban	27%	Lower Middle Class	28%
Rural	20%	Middle Class	36%
Inner City	9%	Upper Middle Class	25%
Gated Community	1%	Wealthy/Affluent	8%

there, and it was like, ooh, the house wasn't as big as I thought, and, ooh, those trees just weren't as large as I thought they were. But, in my mind, they were huge and it was great, and the yard just went forever."

They had paper routes and worked the concession stands at ball games. We asked what they wanted to be when they grew up, and we got the classic litany of middle-American childhood dreams: firefighter, police officer, doctor, cowboy, actor, quarterback for the Minnesota Vikings, pitcher for the New York Yankees, and so on. Few had dreams of fabulous wealth, although they were ambitious in other ways. For example, one aspired to a career in science like his father, telling us, "I thought I could solve a few minor problems like fusion energy and unified field theory."

When we asked how different, or how closely, their life today matched what they imagined it would be, most told us it was 180 degrees from their expectations: "Nowhere near it. I never had that distance. I never thought that far away. I never went to unreachable stars." Even those who aspired to be lawyers and became lawyers, for example, say their lives didn't turn out the way they expected. Entrepreneurship by and large simply wasn't on the cultural radar screen.

The Middle-Class Mind-Set and the Entrepreneurial Path to "Success"

The implications of rising from middle-class backgrounds to wealth through entrepreneurship are profound. This obviously helps explain why today's wealthy feel misunderstood, given public perceptions about who is wealthy and how they got that way. But their middle-class origins also give us tremendous insight into every aspect of their lives, from how they think about themselves to the lifestyles they choose, from their hopes and dreams for their children to the strategies that marketers must adopt to build meaningful connections with them.

The middle-class mind-set, for example, is reflected in the humility with which they talk about their success. Indeed, we started many of our interviews by asking if they considered themselves to be successful. A few definitively said yes, but most hedged; and it was clear that the majority simply didn't resonate to the word *success*. Consider these remarkably humble, and occasionally evasive responses, to the question, "Do you consider yourself a success?":

- "I wouldn't really use that word to describe myself."
- "I've done some successful things."
- "Sort of, I accomplished what I set out to do, I guess, you know? And so lucky."
- "Sort of . . ."
- "Well, I have probably done okay."
- "No. [laughter] I mean, kind of, but. . . . When you look at all the other people that have done big things, like cancer research or AIDS or, you know, really starting new industries— that, to me, is successful. You know, billion-dollar level impact or healthcare impact. I'd say I'm doing okay."
- "I'm financially successful. I mean, I've made more money than I thought I ever might. I have a better family than I ever imagined I'd have. There are some things, personally, I'd like to do differently, that I'm a little hard on myself about. But overall, I'd say that by the normal measurements of a successful person—but there are things that I wish I had done different, or things that I wish I was doing different, today."
- "I mean, in my mind, [success is] a very personal thing. I feel good about what I've been able to do, and contribute to the society, but I don't know whether I'll call myself successful. I never feel successful. You know? I feel good about what I can make a difference in the world. And I never—I don't think I've ever felt successful."

Many would even go on to list remarkable accomplishments, but then conclude by saying that they don't really consider those things as making them successful. Others would question their qualifications for inclusion in our research, telling us, "I'm not in the top one percent, whatever that is." (In fact, they were.)

This humility is not false modesty. It is the combined result of a middle-class upbringing that values modesty while disdaining excessive wealth, and the fact that they largely never set out to be rich or successful. They simply pursued their passions and worked hard. In our interviews, we probed and prodded, giving them "an out" and license to brag a bit by acknowledging, "People are sometimes reluctant or hesitant to talk their special gifts." One particularly insightful respondent chose to talk about her father, an accomplished man in his own right, and took issue with the language we used:

> No, you've got the wrong words. They are not "reluctant," they are not "hesitant to say"—they don't believe, they really truly don't believe. My father absolutely didn't understand what made him so great a man and that's part of the reason he was a great man—because he didn't believe it, he didn't see it. He knew who he was, he knew he was bright and good and competent and all that, and he would often assume that other people operated the way he did and was occasionally disappointed.

The men and women who have built America's technology, software, manufacturing, and services businesses learned their values in middle-class households. Typical of middle-class upbringings in the 1950s, 1960s, and 1970s, their childhoods were infused with the virtue of work, competitive play, school, respect for adults, modesty, independence, and self-determination. These values were prominent when we asked them to set aside any objections they may have to the word *success*, and asked them for the reasons underlying their achievements. Topping the list were middle-class values and the mainstays of entrepreneurial success: hard work, perseverance, treating other people well, and a little luck. They downplayed any extraordinary intelligence, opportunism, networking, or education (see Table 4-2). It also becomes clear why the common perception, among laypeople and marketers, about the dubious ethical nature of wealthy people seems so unfair to them. It's more than just a bad rap; it's a perception that is fundamentally incompatible with their self-concepts and lifelong values.

Table 4-2 **Determination + integrity (+ a little luck) = getting there**

	Wealthy
Keys to Success in Business	
Hard work	32%
Perseverance/dedication	31
Integrity/treating people well	21
Luck	15
Good education	8
Strong social networks	8
Intelligence	5
Drive/ambition	4
Experience	4
Having a plan	3
Common Sense	2

As we have seen, today's wealthy extol the virtues of hard work and dedication, of persistence and of not accepting defeat. Many told tales of seventy- or eighty-hour-plus workweeks. One described returning to work within a few days of having a heart attack. One of our interviews involved a husband-and-wife team who owned a profitable business, and whose definition of "working half-days" meant working twelve hours a day:

Husband: I think a lot of people have a lot more casual and free time than we do. We pretty much work "half-days," twelve hours a day minimum. And about eight days a week. We hardly ever do the 'trip to Bermuda' or . . . I think we went to Mexico once for three days, three years ago.

Wife: And we slept for the first part of it. And then we talked business for the rest of it because we were so refreshed, we had all these ideas.

It is telling that when we asked our respondents for their single favorite word, the responses ran the gamut, including *yes, glorious, savvy, significant, empowering,* and a few we can't print here. But when we asked for their least favorite word, far and away the most common response was *no*, followed by *can't* and *failure*. One described his strongest trait this way: "I rarely take no for an answer because no is the easy way out. Yes is a little bit harder. And I think you can always turn a no into a positive."

Psychological research has shown that hard work and persistence after setbacks are typically found with a constellation of other psychological characteristics, all of which are prevalent among our wealthy respondents:

- *Optimism.* Optimistic people expect positive outcomes and continue to put forth considerable effort, even when initial results are somewhat disappointing. Optimism has been shown to be such a powerful predictor of sales success, for example, that some companies hire only salespeople who score above a certain threshold on tests of optimism.[1]

  Nearly 80 percent of the wealthy describe themselves as extremely or very optimistic about their futures, with virtually all of the rest describing themselves as somewhat optimistic (the main barriers to personal optimism were concerns about their health or their kids). One put it this way, describing the key to his success as "Attitude. Taking everything as being good rather than being bad. I've always been . . . happy and optimistic."

- *A Problem-Solving Approach.* Successful entrepreneurs have been shown to characteristically respond to challenges with problem-solving approaches rather than emotional reactions.[2] The result is less stress and more action. "I'm a solution-oriented person. You give me a problem and I'll tell you how the definition of the solution is contained in the definition of the problem. Then we'll go figure out how to solve it because there's no sense living with a problem. What good does it do to worry about things? Worry doesn't accomplish anything, action does."

- *A Learning Orientation.* Success comes in part from minimizing the inefficiencies of trial-and-error, both through learning from others and from learning from their own experiences of success and failure. "[Success comes from] understanding the good results and the poor results, and the terrible results. Many times . . . you take your successes and you don't look at them, and you dwell on the mistakes. But the better you are able to understand the underlying cause for your success, the more you can latch onto repeatable activities and continue them. So, I think a successful person . . . needs to analyze, every once in a while, both the drivers of success, as well as the drivers for errors."

• *Passion.* At their core, today's financial elite view themselves less as "wealthy" or "successful" and more as people who have worked hard to pursue a passion. They talk at length about the importance of loving their work, about setting personally meaningful goals, and "liking what you do and doing what you like."

"I'm very passionate about putting forth the best for other people. Other people's happiness is as important to me as my own. And when they come to my business, my winery, and they tell me they had just the greatest time—that is the biggest motivator to me. To continue to put forth the effort to make people come out and go 'Wow!'—that's motivating to me. I'm very passionate about that. . . . If I sell crap wine . . . I could be successful and make a lot of money if that's success to you. But, when you make a product from start to finish and grow it and make it and mold it and massage it and kiss it, just do everything you do from start to finish . . . you're giving it your all."

• *Confidence.* Many of our respondents described themselves with terms such as *confident, emotionally strong,* or *willful.* Indeed, 84 percent agree with the statement "I am very good at most everything I do." A few acknowledged that others might consider them arrogant or cocky, and we shall see, the confidence that so often serves them well can lead to trouble when they bring too much of a "do-it-yourself" attitude to complex financial or legal matters.

Regardless, it is clear that confidence and the risk-taking

often associated with it are virtually prerequisites for successful entrepreneurial ventures. It requires an openness to "an alternative career path, . . . willingness to take a risk, willingness to differentiate oneself, willingness to go out on a limb." Although entrepreneurial risk-taking is often analytical and calculated, at some point, one needs to be "willing to bet it all and sleep in the hole."

Beyond determination and its associated cluster of psychological traits, the wealthy attribute much of their success to quality social relationships, and the integrity needed to build and maintain those relationships. Many of the traits the wealthy use to describe themselves reflect both these pro-social values and the implications of them: *loyal, responsible, caring, friendly, communicative, empowering, good-humored, a good listener, fair, respectful*.

Successful entrepreneurs start with a sincere concern for others, and at the risk of using a cliché, they create win-win situations. They share the risks and rewards of their ventures. They are extremely thoughtful about who they hire and how they manage. They often instill a corporate philosophy of putting employees first, with the belief that satisfied employees will then work harder, be more loyal, and extend that sincere concern to clients and customers.

"You've got to like people, and you've got to be interested in them. I made a habit of trying to get to know everybody's names. And as I passed some new young person, I'd say, 'Hi, Joe.' And they'd feel, 'I've been discovered.' They appreciate that. You've got to take care of your people. You've got to be fair with them. [He went on to describe the original founder of the company.] When the company was very small, before they had HR and Employee Assistance Programs, everyone said, 'If you had a problem, the founder was interested.' If you needed a house, he'd go out and help you find one, and help you with the rent, maybe. If you had a sick child, well, he was there to help pay the hospital bills, and so on and so forth. And he really cared. You've got to care for them."

"We surround ourselves with people that are at the same caliber but their position is different. There is no sense in having six quarterbacks on the team. So, let's get the best lineman."

"I tell people what I think and I don't pull punches. I don't go back on my word. I deliver what I say I'm going to or I acknowledge that I was unable to. . . ."

"If you're frivolous with people, you're going to dry up pretty damned quickly, no matter how much money you have. Or you'll be really, really lonely."

"We always would say 'our own people.' Because if we take care of our own people, they'll take care of our clients."

"Getting everybody kind of pulling in the same direction. Team management, motivation, hiring . . . trying to get people that are highly motivated and interested in the chase."

Luck as Necessary but Not Sufficient for Wealth

The wealthy also attribute much of their success to luck. This might seem an odd conclusion for self-made individuals to reach, particularly given the obvious importance they place on hard work and determination. But successful entrepreneurs recognize that unpredictable factors play a role in the success or failure of their endeavors: a chance meeting that evolves into a crucial client relationship, a misstep by a competitor, a technological breakthrough that would have radically different impacts if it occurred six weeks later, or six weeks earlier.

Often, they learn the importance of luck firsthand when they try to repeat initial successes. Consider the story of one successful entrepreneur, who was the son of refugees who lost their homes during the India-Pakistan partition of 1947. After college in the United States, he went to work for a large aerospace company as an engineer. A few years after climbing up the corporate ladder, he was asked to head a task force bidding on a multibillion dollar government contract. He and his team burned the midnight oil for months, and submitted what would eventually become the winning bid. What was the reward for his exhausting role in boosting company revenue by several billion? He and each member of his team got a plaque and a check for $250.

The team members looked at one another, and concluded they needed to chart a different path in life. They started their own company, quietly renting an office next to their current employer, and they operated in stealth mode while maintaining their day jobs. They developed new technologies for Internet routers and servers, and their timing couldn't have been better—it was the early 1990s, the Internet was just taking off, and soon their growing business allowed them to leave the security of their day jobs. Within a few years, they were able to sell the company to a large technology provider for over $70 million, mostly in stock options that proceeded to multiply in value many times over the ensuing years.

For a time, the team members each went their separate ways, enjoying their wealth and pursuing new passions. Some got married. One became a professional gambler and a minor celebrity as a poker analyst on television. But within a few years, they got bored and decided to regroup for another shot at entrepreneurial success. This time, they were seasoned, they had more money to work with, could hire bigger teams, and had even better ideas for new products and services. The market for back-end Internet equipment and services couldn't have been hotter when the new company launched in 2000, but within a year the "perfect storm" of devastating business conditions had taken hold.

The company limped along for a few more years before they were forced to sell their new technology for virtually nothing. Personally they remained wealthy, but they lost virtually everything they had invested in the new venture. Call it luck, timing, chance—the label doesn't matter. The same team, the same hard work, and the same risk-taking that created so much wealth from their first venture were clearly necessary, but not sufficient, conditions for success. Factors outside of their control ultimately determined success or failure.

In recent years, there has been a growing scientific interest in the concept of luck, spearheaded by Dr. Richard Wiseman, a psychologist at the University of Hertfordshire.[3] Dr. Wiseman has recruited hundreds of participants for his research, and they are bound by the commonality that all feel luck has played an important role in their lives. Some consider themselves particularly lucky, whereas others consider themselves particularly unlucky, and those two groups exhibit a consistent pattern of differences.

Lucky people exhibit a characteristic open-mindedness, allowing them to spot opportunities in otherwise chance occurrences. They introduce variety and change into their lives, bringing them in contact with new environments, new people, and new sources of information. They exhibit a stronger sense of creativity. They take chances, and listen to their intuition. They rebound from setbacks, imaging how things might go differently in the future "with just a bit more luck."

Considering oneself to be lucky, in other words, correlates with optimism, risk-taking, confidence, an action-orientation, and many of the other characteristics of the wealthy we have already described. Unlucky people, in contrast, have been shown to be more tense and anxious, creating a broader sense of passivity and risk-aversion, lessening their opportunities to expose themselves to new situations that might give rise to positive interactions or outcomes. As it turns out, Louis Pasteur was right when he said, "Chance favors only the mind that is prepared," as was F. L. Emerson when he said, "I'm a great believer in luck. The harder I work, the more of it I seem to have." The wealthy are luckier, but for the most part, they have created their own luck and they work to increase the number of opportunities they have to benefit from good luck.

The Challenges of the Entrepreneurial Life

The entrepreneurial path, like all life choices, is fraught with trade-offs. It can be personally and financially fulfilling. (Entrepreneurial efforts can also be financially ruinous when they are unsuccessful, as the wealthy know firsthand—over one-fourth have almost "lost it all" financially at some point in their lives.) When a company is successful, the entrepreneurial lifestyle can be all-consuming, and it frequently involves a blurring of personal and professional, of home and business. When we asked about the keys to their personal success compared to their business success compared to their family success, they often found themselves offering the same answers. One woman told us that her business success was due to "hard work," and when asked what enabled her family success, she said with a laugh, "harder work." But at a more fundamental level, they do not make distinctions among their business, family, and personal lives.

> "The key to success in life? [laughter] A happy family life, a positive business life, and being able in your business to provide a service or product for your customers. And then being happy with the service that you provide for them."

> "How would I define success? I'm doing what I want to do in life. It's not monetary. It's not family. It's not work. It's all of the above."

> "[Success in our family life is about] sharing passion. Certainly, that's a big thing for us. Because we are both so committed to [our business], it would be very separating if only one of us was involved in that."

Family is vitally important to the wealthy, and although money may create more time to spend with family after they cash out, the wealthy struggle with issues of balance much like their middle-class brethren. Nearly 90 percent are married or living with a partner, and 60 percent remain married to their first spouse. Only 10 percent have a prenuptial agreement. Three-fourths are parents, and about half have a child under eighteen, a figure that is rising as the average age of the wealthy falls. Although they consistently cite family as the most rewarding aspect of their life, they admit that they split their time equally between family and work (see Table 4-3). And although they have arrived at a comfortable station, the life of the rising entrepreneur and CEO is not an easy one—it takes long hours and consistent sacrifices. Forty-three percent of the wealthy agree that "my

Table 4-3 **Top 3 activities of the wealthy**

Rewarding Aspects of Life*		Areas Focus Time On*	
Family/spouse	47	Family	57
Children/grandchildren	30	Work	54
Work	13	Leisure (non-travel)	39

*Percent of respondents citing each activity as rewarding or as a focus of considerable time in response to open-ended questions.

dedication to business pursuits has come at the expense of my family life," in contrast to just 28 percent of those with income of $75,000 or more.

> My New Year's resolution was to play golf more. I have yet to play. I need to definitely, as many successful entrepreneurs do, stop and smell the roses. And not take it all so personally and work so hard to achieve what you might or might not consider success, but again to do a little bit more of the quality life with my own family. Because I've laid it out on the line, so to speak, and just killing myself in between what little vacations I do take.

Self-Concepts Frozen in Time

As we have seen, despite their tremendous financial achievement, many of today's wealthy struggle to consider themselves "successful," long after they have achieved tremendously by any objective measure. It is almost as if their accomplishments have "snuck up on them." As one president of a large company told us, "I never had to take shortcuts. I never even knew how. I concentrated on being the best. Hell, I didn't even know I had a career until I was running this place."

This aura of unexpected and silent achievement applies to their wealth as well. Most don't "feel wealthy," particularly the 60 percent who have been wealthy for fewer than ten years. Of course they know, intellectually, the status of their bank account. But emotionally, and in terms of their identity and self-concept, it hasn't yet sunk in. Today's wealthy grew up with many of the same misconceptions that we all have about the wealthy, and it takes years for them to realize that their metaphorical ship has come in.

It is almost as if their self-concepts are frozen in their middle-class upbringings, largely untouched by the metamorphosis of their financial situation. This is particularly true because, as we'll see in Chapter 7, many toiled in their businesses for years, earning comfortable salaries, but then wealth struck with suddenness in the form of an IPO or in selling their business. Again, on the whole, today's wealthy tend to think of themselves less as rich and more as people who came from modest means, worked hard, pursued their passions, and achieved some success with the help of luck and good timing.

The middle-class mind-set is pervasive in the attitudes and lifestyles of the wealthy. In Figure 4-2, we highlight some of the grounded values of the wealthy relative to a random sample of households with a total income of a mere $75,000 annually. (Once a common marketing definition of affluent, this income marker now

Figure 4-2 Grounded values of general population and the wealthy (% of those surveyed).

% Agree/Strongly Agree	Gen Pop of $75K+ Household Income %	Wealthy Families %
Confident Conservative		
I am very conservative about how I choose to spend my money	76%	75%
I feel like I deserve every penny that I have	89%	75%
Middle-Class Mentality		
I would still describe myself as middle class at heart	94%	81%
Although I know I have a lot of money, I don't always feel that way	NA	81%
I strongly encourage(d) my children to get a job during their high school years	81%	81%
Money Isn't Everything		
I consider myself a person with simple needs	83%	71%
Luxury items like expensive watches, jewelry, and cars are a waste of money	62%	48%
Money is not important to me	32%	20%
I do not care what others think of me. I judge myself by my own standards	83%	70%
I want people to know I am wealthy	NA	11%

describes a group that is nearly one-third of the U.S. population.) In many respects, the wealthy have similar attitudes to this much broader group—where there are differences, they are modest but telling.

Three-fourths of the wealthy describe themselves as "very conservative" about how they spend their money. And though certainly "very conservative" has something of a different meaning for them, the sentiment does not. Thirty-seven percent of the wealthy are concerned about running out of money, a figure that rises to about 50 percent when we look at the newly wealthy or those who are merely affluent. Remarkably, despite $5 million in liquid assets and $500,000 annually in "spreading around" money, four in five agree that, "I would still describe myself as middle class at heart," and most say that their personality is more middle class than upper class. Forty-seven percent agree that "I don't feel affluent or wealthy." Seven in ten describe themselves as people with "simple needs," and even more want their kids to get jobs during high school. Although as many as 40 percent don't feel wealthy because they still can't buy what they want, the middle-class mind-set derives much more from their upbringing than from the status of their bank account.

Stealth Wealth

Perhaps the single most defining lifestyle element of today's wealthy also derives from their middle-class mind-set: stealth wealth. Eighty-nine percent agree, "I believe in 'stealth wealth'—having money, but keeping it under the radar."

Our conclusion about the prevalence of stealth wealth is very much at odds with public perceptions, and one could argue that these self-reported survey results are simply posturing and false modesty. But in our experience, stealth wealth is far more common than is conspicuous consumption. By definition, conspicuous consumption gets much more, and more exciting, press. Robin Leach's *Lifestyles of the Rich and Famous* had a ten-year run of solid ratings, encouraging us all to aspire to "champagne wishes and caviar dreams." *Lifestyles* went off the air in 1995, but MTV's *Cribs* picked up the baton for a new, more brand-focused generation. (Champagne wishes? Please. For the *Cribs* crowd, it's Cristal or nothing.) These shows only attract viewers to the extent they feature the extreme and the unusual. In a sense, they are popular only because they feature what is unrepresentative.

It's not just entertainment television that perpetuates the stereotype of conspicuous consumption; well-meaning and otherwise savvy journalists in all media play a role because they so often use anecdotal approaches to gathering information for their stories. For example, a journalist writing a story about the wealthy may decide to attend a yacht show in order to meet the wealthy, up close and personal. Once there, he or she will naturally gravitate away from the "mainstream" yachts toward the biggest, the most expensive, the most high-tech, the gaudiest, and so on. The reporter will gravitate away from the "typical" yacht purchaser to the more flamboyant, to those with multiple yachts, to those who buy huge yachts on impulse, and so on.

In each case, the journalist's attention is driven away from the typical and toward the exotic. The exotic, after all, generates the attention-grabbing headlines that sell newspapers and boost television ratings. As *New York Sun* editor John B. Bogart put it long ago, "When a dog bites a man, that is not news, because it happens so often. But if a man bites a dog, that is news." "HAPPILY MARRIED MAN BUILDS A SUCCESSFUL BUSINESS AND LIVES A QUIET, HAPPY LIFE" isn't necessarily news. "RICH GUY WITH MANY GIRLFRIENDS BUYS HUGE YACHT FEATURING BUILT-IN STRIPPER POLE"—now that's something the media can work with.

Certainly there are interesting stories about yachts to be told. There is something of an arms race to build the world's biggest yacht; Russian billionaire Roman Abramovich hopes to win by keeping the length of his under-construction boat a secret, so that someone doesn't intentionally beat him by a single foot. (His vessel is reputed to have a private submarine and two helipads; after all, if you only have one, you might not win the race.) Some yachts do actually come with stripper poles. Others are too big to be moored in traditional marinas and have to "park" among rusting freight ships. Interesting stories? Yes. Representative of the interests and challenges of most wealthy people? No.

Consider a statistic recently played up by the press as an indicator of conspicuous consumption: the fact that orders for yachts over 150 feet have doubled over the past ten years. This tidbit certainly makes it sound like "everyone's doing it." But in fact, that translates to only 200 yachts of that size per year. What about the other 1 million wealthy and 6 million affluent households in the United States alone? A mere 4 percent of wealthy Americans own a yacht, and only 2 percent describe themselves as yachting or boating aficionados. Less than one in five own any kind of boat at all. Certainly that's higher than the U.S. population as a whole, but a yachting obsession is hardly epidemic.

In virtually any category, from cars to houses to jewelry, there are a handful of well-to-do people with an intense passion that relates to intense spending, and in turn, intense media interest. Sometimes this extravagance and media interest serve their own purposes; today's royalty of rock stars and athletes can earn much more in endorsement deals, for example, when they generate their own publicity and become synonymous with opulence. But the resulting media attention creates unrepresentative perceptions about the wealthy. Recall that Leach's show was *Lifestyles of the Rich and Famous*. Simply put, the famous have an agenda that most of the rich don't have or want.

Several cognitive biases and logical errors combine to shape misperceptions of wealth. In reporting on the wealthy, media members are often guilty of what those in the philosophy of science call the drunkard's search—the tendency of people to study phenomena that are easy to see and report on instances that are easy to locate (e.g., someone who has had too much to drink searching for his lost keys under a lamppost, where the light is good, rather than where the person is most likely to have lost the keys). Astronomers, for example, tend to study bright shiny objects such as stars and supernovas because they are easy to see, as opposed to the dark matter or dark energy that many believe actually constitutes over 95 percent of the universe.

Living large is, by definition, an easier phenomenon to uncover than steal wealth. Media reports shape thinking in part through the vividness effect: the tendency of graphic or dramatic depictions of an event to lead people to overestimate how common that event is. Airplane crashes are much less common, and cause many fewer deaths, than car crashes, but the vividness with which airplane crashes are portrayed lead many to falsely believe that air travel is more dangerous than car travel. Vivid depictions of conspicuous consumption have the same effect. The result is a subtle but dramatically wrong leap in logic, as "one must be rich to buy a Porsche" (for example) implicitly becomes "All rich people buy Porsches." This is sometimes called the spotlight fallacy—the tendency to assume that members of group X in the media spotlight are representative of all members of group X.

Stealth wealth, as a television show, would get lousy ratings, but it isn't an artifact of the spotlight fallacy, and it is a very representative description of wealthy lifestyles. It's not just something to which 80+ percent of them pay lip service. Staying below the radar is evident in their clothes, their homes, and their everyday lives. Over half agree, "I still haven't furnished my house in a way that reflects my economic status." Their expensive jewelry spends far more time in the safe than adorning their bodies. Forget high fashion; you are far more likely to encounter the wealthy wearing khakis and a button-down shirt, or a tennis shirt and jeans (no wonder one-third sometimes feel that the salespeople in upscale stores look down on them).

When the wealthy showed us around their homes, we often saw what we described as "theatrical closets." Their clothes are organized around their degree of sartorial conspicuousness, and the types of people around whom they will be worn. There are gala clothes, country club clothes, going-to-the-market clothes, and so on. The wealthy are adept at blending into different social environments, allowing them to come across as a regular Joe or Joanne in each context. Wealth, for all its benefits, has cost them childhood friends and makes them potential targets (for marketers and ne'er-do-wells alike).

Dressing down is one element of stealth wealth; private indulgences are another. The wealthy do indulge—both monetarily and otherwise—but it is typically done privately or in environments where they know they will be surrounded by people of similar financial means. Many have "gala clothes"—designer fashions and high-end couture—but wear them at charity and other social events where these clothes won't mark them as out-of-the-ordinary. Some are passionate about wine and have extensive cellars, but are likely to serve the best wines to their friends at home during private dinners. It is less about serving expensive wine as a public display of wealth, and more about using a high-quality wine as a part of a broader experience that privately expresses appreciation and love for their friends. Similarly, many high-end brands don't look spectacular when viewed from the outside, but offer exquisite phenomenological experiences. Most would not describe Audi automobiles as dazzling or showy in external appearance, but they offer a tremendous experience to drivers and passengers. Luxury brands, and wealth in general, are experiences best savored from the inside out.

Certainly conspicuous consumption does exist among the wealthy, but it tends to happen when they are gathered together behind closed doors and gated walls. And as we'll see in Chapter 7, it tends to be more of a temporary, transitional state. The newly wealthy avoid attracting attention to themselves, while those who have been wealthy for a long time have achieved their own comfort level, with little need to compare themselves outwardly to others. In between is a more insecure state, when the wealthy stop comparing themselves to their humble beginnings and start comparing themselves to the long-term wealthy. Shifting from downward comparison to upward comparison triggers an insecurity that often drives a period that might be called conspicuous consumption.

Middle-Class Demographics and Lifestyles

The middle-class roots of today's wealthy are reflected not only in their values and their mind-sets but also in their demographics and lifestyles. Their average age is forty-seven (and getting younger). Approximately 60 percent are baby boomers and nearly one-third are GenXers. They can be found in every state, but are more heavily concentrated in business hubs: Nearly 20 percent live in the New York/

New Jersey/Connecticut corridor and another 17 percent live in California, leaving about two-thirds dispersed throughout the country.

Nine in ten are college graduates, and they are roughly split between those who attended private colleges and those who attended public ones. Only about one in four attended an Ivy League or similarly elite school, which is certainly higher than the population as a whole, but far short of a defining characteristic or requirement for entry into the elite. Approximately 60 percent of their kids are in public schools, and only 4 percent attend boarding school.

Eighty-six percent are Caucasian, down slightly from just a few years ago; this figure represents less diversity than the general U.S. population today, but is generally reflective of the U.S. middle class forty years ago. Still, there are signs of a growing diversity and inclusiveness in today's entrepreneurial era that were not present in previous eras. For example, Asians (defined broadly to include those from the Indian subcontinent) constitute approximately 8 percent and rising of the wealthy population, compared to approximately 3 percent of the U.S. population as a whole.

Even more dramatic is a growing gender diversity. Whereas wealthy industrialists were almost exclusively male (and the corporate era of wealth was when the phrase "glass ceiling" entered the lexicon), the role of women today among the financial elite is radically different. Although still far short of a 50/50 gender split, a growing number of women entrepreneurs and executives created the wealth in their households; and even among those in which women weren't the primary breadwinners, they have come to hold considerable sway over every aspect of family and financial life.

When it comes to leisure activities, the wealthy generally maintain their middle-class interests, but they find themselves with more time and money to indulge in them (see Table 4-4). Eating out, shopping, movies, and other mall-based, middle-class mainstays remain popular. The wealthy are somewhat, but not dramatically, more likely to engage in what one might think of as "upper-class" activities such as skiing, boating, and working out with a personal trainer. One in four wealthy people play golf, but not particularly well—their average handicap is 18.

The biggest "leisure gaps" between the rich and the rest of the

Table 4-4 **Top leisure activities done on a regular basis**

	Wealthy	General U.S. Population
Go out to eat	80	61
Send/receive personal (nonbusiness) e-mails*	65	—
Exercise	60	38
Go shopping*	48	—
Go to movies	48	35
Go to theater/shows/ballet/opera	46	14
Drink alcoholic beverages	45	37
Entertain*	45	—
Go to museums and art exhibitions*	39	—
Cook new or gourmet dishes for fun*	36	—
Go to live sporting events	36	15
Volunteer	35	20
Attend religious services	31	29
Attend charity events	31	9
Take naps	28	39
Get massages/Reiki	25	6
Play golf	23	8
Run/jog	21	11
Ski	21	3
Boating/sailing	17	7
Yoga/Pilates	15	5
Tennis	14	5
Go to a personal trainer	14	2
Play an instrument	9	11

*Not asked in our general population survey.

population are seen in attending live performances such as theater or sporting events. As a general rule, wealth encourages people to do more of whatever they had done before. Higher-end interests don't replace preexisting habits—they get added on top. A junk-food junkie who becomes wealthy tends to become a junk-food junkie who also occasionally eats at Le Cirque; a Costco enthusiast whose business goes public tends to become a Costco enthusiast who occasionally carries a Prada bag.

There are some exceptions. Attendance at religious services changes little with asset growth. And although the wealthy exercise significantly more, they nap less than the rest of us (they also smoke less—only 7 percent smoke, compared to one-fourth of the general U.S. population, with by far the favorite brand among the wealthy being the decidedly mainstream Marlboro).

A similar pattern emerges in terms of what people feel is missing, and what they would like more of, in their lives. The wealthy generally aspire to the same things as everyone else, but not quite to the same degree. Not surprisingly, the wealthy are most likely to say they want more time, whereas the general population is most likely to express a desire for more money. And both groups are equally likely to want a better body, more patience, and greater fun. But throughout most of the list shown in Table 4-5, the rank order of items is similar, while the wealthy are less likely to have various needs, from security and education to friends and happiness.

The wealthy report watching an average of ten hours of television per week—far less than the typical American, but in other respects their media consumption habits are comparable. Nearly 60 percent have a digital video recorder such as TiVo, and among them, most watch at least half of their television on a recorded (not live) basis, skipping the bulk of the commercials. They spend more than five hours a week reading newspapers or magazines (three-fourths of that time is spent with the print, as opposed to online, versions), with higher-than-average readership of the *Wall Street Journal* and the *New York Times*.

Still, as Table 4-6 shows, they are just as likely to read *People* or *Sports Illustrated* as they are to read *Time* or *Business Week*. Although most read some kind of luxury lifestyle magazine (such as *Travel + Leisure*), readership drops to less than 5 percent for highly specific publications (such as *Cigar Aficionado* or *Yachting*). They spend an average of ten hours surfing the Internet each week, not including e-mail or instant messaging, and as we'll see in the following chapter, the Internet has fundamentally changed their approach to managing and spending money.

Table 4-5 **Top 20 items people wish they had more of (% of those surveyed)**

	Wealthy	General U.S. Population
Time	61	50
A better body	51	52
Patience	40	43
More/better sex*	34	—
Fun	32	39
Money	27	71
Happiness	25	42
Friends	24	38
Intelligence	20	36
Answers/direction for living life	20	32
Freedom	19	23
Security	18	43
Better looks	18	27
Education	17	41
Sense of style	13	12
Respect	12	26
A spouse or partner	11	22
Trendy clothes	7	11
Common sense	7	15
Responsibility	4	9

*Not asked in our general population survey.

A Lot of Money May Buy a Little Extra Happiness

If you ask a random sample of Americans what would make them happier, by far the most common response is more money. But psychologists and other social scientists have tested this intuitive hypothesis many times, and they have typically come to the conclusion that the relationship between money and happiness is much weaker than one might expect. The most common conclusion has been that, beyond a subsistence income, money and happiness are essentially uncorrelated.

Table 4-6 **Top 10 media read or watched by the wealthy (% of those surveyed)***

Read Regularly		Watch Every Week	
Wall Street Journal	29	24-hour news channels	53
New York Times	26	Sports events (football, baseball, etc.)	45
Condé Nast Traveler	22	Comedy/sitcoms	40
Forbes	19	Local news	39
Travel + Leisure	19	Drama/suspense	37
Newsweek	17	History	30
Business Week	16	Documentaries	29
Time	14	Movies and "made for TV" movies	29
People	13	Financial or business news	28
Sports Illustrated	12	Morning news shows	27

*Items within the 5 percentage point margin of error are not significantly different from one another.

Certainly, not being able to pay bills and meet certain basic needs leads to significant unhappiness, but after that, it has generally been thought that more money doesn't make one happier. Lottery winners, for example, feel a brief surge of happiness after their big win, but generally return to their baseline levels of happiness within one year.[4] Globally, people in countries with extreme poverty are less happy than those in more developed countries, but wealthiest countries are not consistently the happiest.

This conclusion that the happiness-inducing effect of money reaches a quick ceiling has been reached by many studies, but is intuitively difficult for many people to accept. The problem with most of these studies is that they typically didn't include the truly wealthy. Most studies using representative samples in the United States today would struggle to get a readable base size of those with over $100,000 in total annual household income, falling far short of what would be considered affluence or wealth today. Our research, and a small body of academic research, suggests that a lot of money does indeed have the potential to make one a little happier.

For example, in our research, 93 percent of the wealthy describe themselves as "very happy," compared to 87 percent of those with household incomes of over $75,000, a slight but statistically significant difference. Two-thirds agree that "as I have accumulated more, I have become happier," and 59 percent agree that "they say money doesn't buy happiness, but I think it comes close." An academic study conducted in the mid-1980s found that members of the *Forbes* 400 described themselves as being happy 77 percent of the time, in contrast to happiness 62 percent of the time among a comparison group.[5]

Perhaps most compelling has been the research of Andrew Oswald and Jonathan Gardner at the University of Wales, who followed 9,000 people throughout the economic ups and downs of their lives. Their conclusion was that it would take roughly $1.5 million to make a very unhappy person become very happy, but even then, how lasting that happiness would be remains an open question.[6] Moreover, most of the wealthy in their research achieved their money from inheritances and lottery winnings, whereas other research suggests that achieving it on your own through entrepreneurship is likely to be more emotionally satisfying.

Taken as a whole, the research suggests that considerable sums of money do have the potential to make one happier, under two conditions. First, you have to use it wisely. Cornell's Robert Frank, a pioneer in the new field of happiness economics, reviewed the research and concluded: "Considerable evidence suggests that if we use an increase in our incomes, as many of us do, simply to buy bigger houses and more expensive cars, then we do not end up any happier than before. But if we use an increase in our incomes to buy more of certain inconspicuous goods—such as freedom from a long commute or a stressful job—then the evidence paints a very different picture."[7]

When we ask the wealthy about the best aspects of having money, the results suggest they are intuitively taking Dr. Frank's advice. Virtually none mentioned high-priced toys or the ability to buy more things. Instead, far and away the most common responses focused on freedom, self-determination, and controlling their own destinies. In short, money has given them the freedom to do what they want, when they want, where they want, how they want. Some specifically mentioned stealth wealth and the anonymity of their lives as fostering this freedom, saying they would struggle with the demands of a more public life. Many point to the freeing effect of money as strengthening a sense of control they already had. For example:

> I don't view myself any different. I don't think that makes a difference. What does make a difference is I have a greater scope of what I want to do and do. And I can do it. I don't have the restrictions. I don't think in the words of "I can't do this, and I can't"—I always had that control as part of my thinking. I still have a value system.

Conversely, the wealthy also appear adept at using money, not just to foster happiness but also to mitigate and manage unhappiness. Indeed, when we asked about the worst aspects of wealth, many struggled for an answer. One laughingly told us it was her golf game. Some mentioned fending off requests for money, but most mentioned simply mundane tasks, the daily routine, or travel (for business or charity commitments, etc.). Our study and others suggest that the biggest emotional differences between the wealthy and everyone else is not so much the frequency or intensity of positive emotions, but rather that the wealthy are able to manage their lives such that they are less likely to experience negative emotions. (A quip generally attributed to Irish comedian Terence Alan "Spike" Milligan sums it up well: "Money can't buy you happiness, but it does afford a more pleasant form of misery.") Similarly, when asked what else they'd like to be doing with their time, many struggled for an answer. This interaction was typical:

> **Q:** Describe three things in your life today where you would like to focus more time.
>
> **A:** That's tough, because I'm spending my time just where I want to spend it. Well, I guess I'd like to spend more time with my grandchildren. I would like to spend more time with my kids too, but my grandchildren first. Three, what else would I like to spend more time doing?

Q: Yes. You don't have to have three.

A: I can't think of three.

Using money wisely is the first key to transforming more money into more happiness; the second is ensuring that money is the result of pursuing one's passion, not an end in itself. Research has shown that people who aspire to wealth and material possessions at the expense of other goals tend to be less happy and less satisfied with life, while suffering more depression and anxiety.[8] In contrast, as we have seen, the wealthy followed paths that interested them, and financial success came along for the ride.

> "To me money is the by-product of professional activity—the passion, the enthusiasm and the knowledge of your subject are the elements that will cause success. The goal has never been about making money. The goal has been about learning, about adventure, about having fun, about sharing."

> "I didn't care to get to the top. I never tried to get to the top, I tried to do a good job and they put me there in spite of it or because of it."

Despite high levels of personal happiness, the wealthy have certainly not been immune to the "emotional recession" that took hold as the Iraq war dragged on and the economy slowed down. As of April 2008, only 23 percent were optimistic about the future of America, down dramatically from 60 percent in 2004. Only 18 percent were optimistic about the future of the world amid geopolitical unrest, global warming, and so on. Still, they are able to manage these stressors and keep them from bringing down their overall emotional well-being. There are, of course, other barriers to happiness, but most of the wealthy appear to have been relatively adept at navigating them.

- *Guilt?* Any guilt over their standing has been assuaged; only one-fourth even feel any occasional guilt about having "more then their fair share of money." They feel they have worked hard to earn it, and that it does not come at the expense of others.

- *Isolation?* Only 28 percent feel that having money can be isolating. (Still, as we'll address in Chapter 7, the newly wealthy often feel isolated, and two-thirds of the wealthy in general would like to connect more with people. Money itself is not isolating, but the change in social circumstances can be until they learn to navigate it.)

- *Complexity?* Less than four in ten agree, "I have too much stuff and would like to simplify" or "the more money I have, the more complicated my life becomes."

- *Ostracism?* Only one-third "fear that I may be judged overindulgent in the things I own and the way that I live."

On the whole, the wealthy are appreciative of what money has done for them. But rather than thinking that wealth makes them happy, they describe themselves as both happy and rich, recognizing that money makes life easier. Their sense of satisfaction comes from their sense of achievement and successful pursuit of a business idea. Money came with this success, but was not their original objective. As one of our respondents put it:

> We worked real hard to build this company, my wife and family and myself. We looked around one day, and my business gave us a lot of things we never dreamed of. But it was the work, and what we were able to do for our customers and the people in this town that made us happy. I guess I can't say that I'd be happy if we were poor, but I don't want anyone to think being able to buy what we want makes us happy . . . being able to do what we want makes us happy.

Summing Up the Myths and Realities of Today's Wealthy

As we have seen, the wealthy are different from many public perceptions of them (see Table 4-7). Whether it is their modesty, the entre-

Table 4-7 **Myths and realities regarding today's wealthy**

Perception	Reality
Conspicuous consumption	Stealth wealth
Social expression	Self-expression
Focused on my brands	Focused on my lifestyle
Trophy wife	First wife
Ivy League	State university
Old patriarchs	Middle-aged families
Lifelong pursuit of wealth	Wealth a by-product of pursuing passions

preneurial source of their wealth, or their focus on pursuing passions instead of money per se, their middle-class values shape every aspect of their lives. But there is an even more defining aspect of today's wealthy, one equally fraught with myths and misperceptions. Simply put, and without irony, we must point out that wealthy people have tremendous amounts of money. We now turn to a deeper understanding of the true role that money plays in their lives.

Notes

1. Martin Seligman, *Learned Optimism* (New York: Pocket Books, 1990).
2. For example, Carl R. Anderson, "Locus of Control, Coping Behaviors, and Performance in a Stress Setting: A Longitudinal Study," *Journal of Applied Psychology* 62 (1977): 446–451.
3. Richard Wiseman, *The Luck Factor* (New York: Hyperion, 2003).
4. Philip Brickman, Dan Coates, and Ronnie Janoff-Bulman, "Lottery Winners and Accident Victims: Is Happiness Relative?" *Journal of Personality and Social Psychology* 36 (1978): 917–927.
5. Edward Diener, Jeff Horzwitz, and Robert Emmons, "Happiness of the Very Wealthy", *Social Indicators Research* 16 (1985): 263–274.
6. Jonathan Gardner and Andrew Oswald, "Does Money Buy Happiness? A Longitudinal Study Using Data on Windfalls." Presented at the Royal Economic Society Annual Conference 2002.

7. Quoted in Steve Maich, "Money Really Can Buy Happiness, Study Shows," *Maclean's*, February 13, 2006. Available at http://www.thecanadianencyclopedia.com/index.cfm?PgNm = TCE&Params = M1A RTM001 2910 (accessed April 11, 2008).
8. Tim Kasser and Richard M. Ryan, "A Dark Side of the American Dream: Correlates of Financial Success as a Central Life Aspiration," *Journal of Personality and Social Psychology* 65 (1993): 410–422.

CHAPTER FIVE

Money Matters

The Myths and Realities of the Wealthy and Their Money

"Let me tell you about the very rich.
They are different from you and me."

—F. Scott Fitzgerald

"Yes, they have more money."

—Ernest Hemingway

ON THE WHOLE, we have to agree with Hemingway. The wealthy are not terribly different from the rest of us in terms of their attitudes, their values, and even in many aspects of their day-to-day lifestyles. But they are radically different from the average American in terms of how much money they have, and in turn, how much they spend. We have seen the public and professional misperceptions about the genesis of wealth and the mind-sets of the wealthy. These, in turn, have led to many myths about how and why the wealthy spend their money.

Myths and Realities of Spending Among the Wealthy

Myth: The wealthy spend freely and take their money for granted. *Reality*: Money matters. For the wealthy, making and spending money is serious business. Very serious. Nearly three-fourths come right out and say, "Money is very important to me." Some of this attitude is simply an extension of the middle-class mind-set. But much of this attitude is rooted in hard financial realities.

The wealthy worked hard for their money, and they easily recall the day-to-day struggles they faced before financial comfort arrived. Indeed, those days weren't all that long ago. Over half have had their wealth ten years or less; 78 percent have had it less than twenty years. Only one in ten say they've been financially comfortable all their lives. More than one-third still worry they could run out of money (rising to more than 50 percent of the affluent). Some have truly ridden a financial roller-coaster, and one-fourth suffered "significant personal financial setbacks in my life, to the extent I almost lost it all." One in five reports that spending, credit card use, and debt are sources of friction in their household.

Myth: The wealthy let accountants and lawyers handle all of their money issues. *Reality*: The wealthy are very "hands-on" in managing their wealth, perhaps too much so. A do-it-yourself ethic is characteristic of many entrepreneurs, and it generally serves them well, in business and in life. But in many respects, wealth brings with it new challenges, new complexities, and new risks, and the do-it-yourself approach that has served them well often becomes a disservice.

Four in ten acknowledge that they are not as on top of their finances as they should be. In fact, about half get no professional wealth management advice, relying only on themselves, friends, spouses, and other relatives. This causes problems in areas as basic as estate planning. Over a quarter don't have an updated will, and they question whether there will be a smooth transition after their death. Nearly one in five expects serious conflict among their relatives after their passing. And consider risk management. Three-fourths know that there are property insurance companies that specialize in the challenges faced by wealthy households. Yet only one-fourth have made a conscious decision to change to an insurance provider with appropriate expertise.

Their relative lack of reliance on professional advice is very much a reflection of the self-reliant and "in me I trust" mind-set of successful entrepreneurs. Moreover, it reflects a considerable lack of trust that has been honed and reinforced for years. In their businesses, they get a steady supply of slick sales pitches from potential partners, vendors, and consultants, and they have learned firsthand that few of these "experts" turn out to be the real deal. With sudden wealth comes a new and steady supply of sales pitches in their personal lives.

For providers of financial services, the result is that it is remarkably difficult to get the attention of wealthy individuals, and once one has their attention, it is even more difficult to gain their trust. The effectiveness of various attention-getting and trust-building strategies differs widely across individuals. For example, one respondent who had remained highly loyal to his financial adviser told us the reason was, "They're strong on the relationship side. They know they need to connect. You want to make me happy? You make me happy through my kids. You invite me to something, fine, but if you invite my kids to something, you got me."

Myth: The wealthy only care about buying stuff. *Reality*: Certainly the wealthy do buy heaping amounts of stuff—so much, in fact, that their houses are sometimes overflowing, and even create an unprecedented secondary market for used luxury goods on the Internet. In apparel-related categories, for example, they typically spend $20,000 to $50,000 annually, with many spending much more (see Table 5-1). Note that in each category, the mean is considerably higher than the median, reflecting a substantial number of extremely high-priced purchases.

But much of their spending is geared less toward accumulating possessions and more toward making their lives easier. This typically translates into considerable spending on personal services. Over 90 percent of the wealthy spend at least some money on regular ser-

Table 5-1 **Typical annual purchases by the wealthy**

	Median	Mean
Designer apparel (excluding shoes)	$5,000	$11,000
Watches	$4,400	$27,000
Jewelry (excluding watches)	$3,000	$15,000
Handbags	$1,500	$ 3,500
Designer footwear	$1,000	$ 3,400

vices, with cleaning the house and maintaining the garden being the tasks most frequently targeted for outsourcing (see Table 5-2). It is remarkable that more wealthy people find value in gardeners and housecleaning services than in accountants and stockbrokers, but again that is reflective of their financial confidence, self-reliance, and hesitancy to trust. The stereotypical "servants" of the wealthy, such as drivers and personal assistants, are far down the list.

Of course, services aren't the only form of "nonstuff" spending in which the wealthy engage. Given their focus on family and fun, it is not surprising that they spend significantly on travel and vacations as well. Indeed, when we ask them what they are most likely to

Table 5-2 **Use of services on a full-time or regular basis**

Service	% Claiming Use of
Lawn maintenance/gardener	66
Housecleaning service	58
Personal accountant	45
Stockbroker	38
Handyman	32
Wealth advisor	31
Travel agent	25
Masseuse/masseur	22
Jeweler	20
Personal trainer	19
Personal Stylist	14
Interior designer	14
Live-in housekeeper/domestic help	13
Psychologist/psychiatrist	12
Nanny/Au pair	10
Personal assistant	11
Personal driver	7
Personal shopper	6
Personal chef/cook	5

splurge on, travel is mentioned more frequently than any other category. They average over five vacations a year, spending an average of
more than $35,000, although many spend much more. Their travel
destinations are diverse and dispersed (see Table 5-3).

Interestingly, their top two domestic travel destinations are the
two capitals of American shopping: New York City and Las Vegas.
Hawaii, the Caribbean, and Europe are common destinations as
well. The wealthy average more than twenty nights annually in hotels
for personal stays; about half typically spend less than $300 a night,
but nearly one in four typically spends over $400 a night.

They are frequent business travelers as well, averaging over eight
trips and twenty nights in hotels for business purposes, giving them
the perks of business travel—frequent-flier miles for free personal
trips and first-class upgrades, hotel points for free personal hotel
stays, and the opportunity to "piggyback" personal trips and experiences onto business trips. If converted to a cash metric, the total
dollar value of their personal trips would be much higher.

On many attitudinal measures, the affluent (top 5 percent) are
similar to the wealthy, but when it comes to travel, the wealthy spend
three or four times as much as those just slightly lower on the economic totem pole. In air travel, for example, the affluent struggle

Table 5-3 **Travel destinations of the wealthy**
(% of those surveyed)

Plan Travel in Next Year (in Lower 48 States)		Plan Travel in Next 2 years (Outside Lower 48 States)	
New York, NY	47	Italy	38
Las Vegas, NV	41	Caribbean & West Indies	36
Chicago, IL	31	Hawaii	36
Boston, MA	32	United Kingdom	34
Los Angeles, CA	30	France	29
San Francisco, CA	27	Mexico	27
Washington, DC	25	Canada	21
Aspen/Denver, CO	25	Australia	17
Orlando	24	Spain	16
Miami	24	Ireland/China (tied)	14

with the psychological trade-offs of paying an extra $3,000 for a few hours in a first-class seat that is just a few inches larger than a regular seat. But for those with true wealth, there is little hesitation.

Myth: The wealthy shop primarily in high-end stores. *Reality:* The wealthy shop everywhere. Their spending is dispersed across a variety of channels, spending roughly as much via traditional retail outlets and the Internet as they do in luxury or high-end retail stores (see Figure 5-1). Just as their channel preferences run the gamut from the everyday to the elite, so do their brand preferences (see Table 5-4). Eighty percent of the wealthy shop at Target and Best Buy, putting them about on a par with traditional high-end retailers like Macy's and Nordstrom. Similarly, just as many shop at Costco as at Saks, Bloomingdale's, and Neiman Marcus. Nearly half shop at Wal-Mart.

A similar pattern of simultaneous high-end and lower-end preferences emerges when we look at their favorite stores (particularly after controlling for the baseline number who shop at each store, reflected in the favorite-to-shop ratio in Table 5-4). Forty-three percent of Costco shoppers consider the store one of their favorites, placing it in a statistical tie for first with Nordstrom. Increasingly, the wealthy are open to buying high-end products in virtually any channel, with 41 percent reporting they would "buy a really expensive item, like jewelry, at a store like Costco or Sam's Club."

Even in thinking about upscale retail experiences, the wealthy

Figure 5-1 Breakdown of the wealthy's shopping by channel.

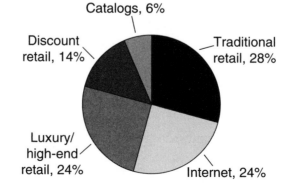

Table 5-4 **Retail preferences of the wealthy
            (% of those surveyed)**

	Shop There	One of My Favorites (among all respondents)	One of my Favorites (among those shopping at that store)
Target	80%	22%	28%
Best Buy	80	17	21
Macy's	76	16	21
Nordstrom	76	32	42
Saks Fifth Avenue	59	22	37
Costco	58	25	43
Bloomingdale's	56	16	29
Neiman Marcus	55	19	35
Wal-Mart	49	9	18
Bergdorf-Goodman	25	9	36

show a decidedly middle-class set of preferences. We presented a list of possible incentives and asked what factors would cause them to respond "yes" to a private event held in a retail store. By far the most commonly cited incentive was discounts of 25 to 30 percent. (In contrast, very few would have been motivated by discounts of just 10 to 15 percent.) Second on the list was that a share of the proceeds go to support a charity. Third, remarkably, was a statistical tie between early access to new merchandise and hors d'oeuvres. Costco and Sam's Club clearly demonstrate that the availability of food draws affection, attention, and staying power in the stores that offer the goodies. The wealthy, like graduate students and everyone else, like free food.

Myth: The wealthy don't care about sales, coupons, or prices in general. *Reality*: See the Target/Costco/Wal-Mart numbers above. Over 80 percent prefer to shop in stores with a reputation for great pricing. Over half look for sales in the newspaper, and a similar number report typically waiting for something to go on sale before they buy it. Forty-five percent shop with coupons "fairly regularly."

Myth: The wealthy are impulse shoppers. *Reality*: Three-fourths plan their shopping trips carefully in advance, and half have a specific budget or price in mind that they won't exceed when shopping for a specific item. Even in traditional luxury retail categories such as jewelry, designer fashion, and shoes, the vast majority of purchases are planned. Only about one-third of designer apparel or shoe purchases are spontaneous or made on impulse. The figure drops to one in four for purchases of handbags, while dropping even further for jewelry and watches.

Instead, there is typically a considerable gestation period during which purchases are weighed and considered. Over half of watch and jewelry purchases are considered for at least a month before purchasing, as well as approximately one-fourth of the purchases in these other categories. Most of the purchasing by the wealthy in these categories is not "shopping for sport." Rather, it is typically driven by special events and occasions, such as charity events, cocktail parties, and weddings.

As they move up the retail chain to bigger ticket purchases, the likelihood of impulse purchasing drops even further. Four percent of automobile purchases are made on impulse; over 80 percent are thought about and evaluated for at least a month. As in lower price-point categories, auto purchasing is largely driven by specific, need-based occasions (see Table 5-5).

Myth: The wealthy are fashion trendsetters. *Reality*: Less than half describe themselves as being on the cutting edge of fashion, and

Table 5-5 **Reasons given for automobile purchases**

Reason	% Responses
Needed to replace or update one I currently owned	55
Wanted to upgrade relative to what I had	23
My automobile requirements had changed, so I wanted a car to serve that	19
Wanted a treat/reward for myself	16
Read an article about it	9
Was just browsing, saw it, and wanted it	8
Saw an ad that made me want it	6
Saw someone else with this particular car or heard others talking about it	5

even fewer try to stay on top of seasonal fashion trends. Less than 30 percent look to celebrities or athletes for ideas of apparel or products. They tend to prefer basic colors and classically tasteful styles, but being too fashion-forward draws unnecessary attention to themselves; moreover, it is largely inconsistent with their middle-class comfort zone and the principle of stealth wealth.

Myth: The wealthy live in mansions, or at least McMansions. *Reality:* A small minority live in palatial estates, but most live in houses that are better described as spacious but modest. The average value of their main residences is about $2 million, with the median being closer to $1.2 million. Depending on your background and where you live, that may sound like a lot. And certainly in some parts of the country, that kind of money can indeed buy a palatial estate. But in New York City or San Francisco, for example, it is more likely to buy a two- or three-bedroom condo in an upscale but not elite neighborhood.

Although their homes are not typically estates, the wealthy are certainly proud of their homes, and they invest considerable time and money in home improvements. In the past two years, 40 percent made significant landscaping upgrades, one-third made major purchases of furniture or appliances, and one-fifth made extensive renovations (see Table 5-6).

Perhaps more telling than home values or repair bills are the words that the wealthy use to describe their homes, which reflect the combination of their middle-class mind-set and their substantial means (see Table 5-7). *Comfortable* is by far the most commonly chosen adjective, followed by *entertaining, friendly,* and *clean.* One-third describe their home as upscale. Their mind-sets may be middle class, but only about one in ten describes his or her home that way. A similar small number describe their homes as showpieces.

One-fourth of the wealthy have a second home, which typically has one-half to one-third of the market value of their primary home, and approximately half are beach houses. Again, descriptions are more psychologically telling than asset values. A typical wealthy person is likely to describe his or her primary home as where his or her heart is, as a place to entertain, and a place to gather with family. In

Table 5-6 **Upgrades to primary home in the past two years**

	% Who Made Changes	Typical Amount Spent (in $1000s)
New outdoor landscaping	40	10–15
Purchased major home furnishings	35	15–30
Purchased major kitchen appliances	29	10–12
Major home renovations	20	40–100+
Major bathroom remodel	17	10–30
Major kitchen remodel	17	25–35
Replaced windows	12	7–15
Put on an addition	7	90–120
None of the above	38	

Table 5-7 **Top 12 ways the wealthy describe the interiors of their primary homes**

Description	% Responses
Comfortable	64
Entertaining-friendly	43
Clean	41
Upscale	34
Traditional	32
Organized	27
Contemporary	26
Cozy	23
Kid-friendly	17
Haven	16
Eclectic	14
Middle class	12
Showpiece	12

contrast, second or vacation homes are far more likely to be described as a retreat, and as a place to go to be anonymous.

Myth: The wealthy have garages full of exotic cars. *Reality*: On average, the wealthy have two or three cars, and their garages are far more likely to have a Ford or Chevy than a Lamborghini or Bugatti. As always, there are exceptions, and there are certainly enthusiasts who do have garages full of exotic cars. On the whole, though, the wealthy are most likely to have premium but nonexotic cars from Mercedes, BMW, and Lexus; ownership of those premium brands is followed closely by vehicles from more mainstream brands such as Toyota, Chevrolet, Ford, and Honda (see Table 5-8).

If we look just slightly further down the economic spectrum, to the 5 percent of the population that is merely affluent, we find that these seven brands are just about equally likely to be owned, with Toyota topping the list. Even among the wealthy, fewer than 3 percent own any of the following: Bentley, Ferrari, Lamborghini, Land/Range Rover, and the original James Bond favorite, Aston Martin. Eighteen percent own a pickup truck, two to three times the number who own a vintage car, exotic car, or hybrid vehicle (although the likelihood of buying a hybrid vehicle is growing strongly). On average, their most recent automotive purchase cost an upscale but not outlandish $50,000.

Table 5-8 **Top 10 vehicles owned by the wealthy and affluent**

Wealthy	% Own	Affluent	% Own
Mercedes-Benz	25	Toyota	21
BMW	23	Ford	18
Lexus	22	Honda	17
Toyota	18	BMW	17
Chevrolet	16	Lexus	17
Ford	14	Mercedes-Benz	17
Honda	12	Chevrolet	13
Porsche	12	Chrysler	9
Volvo	10	Acura	9
Audi	10	Volvo	9

In cars, houses, and many other categories, middle-class tastes persist long after the financial means enable people to buy luxury products and services almost exclusively. One of our respondents summed up the predominant mind-set well, saying "I have a Chevrolet taste on a Mercedes income." But more calculated approaches to self-presentation and stealth wealth are often prevalent as well. A CEO told us that he has a Porsche that he bought ten years ago as his "first toy" after becoming wealthy, but is reluctant to buy another one and drives his Ford Explorer to work: "I don't think you should be showing up at a small public company flaunting your wealth. I think it makes a statement. You pull up, you have a lot of people working for you, and a lot of them don't make a lot of money." He went on to explain that he no longer has company parties at his house because he felt that might create some resentment as well.

The Business of Intelligent Shopping

By now, a common thread has likely become apparent throughout these spending myths and their corresponding realities: The wealthy spend money, sometimes lots of it, but do so thoughtfully and prudently. Managing a household is a complex task, and as wealthy households mature and gain additional assets, they are increasingly run like businesses. Indeed, three-fourths of the wealthy state that "managing my family's finances requires strong business management skills."

Intelligent shopping is indicative of this businesslike approach to spending money, and is also an outgrowth of the value orientation that is central to the middle-class mind-set. Indeed, many wealthy households spend money with a sophistication that a business operations specialist might describe as "just-in-time shopping against the available space." And it can have dramatic bottom-line impacts.

We estimate that savvy purchasing can increase their household income by over 35 percent, freeing up in excess of $100,000 annually in additional after-tax cash flow in many wealthy households (as an example, see the online savings for nine higher-end products in Table 5-9). As an outgrowth of middle-class values, intelligent shopping is generally considered a shared responsibility throughout the house-

Table 5-9 **Retail and online prices for selected higher-end products**

	Luxury Retail ($)	Online ($)	% Savings
6-seat private jet hourly rate (same manufacturer)	2,800	1,275	54
1.5-carat G color, VS clarity quality solitaire diamond (with platinum band)	19,700	11,600	41
Two weeks vacation (Atlantis Resort)	10,340	5,800	44
Gold Cartier LC Tank watch	9,100	7,371	19
St. John's cardigan sweater	285	99	65
High-performance stereo (Bang & Olufsen)	1,325	820	38
Hermès bangle bracelet	345	240	30
Burberry raincoat	575	199	65
Montblanc pen	495	370	25
Total	44,695	27,774	38

hold. It is practiced by both genders, and among other benefits, it becomes a means of teaching children about the value of the money.

In three-fourths of married wealthy households, the wife is responsible for buying groceries and basic supplies, but the responsibility for major purchases is almost always a joint one. Indeed, in households in which the wife does not work, she often takes on the role of de facto household chief financial officer, and the money saved from intelligent shopping is often greater than what she might make working, particularly on an after-tax, after-work-clothing, after-child-care basis.

Smart, savvy decision making is evident in many aspects of wealthy shopping habits. Across many categories, nearly half of the wealthy say they couldn't save any additional money on their purchases regardless of how much more they "shopped around," and the vast majority say they couldn't save more than an additional 10 percent. The opinions of others are important in the purchasing process, but less for social reasons and more as guidelines for ensuring smart decisions. Rather than seeking to impress friends and family, they seek out those experienced with the category or the brands in question. When asked why they hired a new financial adviser, for example, the most commonly cited reason was simply that someone they trusted made a recommendation. Forget about keeping up with the Jones's—the wealthy would rather identify the Jones's strengths and work with them to learn how to leverage those strengths in making smarter decisions.

Smart shopping is also time-efficient shopping. For the wealthy, even more so than the rest of us, time is money, and we've seen how "more time" is the number one item on their wish list. In luxury retail categories, we asked why they purchased the specific items they chose. The number one reason, on a par with quality, brand, and self-expression, was that the item was good enough. In other words, they said, "I was satisfied so I didn't want to spend more time shopping around" (see Table 5-10). Psychologists and economists call it *satisficing*: choosing a product that meets criteria at an adequate level, rather than expending a great deal more time to find a fully optimal solution. Of course, the minimal requirements for adequacy among the wealthy may be quite high in absolute terms, or relative to those of the less well-off, but the principle of time savings as one element of smart decision making is a crucial one.

For both genders, and across every aspect of smart shopping, from time savings to price comparisons, the Internet has been crucial in enabling a business-focused approach to household spending and financial management. Among the wealthy, we found the following:

- *90 percent agree*: "I can get information faster on the Internet than dealing directly with a company's customer service representative."
- *83 percent agree*: "I research the items on the Web I am going to buy to make sure that I am not taken advantage of."
- *85 percent agree*: "The Internet has liberated my shopping."

Also, two-thirds of their trips are booked online; less than 15 percent involve a travel agent.

Certainly, online purchasing itself plays a key role. The wealthy average $10,000 to $40,000 annually in online spending, but the

Table 5-10 **Reasons for purchasing specific items (average of watch/jewelry, fashion apparel, handbags, and shoes)**

Reason	% Responses
I was satisfied so I didn't want to spend more time shopping around	49
Made by a good brand	48
High-quality item	47
Fit me just right	47
Reflected my personality/tastes	43

impact of the Internet on their shopping is even more profound. Averaging across the fifteen key categories that we examined, one-third of the wealthy make online purchases, but over half compared prices and products online, and one-fourth used the Internet to find offline stores.

Philosophically, this growing role of the Internet in purchasing decisions results in a shift from a supply-auction economy, in which companies manage supply through discounts and promotions, to a demand-auction economy, in which individuals "announce" their interest in a product and allow various providers to bid on fulfilling that interest. Moreover, Internet options have dramatically increased the complexity of the price-value equation that people must intuitively calculate when making channel and purchase decisions.

On the whole, for example, the well-to-do tend to choose an in-person retail experience when it involves less than thirty minutes of travel time, when they want to savor the shopping experience, when they are searching for something unique, and when they believe a salesperson will add value. In contrast, they tend to choose online outlets when they cannot afford the time, when their past experience suggests sufficient delivery/fulfillment, and when they are unafraid of fraud. When both sides of this trade-off equation are approximately equal, warranty and exchange privileges often serve as tie breakers.

These trade-offs have been present since the dawn of the Internet, but have become prevalent in higher-end categories only in recent years. As we shall see, the general trends among how people make these trade-offs, and the personality types associated with how people habitually make these trade-offs, are fundamentally reshaping the retail business, particularly in luxury categories.

Passion Shoppers vs. Logic Shoppers

Up to this point, we have been talking about the wealthy and their families in terms of averages. And in truth, wealthy families are homogeneous in many regards. But it turns out that the process of *how* they shop varies significantly. Our statistical analyses revealed two major types of shoppers: passion shoppers and logic shoppers. Passion shoppers seek defined fashions and enjoyable shopping experiences with the help of salespeople and elegant retailers; comprising only 30 percent of the affluent/wealthy market, they are responsible for 50 percent of profits at retail. In contrast, logic shoppers run their households with the precision of a corporate purchasing officer, leveraging the Internet for price comparisons, special discounts, and so on. It is logic shoppers for whom distinct stores like Costco and Sam's Club have a special place in their hearts, and although they are 70 percent of the affluent and wealthy market, they account for much less of the retail industry's profitability. Passion shoppers sometimes engage in the behaviors characteristic of logic shoppers and vice versa, but for the most part, people display one characteristic style across time and across categories.

Passion Shoppers

Reflecting the traditional luxury shopping sales funnel, passion shoppers first become aware of a product, then their passion is aroused, and then they purchase in a store when they want it—at keystone margins (see Figure 5-2).

Indeed, these are the luxury shoppers who truly drive margins in the marketplace. They have a preference for high fashion and high design, uniqueness, and strong brands; in fact, they frequently decide on a brand first, before deciding on the product to purchase.

Figure 5-2 Shopping funnels for passion and logic shoppers.

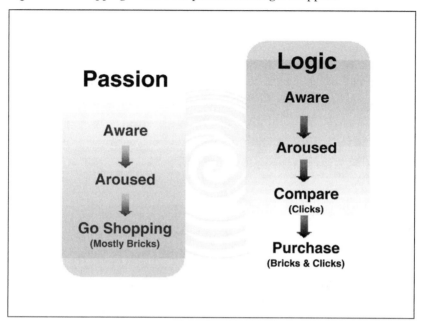

They tend to shop alone, they like interacting with salespeople (for whom they have high expectations), and they feel a genuine enthusiasm for new retail discoveries. For these high-touch purchasers, shopping is a hobby to be savored and an art form to be appreciated, not a chore to be managed. When marketers of higher-end products and services think about "their customers," they typically think in terms of passion shoppers. This would have been a reasonably accurate characterization twenty years ago, but today passion shoppers constitute only about 30 percent of the wealthy population.

Logic Shoppers

The new dominant shopper model, more characteristic of 70 percent of the wealthy, is that of the logic shopper. More strongly shaped by their middle-class upbringings, these people consistently show the characteristics of smart shopping that we described above: a focus on value, taking pride in doing due diligence before purchasing, and leveraging the Internet for information and/or actual purchasing.

They disproportionately use coupon clipping strategies, in-store discounts, sales, and every advantage they can to lower the price (see Table 5-11). They are often willing to make trade-offs for lower prices, including less than perfect service or slightly delayed delivery. As opposed to passion shoppers, logic shoppers' purchasing behavior can be described as deciding on a category's specs and price range first, before they decide on a brand. Logic shoppers may be aroused by advertising; their middle-class days of stretching a dollar have taught them that they can find substantial discounts with just a little added effort.

New Marketing Challenges for New Shoppers

Today's new generation of wealth presents a serious dilemma to the marketers of luxury goods and services. We saw above the dramatic

Table 5-11 **Bargain shopping habits of logic shoppers (% of responses)**

	Passion Shoppers	Logic Shoppers
I prefer to shop in stores with a reputation for great pricing	48	99
I usually wait for something to go on sale before I buty it	21	95
I would buy a really expensive item like jewelry at a store like Costco or Sam's Club	19	51
I look for sales in the newspaper	14	94
I shop with coupons fairly regularly	8	86
Retail Behavior: Stores Shopped		
Nordstrom	54	46
Saks Fifth Avenue	29	15
Neiman Marcus	27	19
Bloomingdale's	30	26
Target	65	82
Best Buy	58	70
Wal-Mart	43	61
Costco	45	51

savings that can be achieved for those willing to make the time and service trade-offs associated with logic shopping, even for luxury products and services; as a result, the number and power of logic shoppers will continue to increase. Currently, logic shoppers are 70 percent of the market, but they deliver less than 50 percent of retail profits. Some retailers will pursue the higher margins and rededicate themselves solely to passion shoppers, aligning inventory, advertising, store design, and in-store services to create a new category of passion-focused elegant shopping. Others will pursue a higher-volume, lower-margin strategy by focusing on the quality and value that drive the logic shopper.

Even approaches to customer service will need to be refined. In a retail context, logic shoppers were likely to tell us they want salespeople who "leave them alone." Although they are certainly open to a friendly "Can I help you?" they definitely don't want someone who hovers and doesn't respect a metaphorical "Don't call me, I'll call you" response. Indeed, salespeople must recognize that they are the end of the logic shopping search process, not the beginning, and the customer is likely already aware of basic product features, price ranges, etc.

The passion shopper is looking for a more emotional connection with a salesperson, relies on them for superior product knowledge, and in short, often considers positive interactions with salespeople to be the make-or-break deciding factor on whether to visit the store again. As expressed by one such shopper:

> The owner can come in and hold up something for me to look at which is something I would never wear in a million years, but one of her salespeople knows the kinds of things I like. When she calls and says, "There's something here I think you'll like," I know it's worth my time to go down there because she understands what works for me. But the person who forever holds up the item that I would never be interested in—I really don't want to even go back because they're constantly shoving things at me that I don't care about.

Regardless of whether retailers target passion shoppers or logic shoppers, they must contend not only with the emergence of logic shopping as a dominant paradigm but also with the fact that a new generation of wealthy individuals is fundamentally reshaping the nature of spending, the expectations of brands, and as we shall see in the next chapter, the concept of luxury itself.

CHAPTER SIX

The New Luxury

The Search for Sublime Value

"LUXURY LIES NOT IN RICHNESS AND ORNATENESS BUT IN THE
ABSENCE OF VULGARITY."

—Coco Chanel

"LUXURY IS NECESSITY."

—John Kenneth Galbraith

REMARKABLY, ONE OF THE MOST significant trends in luxury over the past decade has had essentially nothing to do with the wealthy. Quite the opposite. The social and economic tidal wave that has reshaped the luxury business has been driven, at least in part, by the vast number of people from every age group, class, and category who have fulfilled John Kenneth Galbraith's prophecy. Today, essentially 100 percent of all consumers buy luxury at some time. It is not a question of whether they will buy luxury brands, but how often, and whether they will insist on the real thing. And this is true for the wealthy as well; 34 percent of high-end American households have paid such a low price for a luxury product that they suspected it was counterfeit.

As purchasing luxury is no longer an "if," it requires a greater sophistication in thinking about where, when, in which category, and at what price. This broadening phenomenon goes by many names, including the *mainstreaming of affluence*, the *democratization of luxury*, the *massification of luxury*, and even *masstige*. The democratization effect has brought luxury under criticism from authors such as Dana Thomas, whose book *Deluxe* posits that luxury has "lost its luster."[1] Ultimately, however, this democratization doesn't change the elements that define luxury, or even necessarily lower the bar—it simply reflects a deeper, more pervasive desire among increasingly sophisticated consumers for more frequent luxury experiences. For example:

- Once-exotic items, such as sushi and refined organic products, are now found on grocery store shelves.
- Everyday products are now offered in high-end forms at relatively high-end prices, such as $6 coffee at Starbucks or $14 boxes of chocolate in drug stores.
- High-end designers have expanded into mass market retailers, such as Philippe Starck designs and Isaac Mizrahi pumps at Target; Martha Stewart linens at K-Mart; and Ralph Lauren apparel at Sam's Club. In fact, Costco has become one of America's largest retailers of Dom Pérignon and other fine wines, and it successfully offers high-quality diamonds of five carats or greater in its catalogs.

Sensing a growth opportunity, manufacturers of luxury brands fueled this trend. During the past decade, many iconic luxury brands, whose entire product lines were once extremely high priced and truly exclusive, have rolled out more accessible products (often accessories and jewelry) at price points well within the reach of the mass market.

At the same time, several other trends have been subtly reshaping the luxury industry. Strong merger and acquisition activity has resulted in classic luxury brands becoming conglomerates—a brand portfolio within a growth-focused, vertically integrated commercial enterprise.

Consider, for example, the inelegantly named LVMH Moët Hennessy—Louis Vuitton. Its lengthy moniker is a by-product of the company's strategy of accumulating classic brands through (sometimes contentious) acquisitions. Now with over sixty brands and 60,000 employees, LVMH owns some of the world's most famous luxury brands in a variety of categories, including champagne (Dom

Pérignon, Moët & Chandon), fashion (Louis Vuitton, Fendi, Donna Karan, Givenchy, Marc Jacobs), fragrances (Dior), watches (Tag Heuer), and retailing (Sephora, DFS, eLUXURY.com). LVMH has produced a portfolio that allows its reputation for excellence to penetrate a large number of household categories, thus building its representation both within wealthy households and in other households on a one-off basis.

Similarly, Richemont has built a luxury portfolio that includes Cartier, Van Cleef & Arpels, Piaget, Montblanc, Baume & Mercier, and others. Its strategy has been to own the finest companies in jewelry and accessories that can also operate independently, with Richemont serving as a financing source for elegant and superb manufacturers while protecting each of them from the winds of change.

Finally, the Gucci Group owns the Gucci brand as well as Alexander McQueen, Stella McCartney, Yves Saint Laurent, and a half-dozen others. Gucci's strategy has been to build a brand portfolio of the finest fashion names in the world and to use its strengths in distribution, marketing, and manufacturing as a benefit to all its brands, as well as to consumers who can then choose the brands they like the most.

None of these trends have irreparably tarnished luxury brands—provided the brands themselves have not forever lost the quality and exclusivity that once made them prized and distinctive. It is true that signature brands have products with price points that allow nearly everyone to share in the sense of richness, depth, excellence, collectability, and refined qualities that attend to these sublime brands. However, the fact that more consumers can participate has not necessarily degraded the quality of these brands. What has changed is that the message of these brands is more universally understood and desired. Democratization has simply meant that the receptivity for this message is now part of everyone's taste for things. For some households, satisfaction of that taste is achieved by sacrifice; for others, it is a routine purchase.

None of this, however, changes the fact that traditional luxury brands continue to rule their respective categories in terms of product quality, customer loyalty, profitability, and the value of the companies that own them. Indeed, we believe that in connecting with the wealthy, and with the middle and lower classes as well, branding remains the single most powerful tool in a marketer's arsenal. The challenge is that today's wealthy, with their distinct attitudes and mind-sets, have an evolving set of desires and expectations regarding luxury to which manufacturers must attend.

What the Wealthy Really Want, in Luxury Products and Elsewhere

When we ask the wealthy what they look for in a brand, the top three responses are chosen by virtually everyone and are particularly telling: craftsmanship, quality, and service (see Table 6-1). Again, these were the hallmarks of luxury brands before the past twenty years. And as

Table 6-1 **What the wealthy like in brands (top 10 and bottom 7)**

Rank	Attribute Desired	% of Those Surveyed
1	Reflect high craftsmanship	97
2	Have reputation for the best quality	96
3	Have reputation for service	96
4	Have reputation for technology	87
5	Are valued by spouse or partner	86
6	Have reputation for design	83
7	Have history and heritage	82
8	Allow me to do something good (e.g., support the environment, give to charity, etc.)	79
9	Reflect generosity of spirit	75
10	Reminds me of a special moment in my life	75
19	Communicate to others that I'm successful	54
20	Help me feel privileged	51
21	Are preferred by my children and their friends	49
22	Help me feel trendy	47
23	Communicate to others that I'm loved and appreciated	46
24	Are preferred by my friends	41
25	Help me feel loved	40

we'll see shortly, these aspects remain undiluted in the classic luxury brands that still appeal to the wealthy and are characteristic of the emerging luxury brands that have gained a foothold.

Also telling is item number four on the list: technology. We have asked this particular question in our studies for several years, and this is by far the fastest growing item on the list. This represents a sea change in the attitudes of the wealthy. Twenty years ago, the wealthy had others who "did tech" for them. Today, 80 percent believe that technology has been important to their success, and a similar number describe themselves as "technologically intelligent." Their homes, and their cars, are wired (see Table 6-2). At the higher end, technology as an element of luxury is obviously about quality and performance, and it is also about sleek design and ergonomics. But there's an important emotional component as well. The utilitarian features of a $600 iPhone or $3000 Sony laptop can be obtained for much less money, but these products and brands are about expressing one's commitment to and passion for technology, even though their objective value declines from the moment of purchase.

The bottom of the attributes list in Table 6-1 is just as revealing. The social and status-oriented aspects of brands are among the least potent motivators, particularly the notion of brand as a badge and

Table 6-2 **Technology ownership among the wealthy**

Technology	% Who Own Item
PC with broadband Internet access (Cable or DSL)	77
Portable MP3 player such as iPod	61
High-definition television (HDTV)	72
Television larger than 40 inches	69
LCD or Plasma Flat Screen TV	63
Digital video recorder (DVR, TiVo)	59
Surround-sound speaker system	51
XM or Sirius Satellite Radio at home or in your car	36
Centrally wired system to distribute music throughout house	28
Direct TV	25
Dedicated in-home theater room	23

public indicator of wealth. Taken as a whole, the picture becomes clear that luxury for the wealthy is much more about quality and self-expression than it is about specific brands and self-congratulation (see Table 6-3).

Luxury for a New Generation: The Search for Sublime Value

Pulling all of these insights together brings us to a new definition of luxury, and the people with a passion for it:

> *The word* Luxury *describes products and services that offer consumers sublime quality, performance, and emotional connections.*

> *The term* Luxury Market *describes people who value taste, emotional resonance, quality and artistic merit in the things they choose to buy and possess.*

One of the key words in these definitions is *sublime*. True luxury is not about logos, but about high quality combined with subtlety and tastefulness. Someone with a stealth-wealth mind-set and a hunger for the highest quality would seek precisely this combination of attributes. Recall the quote from pioneering designer Coco Chanel that opened this chapter: *"Luxury lies not in richness and ornateness but in the absence of vulgarity."*

Table 6-3 **Meanings of luxury for the wealthy**

Luxury Is . . .	Luxury Is Not . . .
• **Quality:** 90% agree, "I don't care about most luxury items per se, but I am into having items that are the best quality and craftsmanship."	• **Specific brands:** Only 34% agree, "it is important to wear the right brands."
• **Self-expression:** 76% agree, "Expressing my personal style is very important to me."	• **Self-congratulation:** 25% agree, "I enjoy subtle clues like exclusive designer apparel or an expensive watch to remind me of what I have attained."

From a quality perspective, what separates truly elite products from merely good ones is subtle, indeed sublime, distinctions. The fact is that the vast majority of the products in any category are, for all intents and purposes, functionally interchangeable. But at the same time, every category has a point at which very subtle distinctions have a huge impact on perceived quality, as well as on profit margins. These points of sublime distinction are the essence of true luxury.

Consider the sublime qualities of the product that probably best exemplifies "old-school" luxury brands: the Hermès bag. It falls into the "if you have to ask how much it costs, you probably can't afford it" category. Prices start at about $6,000, but can easily run into five or even six figures. Hermès's clientele includes Oprah Winfrey, Argentinian President Cristina Fernandez de Kirchner, and a long list of actresses, models, and singers. Martha Stewart was criticized by some for walking into her trial with one. Victoria "Posh Spice" Beckham is reported to have over 100 Hermès bags valued collectively at over $1 million.

But the appeal of the Hermès is less about who has one and more about the quality and authenticity of the product itself. There can be no doubt that people who have them get noticed by people who know about them. With a few exceptions, each one is custom made. You don't typically walk into a store and buy one. You order one. You choose the material, the hardware, sometimes even the stitching. Want a diamond-encrusted ostrich bag with stitching on the outside? No problem. Today's wealthy aspire to self-expression, and Hermès delivers. The bags are handmade by artisans who graduate from France's premier trade academies and serve two-year apprenticeships with the company before graduating to work on a Hermès bag. Each bag takes anywhere from fifteen to fifty hours or more to create. The company has grown but has resisted all efforts to mechanize the process, outsource the production, or become the centerpiece of a multi-billion dollar conglomerate.

One result for Hermès is an authentic scarcity: It produces fewer than 150,000 bags a year, with waiting lists of a year or more—as long as you agree that 150,000 bags a year is scarce for a bag that lasts forever (remember, that's a million-and-a-half bags every ten years). The rhythm of the business is set, not by what they can sell, but by what they can manufacture to their standards. Is there a physical difference between a Hermès bag and some other quality bag? Yes, but it isn't necessarily obvious to the uninitiated. It takes experience and learning to understand the sublime differences. But even then, owning a Hermès bag is less about product features and more about emotional benefits. In a sense, it is not so much about talking to others, but about talking to oneself. The virtues of the bag reflect on the person; the authenticity of the bag validates her own authenticity. As Marc Jacobs, creative director for Louis Vuitton, put it: "The way I define luxury isn't by fabric or fiber or the amount of gold bits hanging from it. . . . That's the old definition. For me, luxury is about pleasing yourself, not dressing for other people."

Each category has its own luxury pinnacle—an Hermès equivalent, if you will. For example, in 1623, in the heart of the Ottoman Empire, Avedis Zildjian invented a new method of making musical instruments by fusing copper, tin, and silver. Nearly four centuries later, the alchemical formula he created remains a secret, but the cymbals that bear his name are the hallmark of excellence among drummers around the world. In point of fact, if you claim to be a drummer, and you don't play Zildjians, you are not.

Remarkable brands such as Hermès and Zildjian result from transcendence in five key aspects: *history, scarcity, design, clientele,* and *materials.* Such brands come to be characterized by a consistency of meaning across time, and a consistency of experience. In this context, *meaning* refers to the brand becoming synonymous with a trait of human behavior, consciousness, or style, so that possession of the brand reflects the importance of the trait to the individual. By *experience*, we mean that people who have been-there done-that are allowed to "wear the adventure," or display the cultural symbolism of the experience as a merit badge in life. The notion of a "life list" of things to do before kicking the bucket refers to the stipulation of these experiences as a necessary component of living well. Products become obsolete, but brands that become imbued with meaning, and become synonymous with valued traits or experiences, persist. Consider that nineteen of the twenty-five brands that led their category in 1925 still lead their category today. Excellent brands can easily lead their categories for centuries. Beretta is one of the oldest companies in the world and has made the world's finest firearms for nearly half a millennium. Royal Delft has been in the pottery business for over 350 years. Christies has been conducting auctions since 1766, one year longer than Hennessy has been making cognac. Cartier has been in the superb diamond business for over 150 years. The list goes on.

We did a study several years ago for Shell Oil in which we answered the question, "Is Shell a great company?" in part by examining brands that lasted more than 150 years. We found that companies displaying such longevity tend to have the name of a founder on the door, adapt to technological change effectively, and adapt to—if not lead—changes in style. But perhaps most important, they were *not* likely to be in the same product business in which they began, while still operating with the same spirit and commitment. The values of a founder transcend time in great products and brands, and those values continue to convey meaning across centuries.

These great brands exhibit tremendous resilience, surviving product faults, marketing missteps, and the natural vacillation of business cycles. Strong brands can endure a potentially brand-diluting influx of lower-quality, lower-priced products. To use a fine-art metaphor, simply because Picasso produced perhaps the greatest *quantity* of art in the modern era, including many relatively "low quality" pencil drawings, does not tarnish the fact that his greatest works are among the most desired in history (and from a purely monetary perspective, have held their value remarkably well). Mercedes suffered from several brand-diluting missteps, including the disastrous launch of its too-low-end 190 series and its ill-fated acquisition of Chrysler, but its brand has been strong enough to rebound. (Although not a luxury brand in the traditional sense, IBM's experience is instructive as well—its brand came to have several negative connotations during the 1990s but has rebounded while many of the upstarts that challenged it have fallen by the wayside).

A sixth characteristic of great brands is what we call the transitive property—the reliability with which the brand delivers its primary emotional or experiential connotation. Coca-Cola has delivered the same experience to consumers over and over again, no matter what country they are in, and has done so for decades. However many billions of bottles Coca-Cola produces, it still offers, without fail, a *moment*. It is the moment in which you may be driving across the Mojave Desert (or at least you feel that thirsty), you bring a cold Coca-Cola to your lips, and you experience a refreshment that transcends your thirst. The entire experience instills the feeling that "they made this just for me." Indeed, like Coca-Cola, top luxury brands serve a risk-management function, guaranteeing core benefits that mitigate downside risks of making a poor purchase and being dissatisfied. Generally speaking, the more a brand mitigates risks, the higher the price and the profit margin.

The transitive experience of brands serves as a powerful cohesive force for employees as well, helping to define the culture of the organization across decades and even centuries. In every generation of a luxury brand, managers have the opportunity to maximize short-term profits with any number of brand-tarnishing initiatives, but the best managers recognize that protecting their brand means protecting the interests of their customers and ensuring that they deliver the same high-quality experience on every occasion.

The origin point of great brands, and the genesis of their transitive experience, as we mentioned above, is often found in individuals, from Coco Chanel to Walt Disney. Her and his obsession with the sublime detail, and the artistic merit with which one implements sublime detail, causes key decisions about style and meaning to be made early in a company's history. Chanel's choices are characterized by outstanding quality in materials, extraordinary expertise in production, superb design, and marketing and sales people who embrace her vision. These choices form patterns that are embedded in a business's cost structure and market appeal. They become part of the legend and reputation of a company. They strongly influence the selection of successive managers. Locking in a preference for perfection over cost, and an uncompromising insistence on the sublime, creates collectability and benchmarks luxury. That is why the very great luxe companies—Cartier, Beretta, Hermès, and so on— transcend time. They last a long time because their need to produce the sublime is not a nicety but rather a necessity that is a cultural virtue of the organization. Excellence is in their DNA.

A variety of other benefits derive from strength in history, scarcity, design, clientele, and materials. Obviously, profit margins are strong, both on each individual sale and because of the intense loyalty that such brands typically inspire. A luxury automobile brand with a 60 percent repurchase rate, for example, has 60 percent of its sales for the year essentially locked in on day one, dramatically reducing sales and marketing costs. But at their core, profit margins and loyalty both stem from perhaps the most potent force in luxury branding: intense emotional connotations and connections. Consider, for example, Cartier, a brand that is truly distinctive on all five dimensions of history, scarcity, design, clientele, and materials. Its transitive nature and consistency of quality minimizes downside risks. But giving Cartier as a gift, in its famous and emotion-laden red box, is less about product quality per se, and more about making the statement that "you deserve something of exquisite beauty and the highest standards."

Consider this simple test of the importance of emotional connections: Suppose you could own all the physical aspects of Mercedes-Benz—the manufacturing plants, the distribution pipeline, the dealerships, and the customers. Or you could own the name Mercedes-Benz. Which would you choose? Of course you would choose the name. All the physical assets of the company could reliably be replicated in relatively short order with enough money. The name, however, and all the rich emotional connections with it, could only be reconstructed with decades of effort, dedication, and consistent performance.

The Sublime Art of Learning Sublime Distinctions

In any category, there are true enthusiasts—passionate, emotionally involved savants who appreciate the fine details of distinction that create the auction markets that in turn define the true range of value in any category. A two-seat Nash Rambler that sold in the 1950s for $1,200 sells today as a luxury car in auction markets for $22,000, representing a five- to six-fold increase in value, after adjusting for inflation. Was it a luxury in the beginning? No, but today it is because its uniqueness has rendered it an extraordinary collectable available only to the few who can appreciate the special ambiance of that strange little car. Opinion counts, and luxury is in the eye of the beholder. This rare people-mover fits the definition of luxury for its unique category in terms of design, scarcity, transitivity, emotional connection, and so on. For the enthusiast, it simply rocks.

Learning these qualities and details takes time and experience, and for the majority of wealthy consumers who come from the middle class, familiarity with these details is not part of typical household communication. Furthermore, no one has the time or interest to learn all the distinctions in any given category. Brand partially offsets that ignorance, particularly in categories in which one doesn't care to develop expertise.

For example, if several of the finest wines in the world were placed in a blind taste test with forty other varietals across the price spectrum, the typical wine drinker could not tell the difference among them. Differences in taste and bouquet are incredibly subtle. Indeed, one recent study found that people could not tell the difference between $5 bottles of wine and $90 bottles of wine, even though they believed they could. However, if price tags are attached, they report liking wine labeled as $90 more, even if it was just the $5 bottle of wine with a $90 price tag placed on it.[2] A wine enthusiast may be able tell the difference, but this extra mile, this sublime final step up to the top of the taste and quality hierarchy, is discernable only after considerable time and education. The budding enthusiasts learn, however, that price and brand are good predictors of quality. It is assumed that experts have set the price, and that a respected brand reflects the best in manufacturing, distribution, and taste. They are confident they will not be judged as inexperienced or poor hosts by placing a great wine in front of their guests—moreover, the act of choosing well expresses affection. Except for the true connoisseurs, most of the wealthy derive this form of pleasure and satisfaction from their experiences with fine wines.

The knowledge of the sublime takes time to acquire, and the wealthy learn these distinctions one category at a time, proceeding in an order based on their needs and interests over a period of roughly twenty years, starting with their first significant liquidity experience. The process covers more than 500 categories wealthy people shop and interact with, running the gamut from scheduled insurance policies, to fine wines, to extraordinary automobiles, to fine fabrics, to interior design, and even to the selection of the proper swimming pool manufacturer (see a small sample in Table 6-4).

The journey begins with a learning process in which one learns *how* to learn. The process typically begins in American public institutions where the real art of education is teaching people how to learn on the fly. But from that process the wealthy learn to distinguish details, and it is the details that separate the wheat from the chaff in luxury products. Specifically, the wealthy learn to weed out errors of commission (in statistical parlance, "Type I errors") from errors of omission (Type II errors). The luxury consumer relies on retailers, brands, reputations of excellence, and personal agents to avoid making a mistake in the selection of tastes and values. An agent can be a professional like a decorator, an art buyer, a personal shopper, a broker, or even a maven. The expert influences choice through wisdom and experience, and helps people avoid errors of commission— the selection of an underperforming product, a service ill-suited to their lifestyle, etc. Errors of omission are avoided through the process of observing the lives of other wealthy people and paying attention to the advertising about what "ought to" constitute the wealthy life. Through that process, the wealthy make decisions about what they will own and the roles those things will play in their lives, largely filtered through the lens of what they believe will appeal to them personally—from private jets and clubs to exotic vacations on the tip of South America. Errors of omission are avoided by listening carefully, watching others, and letting their senses do the talking.

In each category, the enthusiast learns to enjoy and appreciate

Table 6-4 **A small sample of categories in which sublime distinctions must be learned**

Luxury Items	Travel	Around the House	Services
Jewelry	Hotels	Food	Investment firms
Watches	Cars	Wine	Private banks
Clothing	Private jets	Appliances	Charities
Handbags	Boats	Dishware	Housecleaning services
Wallets	Motorcycles	Glassware	Dry cleaning
Art	Bicycles	Decorating	Gardening services

the subtle distinctions. But as we have seen, just as important are the emotional benefits that derive from appreciating these distinctions. For some, a dress by Chanel takes them back into the glamorous life of Coco Chanel herself. For others, a dress by Stella McCartney does the same. A music enthusiast savors the craftsmanship and feels connected to the history inherent in a $7,000 Wurlitzer jukebox, even if an iPod can deliver the same sound quality. (By the way, the enthusiast probably has an iPod too, which he appreciates for its own design elegance.) Buying a jet from Challenger, Lear, or Gulfstream is about getting an excellent product with an outstanding safety record. At the same time, it is about appreciating the engineering commitment and excellence of the companies that make them. About 10 percent of the wealthy consider themselves art connoisseurs, but that's been enough to create a boom in the $5 trillion art market over the past decade. The problem is that only superb works by superb artists gain value. So you can either devote yourself to understanding the subtle distinctions in fine art, or you can invest in an art hedge fund and trust the fund manager to understand those distinctions for you.

When we asked our respondents about their favorite objects in their houses, many responded with enthusiasm, and their detailed knowledge of the sublime distinctions in categories of interest shone through, along with the emotional connections that truly unique objects can create. For example:

> "My John Henry Belter cabinet in my bedroom from 1840. I wanted a piece of Belter's for years. He was the finest in laminating rosewood. He didn't discover the lamination process but he perfected it. He took ten to twelve layers of rosewood averaging 1/600th of an inch thick, he put them at 90 degree angles, and glued them in a very sophisticated way. The resulting backing is in ten to twelve layers, and it's the most exquisite, wonderful thing . . . there's a feeling I have when I'm around that kind of furniture, a feeling of comfort, safety, sereneness that I get with nothing else."

> "I have a Wolf [professional-quality oven] in my house. . . . It's the sexiest thing in the whole wide world. And yet it

functions beautifully and it gives off that look. Our deal is all about looking spiffy and having edge and being just a little bit, you know, commercial, out of the home, thinking out of the box. . . . The Wolf is all of that."

[Describing his world-class collection of Native American art] "I didn't buy things that were made today because those objects were made for sale. Ninety-nine percent of everything I have was made for ceremonial or utilitarian use and has a real soul to it, because it's from a real person and a real culture and a time and a place and conditions that I have tremendous respect and admiration for. I love the heartiness and ability of these people to be so intelligent and to express themselves with their hands and to believe in the things they believed in. I love every bit of it and have traveled extensively, read extensively, collected extensively, have been in the basements of museums, known the leading museum directors and curators and writers and experts all over the world."

Sophisticatering: The Art and Science of Teaching Sublime Distinctions

When sublime distinctions come to define luxury, then the essence of effectively selling luxury products is helping customers become more sophisticated about the sublime distinctions in the category. We call it *sophisticatering*, from *sophisticated*, meaning "cosmopolitan," "refined," "complex," and "cerebral," and from *catering*, meaning "to be attentive," "to minister to the needs or wants of."

The associates in high-end jewelry stores, for example, are trained extensively in explaining the sublime differences between their offerings and more mainstream ones. Saks Fifth Avenue gives tours for the newly wealthy in how the store is laid out, how they can access its more sophisticated shopping services, and so on. Many of our sales training programs focus on educating sales staff on the realities of today's wealthy, precisely so they can build more rapport and do more effective sophisticatering. When we ask the wealthy what attributes they want in a salesperson, product knowledge is by far the most important. Sales excellence in luxury markets is much less about creating a welcoming feeling or a luxurious atmosphere and much more about understanding the sublime distinctions. In a sense, today's wealthy want a retail docent.

Marketing and advertising of luxury products often miss the mark in terms of sophisticatering. Much of it still relies primarily on celebrity endorsements, which generally fail to explain sublime quality and are not terribly persuasive among the wealthy. Other attempts rely on assertions that provide little in the way of education or true differentiation (e.g., a private jet company that asserts without evidence that its planes are fast, safe, and luxurious, just like the assertions from all the other jet companies).

Some companies, however, have navigated these challenges quite effectively. Breitling's watches, for example, were initially designed for aviation professionals, and the company has been adept at communicating how its watches go a step beyond in terms of quality, ruggedness, sophistication, and accuracy. (For example, the proprietary Superquartz is supposedly ten times more accurate than a standard quartz watch movement.) Some models even have a truly unique feature—an emergency radio transmitter—that has saved the lives of some pilots, and is available to nonpilots only upon signing a waiver stating their willingness to pay for rescue services if they accidentally trigger the transmitter. As a result of this sophisticatering, the company has acquired a loyal following among watch aficionados, including Brad Pitt, Jerry Seinfeld, and Tom Cruise.

Obviously, Hollywood celebrities generally don't *need* aviation-quality timepieces (although they may at some point benefit from the emergency safety feature). Instead, their affinity for the Breitling brand comes from the fact that they are sophisticated collectors of jewelry, and they have an appreciation of what makes these particular watches truly unique. They can realize the artistry, the precision, the history, and the uniqueness of the product, even if its most obvious utilitarian features aren't directly relevant for them. The fact that Breitling has celebrity users is an outgrowth of its product excellence, rather than the main thrust of its marketing efforts—in a sense, its elite clientele becomes a proof point for its claims of sublime quality.

Those retailers who have successfully marketed luxury products online have learned the art of Internet sophisticatering. Natalie Massenet, creator of Net-a-Porter.com, has built one of fastest growing online luxury retailers in large part by emphasizing Vogue-like articles over Amazon.com–like product descriptions. With articles like "A to Z of Spring: 26 Ways to Start Afresh in the New Season" and "Fashion Resolutions: Commit Yourself to a Chic and Fashionable New Year," readers are engaged and understand the relevance of luxury items to their lives. And along the way, they learn the subtleties that differentiate those items. As Massenet puts it, engaging stories "tell readers what makes the items for sale so special. You have to keep the magic. If you reduce it to a garment, you are missing the point of what that garment is all about. It becomes a generic item."[3]

The Opportunity for New Luxury Brands

In many respects, there has never been a better time to launch a new luxury brand. The gravitational pull of wealth has concentrated ever more money in the hands of fewer people, making targeting easier. A variety of brand-related dynamics make the opportunity even more promising.

Brands per se are less important than quality. We saw earlier how the vast majority of the wealthy are looking for quality and self-expression over brands and public expression. Although classic luxury brands are still valued, they are by no means a requirement for high-end purchases. In fact, in many categories, consumers arrive at the moment of purchase understanding the product options they want, but being open to any number of brands (see Table 6-5).

Repeat purchasing is strong. Brand loyalty may not be the right phrase, as that implies an emotional commitment to staying with a brand regardless of circumstance. But there is a definite three-stage pattern to luxury purchases: discovery, experimentation, bonding. We've seen the openness to new brands, which brings with it a certain thrill of discovery. Next, experimentation sets in as the buyer tests different brands in different contexts, both through his or her own experience and those of others. Finally, buyers become bonded to certain brands, often after they achieve firsthand experience of the

Table 6-5 **Brand openness in traditional luxury categories (% of responses)**

	Jewelry/ Watch	Designer Apparel	Shoes	
I knew the exact brand and options/details I wanted from the very beginning.	19	15	18	30–40% know what brand they want
I knew which brand I wanted to buy, I just needed to decide on the final options/details offered by the brand.	23	12	15	
I pretty much knew what options/details I wanted in a product and I just needed to decide on the final brand.	36	40	35	60–70% are open to brands
I bought on impulse, without really knowing the brand or options/details I wanted in advance.	23	33	31	

sublime distinctions at the high end of the category. Once someone has bought their first Cartier watch, for example, he or she tends to buy another.

There is a window of opportunity in cause-related marketing. Recall the drivers of brand enthusiasm in Table 6-1. There are two key drivers we have not yet addressed: 79 percent look for brands that "allow me to do something good (e.g., support the environment, give to charity, etc.)," and 75 percent like brands that "reflect a generosity of spirit." As we'll see in a later chapter, the wealthy are involved in philanthropic endeavors in a very hands-on way, and that extends to their purchasing. Two-thirds are willing to pay premium prices for brands that support charitable causes. But in this respect, there is a huge gap between the desires of the wealthy and what luxury brands are delivering. We gave our respondents a list of thirty-seven of the top luxury brands in the world and asked them which ones are doing a very good job at being involved in significant ways with charitable causes. The top scoring brands? Donna Karan and Ralph Lauren tied for first place, with a mere 6 percent of those surveyed giving them favorable ratings. Stella McCartney and MAC Cosmetics tied for second place, both with 5 percent. Seventy-nine percent of the respondents said none of the brands walked the walk in terms of charity and causes. Many brands fared poorly because cause-related associations are often seen merely as casual promotional tie-ins. To effectively leverage what is clearly an opportunity for new brands seeking to gain a foothold in the luxury space, the charitable cause must be closely and meaningfully associated with the brand itself. For example, a private jet company may be seen as authentically connected with an organ donation charity (requiring rapid transport of organs to recipients in need) or a charity that provides dream vacations to terminally ill children (who need close medical attention during their travels).

Given this confluence of factors, it should come as no surprise that new luxury brands are emerging each day. Some are older brands that have become "new" again, but what defines them all is that they mostly fly under the radar for average consumers. Indeed, one of our colleagues jokingly calls these "Palm Beach brands"—if you're not part of the wealthy elite in Palm Beach (or Greenwich or Aspen, etc.), then you probably don't know them.

For example, Belgian shoes are hand-sewn, long-lasting, and incredibly comfortable; their casual, nonconspicuous designs are making them a favorite among today's wealthy. Stubbs and Wootten shoes are also well known among the wealthy, but much less so among the aspiring middle class, and the company takes a more obviously upscale tack. According to its Web site, its "gamut of shoes will take you from easy mornings, to lunches at the club or on the boat, to white-tie benefits for the little lady's favoritest [sic, intentionally and ironically] charity. We know the drill." They are perhaps best known for the custom slippers they created for the Pope and the British Royal family (and for you, starting at $900 a pair).

Those who spend $75,000 for a Range Rover, but use it only to drive to the supermarket are also likely to spend $500 for a high-quality yet inconspicuous Barbour barn jacket. New luxury clothing brands include J. McLaughlin, Lilly Pulitzer, Escada, Emilio Pucci, and St. John's. You can accessorize those outfits with eyeglasses from Oliver Peoples, and jewelry from Seaman Schepps and Helga Wagner. Top them off with evening attire from Badgley Mischka, lingerie from La Perla, and linens from Schweitzer. After the kids come along, dress them with the best from Jacadi and Spring Flowers. Each of these brands provides the sublime qualities of true luxury, while helping to maintain a stealth-wealth lifestyle.

The Journey of Wealth

As we've seen, discerning the subtle qualities of high-end products takes place, category by category, over a considerable period of time and with considerable education. That's not the only element of wealthy lifestyles that evolves over time. In fact, just about every aspect of living with abundance is a learning experience. Those who have had money for many years are very different from those who have just recently had their first liquidity events, and every aspect of the marketing and product mix should be refined accordingly.

As we work with companies looking to build relationships with wealthy individuals, we have found this simple concept to be one of the biggest "Aha's." The common, yet implicit, assumption that "if a person has money, then he must be good at managing money and buying things" is simply not true, particularly not at first. Wealth, as it turns out, is a journey, not a destination.

Notes

1. Dana Thomas, *Deluxe: How Luxury Lost Its Luster* (New York: Penguin, 2007).
2. Hilke Plassmann et al., "Marketing Actions Can Modulate Neural Representations of Experienced Pleasantness," *Proceedings of the National Academy of Sciences* 105, no. 3 (2008): 1050–1054. Published online on January 14, 2008, 10.1073/pnas.0706929 105: http://www.pnas.org/cgi/content/short/105/3/1050
3. Quoted in Dana Thomas, *Deluxe*.

CHAPTER SEVEN

The Journey of Wealth

The Arc of Maturation

"WE GOT RICHER INSTEAD OF POORER, AND WE GOT GOOD AT
LIVING RICHER. BUT IT SURE PUT A LOAD ON US
TO FIGURE IT ALL OUT."

—One of our wealthy research participants

AMERICAN WEALTH TODAY typically occurs in lump-sum distributions. Whether you are a Goldman Sachs investment adviser, a McKinsey partner, a number one overall football draft choice, or a successful entrepreneur, real wealth is not so much accumulated by patient saving as it is delivered in lump-sum checks. It does, however, typically come after years of hard work and comfortable but not affluent living. This is particularly true for the successful entrepreneurs who make up the bulk of today's new generation of wealth.

Most new companies are "bootstrapped"—that is, they are financed on a relative shoestring, using personal savings, credit cards, and loans from family or friends. Founders often go without salaries during the early years, they mortgage their houses, they tap their retirement funds, and they take considerable risks to get ventures off the ground. In retrospect, the "origin stories" of successful companies take on a certain romance, but at the time they are often scary, potentially family-jarring leaps into the unknown. A successful vine-yard owner described his leap this way:

> My transition from the corporate workaday world to [running a successful business] involved, first, giving it all up, sacrificing, and living on a vineyard without electricity. Without running water. Without a toilet. In a double-wide mobile home. With an eighteen-month-old and a three-and-a-half-year-old. With no income, no cash flow, no nothing. Nose-diving into debt. All to get this thing up and running.

Even those few entrepreneurs who manage to get venture capital funding tend to live in modest comfort for many years while the company builds toward acquisition or an IPO. Venture capitalists like to keep founders and managers hungry, avoiding early liquidity events that might sap motivation or lead the team to dissolve prematurely.

After a middle-class upbringing and years of striving, lump-sum wealth leaves most woefully unprepared for the challenges of living with abundance. These challenges may not bring much sympathy from the average American, and they are challenges we would all like to face, but they are formidable in their own right, nevertheless. Remember, they grew up middle class, with fathers and mothers extolling the virtues of hitting the books, getting a job, and always doing the right thing so as not to tarnish the family name. They were not learning the art of discerning sublime distinctions between Cartier's tank watch and Bulgari's solid gold competitor; they were not learning to tactfully rebuff a distant family member's request for a handout; they were not learning how to run the renewable family charitable foundation. The Rockefellers, Carnegies, and Mellons trained their children in the arts of sophisticated spending, investing, and philanthropy. Middle-class kids were told to save a third, spend a third, and give a third. For example:

> My husband and I are "first generations" to the wealth that we have created, so there are lots of surprises along the

way—things you don't expect. And there's nobody putting their arm around you, helping you figure things out. For instance, when we took the company public, nobody said: "Here are five things that you need to really think about." Even with both of us being people who go out and really seek advice and counsel and help, there were a lot of things . . . that I was absolutely broadsided by. . . . I really got educated after the company went public. And we spent a lot of time in New York with [our financial adviser] and it was quite an education; quite a broadening of our horizons . . . there is an incredible learning curve when you come from a background in the humanities or psychology.

Wealth, then, is a journey. Psychological research has shown that all change is stressful, even positive changes like sudden wealth; and the fact is that money brings considerable change to every aspect of life. Eighty-three percent of the wealthy describe having money as "a real learning process." Half agree that, "As I have gained more affluence, it seems that my social network has changed with it." Half have been, in their words, "ripped off." For good and bad, living with abundance is a process of change and maturation.

The length of time people have been wealthy is one of the most powerful predictors of not only how they spend money but also how they view themselves and live their lives. Years of being wealthy brings depth and experience—and new challenges. Living with abundance is a journey that requires evolving middle-class values, tastes, and aesthetics into a life that accounts for both wealth *and* a solid value system. It is a transformation we call the *arc of maturation*. This process of maturation begins suddenly, often on one specific day.

Liquidity Events and Lump Sums: The Day Wealth Happens

In his autobiography *Made in America*, Wal-Mart founder Sam Walton reflected on the lessons of his life: "Somehow over the years, folks have gotten the impression that Wal-Mart was something I dreamed up out of the blue as a middle-aged man, and that it was just this great idea that turned into an overnight success . . . Like most other overnight successes, it was about twenty years in the making."

Wealth typically dawns in a sudden, liberating, head-spinning moment, after years and decades of hard work. The story of Jim McCann is typical. McCann, like so many others in the top 1 percent of the wealth distribution, did not set out to be rich. But he did have an unquenchable thirst to build something and a desire to make a difference in the lives of others. His father was a painting contractor, a small-business owner rather than an entrepreneur. He did reasonably well, but had none of his son's fervor to grow his company.

McCann's first career was as a social worker and he found himself as an administrator at the St. John's Home for Boys in Rockaway, New York. He worked there for fourteen years, helping troubled and underprivileged kids who were seeking to overcome the effects of poverty, drugs, and emotional distress. "I was horrible at it," he told us. "I was worried that a kid in my care would be hurt or killed, or that I would be hurt or killed myself. But the Brother who ran the Home became my mentor. I came to understand how much people need social intimacy and connectivity, and my experience there greatly influences the management style I use in the business today."

In 1976, while he worked as an administrator of the Home for Boys, he purchased a flower shop in Manhattan for $10,000 and called it Flora Plenty. He continued to operate his flower shops on the side for the next ten years while working at the boys' home. Like most small businesses, he got the funding through his own savings and borrowed a little from family and friends. He overcame his lack of financial savvy (at first, he said he was "running a cash business with a cigar-box mentality"), and grew it into a moderately successful chain of fourteen shops. In 1987, he leveraged his personal assets, mortgaged his house, and sold ten stores to purchase 1-800-FLOW-ERS, a nearly bankrupt Dallas-based company, because he believed that toll-free telephone shopping would be the next logical step for the industry.

In a process that Jim calls "due negligence," he paid $2 million for the 1-800-FLOWERS business, and discovered only later that he would need to spend another $7 million covering debts and liquidating assets. His decision making was driven as much by his values and his upbringing as by purely financial concerns. "Most of the debt was owed to florists who had done business with 1-800-FLOWERS under its previous ownership," he told *Inc.* magazine. "People advised me to just give up and file for bankruptcy, but that was not an option for me. Morally, I think bankruptcy is wrong, and I knew that our bankruptcy would have had a severe impact on florists all across the country. Instead, I said: 'Look, we've made a mistake. Now, to pay off our debt, we'll just have to expand our plans, play on a bigger stage, and be successful sooner.'"

Five years later, McCann was out of debt. Next came what he modestly called a series of "logical next steps"; others might call them a series of remarkably innovative and savvy growth strategies. In January 1991, he began advertising on CNN and gained tremendous exposure there during the first Gulf conflict. In 1994, McCann became the first retailer to partner with a little-known start-up called America Online. He instituted consumer-friendly policies, such as a seven-day freshness guarantee, a 100 percent satisfaction guarantee, and a frequent-buyers club. He created a "documercial"—a flower industry–first combination of infomercial and documentary. As the 1990s drew to a close, 1-800-FLOWERS had become a $300 million business. He was financially comfortable, but far from wealthy: he and his wife had a combined net worth of perhaps a few million. Then came the day 1-800-FLOWERS went public.

McCann's investment banker—Goldman Sachs—put the offer to the market at 10 A.M. on August 2, 1999. At lunch that day, Jim was escorted into the private dining room of the chairman of Goldman Sachs. Imagine the room, if you will. It's a theatrical setting for business elegance: paneled in oak, with shelves of books and expensive glass objects surrounding a table covered with a snappy linen tablecloth. Four chairs were at the table, one for Jim, one for his brother (who had become Jim's right-hand man in running the business), one for Goldman Sachs chairman, and one for the lead banker. An extremely efficient waiter attended to the food. The environment was seeped in old money—wealth, power, and majesty. It was a place where great moments occurred routinely.

Jim was escorted to his chair. Lunch was served. And the chairman of Goldman Sachs told Jim how proud they were to have 1-800-FLOWERS as a client. He explained that the offer hit the street at 10:07, it was oversubscribed (a good thing), and all the shares were sold by 11:15. He then handed Jim an envelope, explaining that it contained a check with his share of the proceeds after taxes. Jim took a peek—millions beyond his dreams . . . an envelope filled with freedom. In a moment—the snap of a finger, the blink of an eye—Jim went from a comfortable, affluent middle-class life to real money. And everything wanted to change, but Jim wanted to keep his life as ordinary as possible. As we shall see, much of the lives of successful men and women is spent managing this dilemma.

Today, you might mistake Jim for a middle school teacher or your local pediatrician, but his stake in the company has been valued at upwards of $400 million. As he recounts the story of that day, he still can't quite believe it. Nothing had prepared him for that moment. Jim, in an instant, was thrust into apprenticeship.

Apprenticeship: Caution in the First Five Years of Wealth

Those who have been wealthy for five years or less, we call *apprentices*. They still struggle with the feeling of unreality, with the sense that their sudden wealth might just as suddenly disappear. They still have an unadulterated middle-class appreciation of wealth, which translates to a pervasive sense of caution.

Financial Caution

Despite their tremendous wealth, 43 percent of apprentices worry that they will run out of money (a figure that drops dramatically as the tenure of wealth increases). They are price-conscious shoppers and conservative investors. Their business is still their primary source of income, and they know firsthand how quickly business fortunes can reverse. No wonder they prefer defensive portfolios, resist the temptation to indulge, and continue to abide by their mantra of living within their means. As one apprentice told us, "We don't overspend, we always save and we think really hard about how we will spend our money."

Interpersonal Caution

For all its benefits, wealth can be isolating, particularly for apprentices. Old friendships and family ties often get disrupted; new acquaintances have uncertain motives; requests to fund (sometimes ridiculous) pet projects come at them from all angles. This ensuing interpersonal caution is one of the core roots of stealth wealth. As one successful Wall Street financier told us, when he "struck it rich," he lost most of his childhood friends and felt disconnected from his family. "The first call I got was my brother-in-law looking for a loan. My friends thought I had changed. It's no wonder I spend much of my time disguising my success."

Apprenticeship is also characterized by concerns that the money will strain relationships with the children. Apprentices believe that merit and hard work brought them to the top, and they fear that their kids will be ruined by wealth, as they may fail to learn the value of hard work or the modesty so important to middle-class living. Although proud of their success and excited for their futures, apprentices often feel very much alone, and they are unconnected to the networks that will eventually serve as their community and their confidants.

Moral Caution

The anxiety felt by apprentices is, at times, more diffuse and existential than concerns about money and friends. At a fundamental level, they fear losing their sense of self—their character and their values. After a lifetime of striving and dedication, the main thing the wealthy want is to be judged by their character, not their money. Suddenly, they have the money to do the wrong thing on a big scale, if they choose.

Hollywood is typically filled with cautionary tales of actors or musicians who lost their moral framework after financial success.

The prevalence of these stories in the media overstates how common this dynamic is, but it nevertheless remains a concern and source of caution for the newly wealthy. They don't want money to change them, although it inevitably will; they struggle to ensure that it doesn't erode their moral fiber.

Shopping Caution

As we've seen, the newly wealthy spend, but they do so in a relatively cautious and price-sensitive manner. They are particularly cautious when it comes to big-ticket and luxury items. They are only starting to become educated about the sublime qualities that differentiate high-end products. Instead, they use price and brands as heuristics; more often than you might expect, they avoid the highest-end products altogether. Beyond concerns about price, apprentices are reluctant to buy anything that might be construed as a status symbol because their still-prevalent middle-class mind-set associates these with the indolence and self-indulgence of traditional aristocratic wealth.

It is certainly too strong to call apprentices naïve. They are sophisticated and successful people. And when it comes to luxury products, they know their limitations—in a sense, they know what they *don't* know. If we were to offer a completely unfair caricature of an apprentice, it might be Buddy Ebsen's character Jed Clampett from *The Beverly Hillbillies*. Sudden wealth from an oil strike landed him and his family in a posh Hollywood suburb. Each episode explored this fish-out-of-water premise, in which Jed and his family were confused and overwhelmed by the trappings of wealth. Certainly today's entrepreneurial wealthy wouldn't call a swimming pool a "cement pond," but they find themselves initially confused by unfamiliar tax laws, complex financial instruments, the subtleties of managing household staff, and the sophistication required for truly high-end purchases.

From Apprentice to Journeyman

As apprentices mature in their education, they become journeymen. Multiple liquidity events and greater net worth reduce their price sensitivity and sense of risk. Their growing network opens their eyes to diversified investment opportunities beyond equities. They become aggressive in investment markets as their pool of assets grows more significant. They begin to dabble in real estate, both personal and commercial, and often buy second homes.

Journeymen learn to appreciate the status value of objects, and they feel the tug of rewarding themselves for the hard work and sacrifice it took to make it. They purchase collectables and become connoisseurs (see Figure 7-1). They buy their first seriously expensive toys. They see the toys of their newly made wealthy friends and ask, "Where did you get that?" And so, the journeymen begin experimenting in the power of wealth. They begin to join clubs and begin to have friends who are similarity situated. They also start serving on boards, and they become active politically and philanthropically. To the extent that today's wealthy indulge in conspicuous consumption, it tends to be during this phase, when they are transitioning from psychologically comparing themselves with their humble upbringing

Figure 7-1 The wealthy as collectors and connoisseurs.

| | Total | Length of Time Wealthy | | |
		Apprentice 5 years or less	Journeyman 6–14 years	Master 15+ years
Fine art	33%	19	35	57
Fine wines/champagne	32%	26	38	26
Antiques	21%	15	24	26
Watches/jewelry	19%	14	22	23
Books/rare books	14%	6	20	16
Stamps/coins	11%	15	9	11
Cigars	7%	8	9	3
Vintage cars	7%	5	8	9
Vintage watches/jewelry	6%	3	8	11
Yachts/boats	4%	3	2	8
Thoroughbreds	2%	1	2	4
None of these	34%	46	29	26
Have spent more than $10,000 in at least 1 category	51%	39	56	64

to comparing themselves with wealthier and more sophisticated masters.

From Journeyman to Master

The next inflection point in the journey of wealth occurs after approximately fifteen years, as journeymen evolve into masters. Masters are both conservative and aggressive—in a sense, they are very aggressive about being conservative.

Financially, the source of their wealth has shifted from their business to their now diverse portfolio of investments. They have an orderly approach to charity, family, estate management, and business participation. Many, but certainly not all, have the interests and accessories of the classic aristocrat: clubs, commercial real estate, multiple houses, business jets, and a healthy respect for distribution. They become comfortable with the idea of being wealthy and the role it will have in their family. They are networked and fully realized members of the wealthy class, and will remain so. They are living the good life, or at least what society says the good life ought to be.

The distinct attitudes of masters are driven not only by their decade-plus experience with wealth but also by the fact that their wealth has grown dramatically. Simply put, wealth "snowballs" over time, as the gravitational pull of money showed in the first chapter (also see Table 7-1). From apprentice to master, income grows from an average of $1 million to $3 million per year. Average assets rise from $9 million to nearly $75 million. The percent of income from their business declines from 67 percent to 49 percent as the com-

Table 7-1 **The snowballing of wealth across the arc of maturation**

	Wealth Maturation		
	Apprentice	Journeyman	Master
Mean Household Income ($MMs)	1.0	2.1	3.3
Mean Value of Assets ($MMs)	8.9	27.5	74.6
% of wealth from work	68	63	49
Average Age (years)	48	56	61

pounding effect of investment returns takes place. While masters are the smallest segment, they hold nearly 50 percent of all the assets of the wealthy elite.

Masters are older (thirteen years older, on average) and wiser. Other than fostering a growing suspicion that more people want to associate with them because of their money, their lives become less complicated and they become happier. Their attitudes about children, time, and wealth itself become less intense and, in some sense, more worldly and sophisticated. The capacity to spend, and the willingness to pull the trigger, also grow over the maturation curve.

Purchases of fine art, antiques, and jewelry go decidedly uphill. Among masters, roughly two-thirds spend over $10,000 per year in a "category of passion," one-third have a boat, and one-quarter own a vintage car. Significant increases are also seen in the two major sources of "splurge" spending—home and travel. On average, masters spend twice what apprentices do on home renovations, three times as much on personal travel, and four times as much on home furnishings.

For the most part, new interests and purchasing patterns tend to be "added on top of" existing mind-sets and behavioral patterns, rather than replacing them. Middle-class attitudes, for example, weaken across the arc of maturation, but they are still prevalent even after two decades of wealth, and they remain characteristic of over half of the masters surveyed (see Table 7-2). Although many atti-

Table 7-2 **The gradual weakening of middle-class attitudes**

	Wealth Maturation		
	Apprentice %	Journeyman %	Master %
I would still describe myself as middle class at heart	92	77	68
I consider myself a person with simple needs	75	70	64
I do not care what others think of me. I judge myself by my own standards	72	72	60

tudes and interests remain largely unchanged by wealth, it is also clear that years of education and sophisticatering deepen their understanding of money and their appreciation of aesthetics.

For marketers and people in service occupations, successful relationships with the wealthy are often built on helping them navigate the arc of maturation faster and more gracefully. One interior decorator, who became quite successful in her own right by catering to the wealthy, described the key to her success as helping clients "gain connoisseurship." Another described a similar skill in helping the recently wealthy achieve a new level of sophistication in décor and in appreciating the differences in refinement between two pieces of art that ostensibly focus on the same subject matter. As she explains:

> The newly wealthy are playing catch-up. They are into the quick fix—buying in their minds what seems to be a level of refinement. They buy lots of marble and mirrors, thinking that's fancy or popular, but the architecture and the interior just don't have the classic elements to it. [Masters] really understand refined classic country estates and beautiful antiquities and the refinement of art and culture. [An apprentice might buy] a piece that's cranked out by a contemporary artist that doesn't have nearly the refinement of a piece like Thomas Moran's classic painting of the Grand Canyon or something that's done of the Santa Fe Railroad in 1912. They might buy something of the same basic size, the same basic foreground, the same basic subject matter, but the difference between the two objects is night and day.

We've seen some of these general trends and tendencies evolve as people acclimate to financial abundance, and these are the most common differences among apprentices, journeymen, and masters. There are, of course, other "flavors" of wealth, and many other ways of segmenting this population. Some differences are based on basic personality traits, such as extraversion or anxiety, that remain relatively unchanged by wealth, although additional time and resources may exacerbate or quell their expression. Still other approaches focus on reactions to wealth. Some respond to abundance by trying to accumulate more; others respond by giving it away. As we have seen, most live quietly, almost under the radar of marketers and media. As we have also seen, different groups make distinctly different choices when it comes to lifestyles, purchasing habits, and brand preferences. We now turn to understanding these flavors of wealth, and see how they are shaped by a combination of personality traits and lifestyle choices.

CHAPTER EIGHT

Flavors of Wealth

The Five Lifestyle Choices

"IF YOU'RE NOT THINKING SEGMENTATION,
THEN YOU'RE NOT THINKING."

—Theodore Levitt, Harvard Business School

WE'VE PAINTED A portrait of today's wealthy, from their middle-class upbringing, to the sudden onset of lump-sum wealth, to their journey from apprentice to master. This portrait is data driven and highly accurate, but it also represents a portrait of the "typical" wealthy person, based on averages and common tendencies. There are, in fact, many flavors of wealth, reflecting different types of well-to-do individuals from different backgrounds with different needs, attitudes, and aspirations.

In our studies, we used a series of advanced statistical techniques (described in more detail in the Appendix) and identified five groups with distinct reactions to the value and purpose of money from personal, familial, and societal vantage points. We've called them *neighbors, wrestlers, patrons, mavericks,* and *directors.* As the overview in Table 8-1 shows, these segments also differ in terms of their size, the tenure of their wealth, and the magnitude of their income and their assets.

Table 8-1 **Overview of the five lifestyle segments**

	The Neighbors	The Wrestlers	The Patrons	The Mavericks	The Directors
% of Wealth Population	18	24	15	13	30
Average years been wealthy	6.7	7.6	17.4	12.0	8.3
Mean Income ($MM's)	1.1	1.1	1.8	3.2	2.4
Mean Assets ($MM's)	16.9	19.5	24.9	37.6	39.6

These segments don't differ much in terms of traditional demographic characteristics such as gender (80 percent are male), marital status (80 percent are married), or education (90 percent are college educated, roughly split between public and private colleges). The fact that people in these segments are so distinct in their lifestyles and financial attitudes, yet are similar demographically, highlights the old adage "Don't judge a book by its cover" and underscores the need for marketers to look beyond traditional approaches to understanding differences among the wealthy.

The wealthy differ from one another particularly dramatically on two key dimensions. The first is their philosophical perspective on how money fits into their lives generally. This is an affective response, ranging from emotional comfort with their wealth to fear or anxiety associated with how wealth may influence their lives (the horizontal axis in Figure 8-1). The second dimension is more cognitive in nature, ranging from those who mentally associate money with responsibility and the things that money can accomplish, to those for whom money is less of an objective and more an incidental product that will not be allowed to impact their self-perceptions of character (the vertical axis in Figure 8-1). Combined, these two dimensions offer a broad overview of the personalities of people in each segment and how they differ from one another. Note that on this map, our survey questions are reflected as statements, and the closer a statement is to a segment, the more it describes how members of that segment feel about themselves; conversely, the further a statement is from a segment, the less it is associated with their self-perceptions.

Figure 8-1 Perceptual map of the five lifestyle segments.

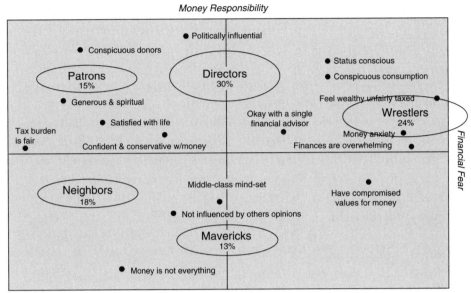

Neighbors

"My life does not really need to change as a result of having money."

Neighbors are at the far left end of the segment map in Figure 8-1, and are characterized by their extreme comfort with the role of money in their lives. Money does not define them; in as many respects as possible, they have tried to ensure it does not change them. About one in five wealthy individuals are neighbors, but in many respects, they are the easiest to miss, as they are most likely to blend in with mainstream America. These are the successful small-business owners often found in little towns and suburbs who have grown incrementally successful over the years, but remain largely committed to living the same life as they had before accumulating wealth. Money happened to be an outcome of hard work, something that could be valuable for a rainy day, but has incrementally less significance and impact on their lifestyle and self-perceptions than on any other segment.

Their more grounded reaction to money may also be because they are among the newest to it (59 percent are apprentices) and tend to have less of it than the other segments (three-fourths have total assets of $5 to $10 million, with an average before-tax income of a "mere" $1.1 million annually). Of all the segments, they are the exemplars of having grown up in middle-class households and retaining that mind-set despite their wealth.

From the outside looking in, we find few cues to their wealth, as neighbors epitomize stealth wealth. They may appear a bit better off than those who live around them, but not dramatically so, and they are far more conservative in spending and displaying money relative to the other segments. Neighbors are likely to have one of the nicer houses in town, but its average value of $1 million is about half that of their wealthy peers. They drive nice but not ostentatious cars, often American made. For their next car purchase, they are most likely to consider a Lexus (as do the wealthy in most segments), but beyond that, they are just as likely to choose a Honda or Volvo as they are a Mercedes or BMW. They take nice vacations, but their average of four per year for less than $30,000 ranks lowest among the segments in terms of both frequency and dollars spent. Eighty-eight percent traveled internationally in the past year—the lowest of any segment, but obviously high in absolute terms—although they are least likely to fly first class or by private jet.

They aren't particularly "television people"—only one-third have a digital video recorder, and a similar number have a high-end television. Relative to the other wealthy segments, neighbors watch the least television, particularly in terms of news and historical documentaries, preferring more middle-class mainstays of sports and sitcoms. Instead, they are the heaviest Internet users and the heaviest magazine readers, where their interests skew toward finance (*Barron's, Forbes, Money*), news, and sports, and away from titles focused on food, travel, and luxury. They are most likely to read the *Wall Street Journal*, but least likely to read the *New York Times*. They are least likely to be connoisseurs or collectors; only one-third have spent more than $10,000 in the past year on a category of passion (in every other segment, over half have done so). When they do collect, their interests skew toward wine, coins, stamps, or antiques rather than jewelry, watches, or cigars.

Their ideal shopping experience is less about an exclusive or luxurious sales environment, and much more about good prices and getting advice from a skilled product expert; their favorite city to shop in is not New York or Paris, but rather their hometown. They have the lowest ownership of traditional luxury brands, although half own a Tiffany product and one in four owns something from Hermès (on the other hand, nearly as many have never heard of Hermès).

Another factor in the neighbor's approach to wealth is that they have, in a sense, "become one with their business." Many operate family businesses, and are often so comfortable and satisfied with their life's work that they don't plan major changes any time soon. Of course, that is not to say that they haven't thought about the future of their businesses. To the contrary, they are highly likely to have a well-defined, well-communicated exit plan for their business, which often involves selling it or turning it over to their kids. They are also the most likely to have an explicit succession plan for their business in the event that they suddenly pass away or become too ill to manage it. Clearly, they have exit plans and contingency plans— they just don't plan to execute either soon, as they are quite content to continue doing what they are doing. Table 8-2 provides an overall picture of typical neighbors.

One realtor we know, who not surprisingly prefers to remain nameless, is a perfect example of a neighbor. A few years ago, John (not his real name) sold his real estate company to one of the national chains for a significant amount of money. He now has enough financial wherewithal to retire, buy a bigger house, and live the good life. The reality is he has not. In his early fifties, John still lists real estate, advertises himself in the local paper, and is as responsive and tuned into the market as he ever was. He is equally committed to showing a $5,000 rental as he would a $5 million mansion. The reality is that John would have lost the quality of life that he holds nearest and dearest if he had let money change him or the lifestyle he presents to the community.

Yes, there was an addition to the house and new furnishings, but

Table 8-2 **Characteristics of neighbors**

Neighbors Are Not Likely To . . .	Neighbors Are Very Likely To . . .
Feel that money or their business pursuits have hampered their values or relationships	Be emphatically middle class at heart
Be intimidated by all the investment options available to them	Describe themselves as "on top of their finances" and very conservative about spending money
Use high-end products to remind them of what they have attained	Be a discount shopper, believing "luxury" is a shallow waste of money
Shop for sport	Shop for a reason
Be concerned about their children's work ethic	Have had a very close relationship with their parents when growing up
Feel their life has become too complicated	Describe themselves as someone with "simple needs"
Believe money can buy happiness, or at least come close	Describe themselves as a spiritual or religious person

his demeanor, his apparel, his friendships, and his sense of self did not change. By most people's standards, he also takes some very nice vacations, and while on those vacations he may indulge in exceptional dinners out, take some unusual excursions, and do some serious shopping, but these tales don't make it to his general friendship network. He carefully chooses whom he can safely share his stories with and whom he cannot. Telling stories beyond the means of the average person could make everyone uncomfortable, and he is far too sensitive to the feelings of those around him to be so thoughtless. Indeed, his sensitivity and acuity to those who work with and for him have been major factors in his success. None of his friends knows for sure just how much money he really has.

Whether it is a conscious or unconscious decision (we suspect both), there would be real risk to John if he were to adopt a more flamboyant lifestyle. An expensive car, more expansive estate, or fancier clothes would all signal that he had taken advantage of or used the people he has served his entire life. Rather than being a just reward for a lifetime of working hard and well, his own definition of overindulgence could cause John embarrassment in his life's work or, at the very least, change the ease in relationships he has come to value over time. For John, this is a simple and easy choice because it does not feel like a sacrifice to have the life he has always enjoyed. We suspect John will be joyfully selling real estate for the rest of his life.

An additional reason the lives of neighbors don't tend to change is that they don't switch their social network and are less often introduced into the next echelon of real wealth, as their businesses tend to be local in nature. Even as they sell their enterprises, the experience will not typically involve extended exposure to venture capitalists or corporate executives from large companies, who hold the business and subsequent social networks often associated with reaching the next stage of affluence.

The reality is that the degree to which a wealthy individual will adopt prestigious brands and lifestyles often depends on the new network of business associates and friends he or she encounters with the transaction of the business and the new life it can bring. If the business is local in nature, it is more likely that the entrepreneur will maintain his or her existing lifestyle because exposure to large corporate wealth and venture scenarios is limited. As we have mentioned before, living with wealth is a learned experience, one that can involve social pressures to step up to a higher standard of living. Neighbors are far less likely to encounter these forces.

A few neighbors will choose moments to live a double life during the course of a year, just to experience their wealth. One participant we spoke with had built a successful sign company that was worth tens of millions of dollars. On one trip west he decided to try a high-end luxury hotel to see what it was like. In the course of that trip, the concierge noticed that he looked as if he were lost and began to introduce him to the many services available at the hotel. He got into the best clubs and the best restaurants and was introduced to other extremely wealthy and successful people. He now leads a regular life in the small town where he lives, but when he travels, he makes it a point to get into the best clubs and reports back his experiences to his new friends.

Wrestlers

"It's still a bit of a struggle."

In contrast to the simplicity and contentment that neighbors seem to enjoy, life for wrestlers is more conflicted, as they find themselves struggling to deal with the paradoxes of wealth. Wrestlers worked hard, buying into the American cultural belief system that financial achievement is the ultimate destination for inner peace, self-actualization, and freedom. But to their surprise, money has magnified, rather than lessened, the anxieties and insecurities of life that existed before wealth. They have brought their old problems with them; they have learned, to borrow a phrase from John Kabat-Zinn, "Wherever you go, there you are." Even worse, money has added new problems on top of their old ones, causing some wrestlers to lose their sense of purpose and identity. As one wrestler put it to us, "I was in my comfort zone in the fight to get money. Now that I have it, I'm not sure who I am anymore or what I'm supposed to be."

Although they wrestle with the feeling that money has created as much conflict and anxiety in their lives as it has relief and enjoyment, that is not to say that they want to give all their money back. In fact, they are most likely to say that money is important to them, and they are fully aware of how it has made their life easier as well as harder. But while neighbors feel grounded by their connections to their businesses, and confident in their knowledge of how to handle money, wrestlers are, metaphorically speaking, left flapping in the wind without these solid personal or professional groundings.

Professionally, they are least likely to have a solid exit or succession plan for their business. On a personal level, three-quarters feel they are not as in control of their finances as they would like to be—by far the highest of any segment. Many struggle with the fear that they could lose all their money and have to start rebuilding their lives all over again, despite their average of nearly $20 million in assets. Less than one in four feels he or she has an organized estate plan and many believe that the distribution of their assets will be a major source of family turmoil and conflict after their death. Virtually none of their kids have a good understanding of the value of their estate. Heck, forget the kids—over half of wrestlers haven't told their spouses of the degree or nature of their financial empire!

On average, wrestlers aren't miserably unhappy; 88 percent describe themselves as "very happy," although this is the lowest of any of the five segments. But their anxieties, insecurities, and struggles with the contradictions of wealth are pervasive and far-reaching. Although it is always tenuous to play armchair therapist, we can't help noticing that their insecurities appear to be deep-seated as well. They are least likely to report having had a close relationship with their parents while growing up, and qualitatively many told us that their motivation to achieve came in part from compensating for more challenging childhoods. Whether it was less approving parents or difficult peer relationships in school, wrestlers often have something to prove to themselves and the world around them, and their financial success is one symptom of this insecurity-driven, validation-seeking striving. Table 8-3 gives an overall picture of typical wrestlers.

Behaviorally, the inner conflicts of wrestlers manifest themselves as yo-yo spending, sometimes spending with abandon, sometimes

Table 8-3 **Characteristics of wrestlers**

Wrestlers Are Not Likely To . . .	Wrestlers Are Very Likely To . . .
Feel a sense of alignment among their values, interests, attitudes, and actions	Feel anxious, conflicted, and that they never have enough time for themselves
Feel luxury items like expensive watches, jewelry, and cars are a waste of money	Enjoy using subtle cues like exclusive designer apparel or an expensive watch to remind them of what they have attained
Feel that money has made their lives simpler and less stressful	Fear being judged, resented, or running out of money
Have had a very close relationship with their parents when growing up	Be concerned about their children's work ethic because they have always had money
Describe themselves as content, religious, or spiritual	Buy sporadically into luxury brands—enjoying them, but wondering if they overdid it
Be emotional, carefree shoppers	Shop for status objects, rareness, and uniqueness

denying themselves and their families. Sometimes they pursue stealth-wealth strategies, liking the anonymity, but miss the acknowledgement of their status. On other occasions, they indulge in conspicuous consumption, but that brings conflicts as well—they are most likely to say that they want other people to know they are wealthy, but they are also likely to acknowledge that many people want to be friends with them simply because of their wealth.

Their approach to luxury brands conveys a similar sense of contradiction and vacillation. For example, wrestlers admire luxury brands, and like the *idea* of buying them, but they are only about average in terms of actually purchasing or owning luxury brands. They are torn between the desire to reward themselves and the feeling that it is being overindulgent. They are torn between liking the perceived status that comes with high-end brands and the fear that others will judge them, or possibly even consider them targets. They find conflict in the knowledge that they can now afford a $250 shirt—and will even buy it and feel good wearing it—and then in the next moment wonder if they have lost their character and sense of values for doing so.

They struggle with the idea of indulging themselves when so many in the world have so much less, yet they have worked hard to achieve what they have—haven't they earned the right to enjoy their money? They are certain that their spouses and families have sacrificed (as they have) to attain financial success. A wrestler will indulge his wife with a three-carat flawless diamond ring for being there all these years one day, enjoy the gift briefly, and then wonder if he has lost his mind for having spent the money.

In a sales context, the wrestler's insecurity translates into the search for encouragement and reinforcement. When asked about their ideal shopping experiences, wrestlers are most likely to feel the sales process is of critical importance. But they are less focused on utilitarian product knowledge. Compared to other segments, wrestlers are most likely to cite the importance of having a salesperson who makes a personal connection with them, making them feel like "the most important customer they have." What really turns them off? Interacting with a salesperson who treats them like any other person off the street, or who might look down on them for their lack of knowledge in the category. They want to spend more and will spend more; they just need to get better at it.

One might think that contributing to charity is a relatively unambiguous good thing to do, but for wrestlers, even that action is fraught with anxiety and paradox. Although they donate about as much as other wealthy people, wrestlers struggle the most in deciding which charities to contribute to and are most likely to feel that charities are inefficient in how they use their resources. They primarily support charities that serve issues or tragedies that have affected their own lives, which is certainly rewarding, but also serves as a reminder of their struggles and setbacks. They are least likely to have their own charitable foundations, but have the highest intention to do so "someday."

Anxiety and contradiction pop up in many areas of the wrestlers' lives. They like international travel, but are cautious of the risks involved, so they tend to do it close to home, with higher than average visitation to Canada, Mexico, the Caribbean, and the United Kingdom. They understand the risks of not diversifying their investments, but at the same time, they look to simplify their decision making and are most likely to be comfortable having a single wealth-management company manage all of their money.

They appreciate their wealth, but are most likely to feel unfairly treated by the government in terms of their tax burden. They are most likely to be intimidated by the investment options available to them, but they are least likely to read the financial magazines that can help. Like neighbors, they aren't big television watchers, although they do like news and documentaries. Perhaps most telling, they were among the heaviest watchers of popular "escapist" dramas—in our 2005 survey, for example, these included *24*, *Boston Legal*, and *Desperate Housewives*. These might be considered "televised cotton candy"—momentarily satisfying, followed by the feeling of "I can't believe I just wasted an hour watching that." (Not that we're judging—at least one of the three authors has continued his own guilty pleasure addiction to *Desperate Housewives* long after many felt it had reached its peak.)

In the meantime, wrestlers like to buy things that can reinforce their sense of style, technical sophistication, financial means, and competence. One particular area of indulgence is the home, where they spend far more than any other group on remodeling projects, landscaping, and furnishings. They particularly love home electronics, where they have indulged their interests in plasma TVs, surround-sound systems, home theaters, high-speed Internet access, high-end MP3 players, and DVR technology. They are far more likely to be driving BMWs, Acuras, Porsches, and Audis than the other groups, but they are least satisfied with their vehicle, regardless of its year or make. For their next car, their most likely choices are mainstays of the wealthy population as a whole—Mercedes, BMW, Lexus—but are significantly more likely than others to be thinking more exotically, like an Aston Martin, Porsche, or Bentley.

Wrestlers are the youngest segment, with most in their early to mid-forties, although many are considerably younger. Their success at such a young age, while their interests and values are still forming, no doubt contributes to their anxieties. Another factor: Like neighbors, wrestlers are relatively new to money—43 percent are apprentices and 44 percent are journeymen—and their profile is similar in many ways to that of journeymen we highlighted in the previous chapter. For example, when they come to a collegue's office, they are most likely to notice objects of art or unique personal significance and ask, "Where did you get that?" Objects that convey status are of particular interest to them, and like many journeymen, they are heavy spenders on collectables, particularly fine art, watches, and jewelry. They also tend to be particularly avid readers of publications such as *Vanity Fair* and *Wine Spectator.*

They fear the consequences of wealth, particularly for their children. Part of the motivation to acquire wealth was to create a better life for their children—to give them access to enriching experiences and finer things. Yet in the process, they are very concerned about how access to such an affluent lifestyle will ruin their children's work ethic, their family connection, and sense of middle-class values that they hold so dear. The ease with which their kids can get new toys, new designer clothes, and premier vacations are all in conflict with the middle-class sense of values most of these individuals carry. Indeed, three-quarters of wrestlers express concern about their children's work ethic, and 94 percent strongly encouraged their kids to get jobs during their high school years. Many find it difficult to accept that their children are growing up wealthy and cannot seem to find a way to enable them to be both comfortable and responsible. Many would like to believe that their children could grow up with the middle-class values they held. As one of our interviewees, who grew up in poverty, put it to us:

> I haven't made many lifestyle changes at all, because I want my daughter to grow up just the way I think people should grow up. I'd rather have her grow up as a normal child, and face the world the way everyone sees it. I want her to go to privileged schools, the best private schools, but I want her to feel like she's just like everyone else. I want her to have the hunger, just the way I had.

If wrestlers can overcome their childhood insecurities and frailties, they may move into the ranks of the mavericks, patrons, or directors. The shifts in attitudes will be significant, but at the same time, it's not difficult to imagine their evolution once years of experience and comfort kick in. One of the most telling statistics about this segment—which reflects how widespread the challenges of wealth are—is the fact that they are the second largest segment, representing 24 percent of the wealthy elite.

Mavericks

"In Me I Trust."

Every few years, one maverick we know (we will call him Jason) divests himself of his material possessions and his profession, so he can start again with a clean slate. He has the freedom to do that primarily because he's worth hundreds of millions of dollars—and so, no matter what he sheds, he can buy again anything he wants or needs.

When Jason was his early twenties, he had no thoughts of wealth. He was more focused on indulging his passion for alternative music. In 1993, a friend asked him if knew anything about creating an obscure and little-known thing called a Web site. (A year later, Jeff Bezos founded Amazon.com, and as he told colleagues about his idea to sell books on the Internet, the most common question he heard was, "What's the Internet?") Jason was intrigued, and as always, followed his curiosity. He and his friend founded one of the first dot-coms, and with plenty of hard work and great timing, they built it into a thriving enterprise. As the new millennium arrived, so did their initial public offering, and lump-sum wealth arrived as a reward for years of dedication.

Today, Jason enjoys tremendous financial success and is a widely respected industry leader. He is routinely named in lists of the most influential people in his industry. In his early forties, he believes he's just getting started. He is probably right.

Today he remains chairman of that company he founded a decade and a half ago and works long hours out of passion, not financial need. He takes his hobbies, such as his passion for music, just as seriously. In his "spare time," he owns blues clubs and produces music festivals. Some might think that blues, incredibly hard work, and a multimillion dollar net worth are an odd combination. He doesn't care. In fact, that's what makes Jason a prototypical maverick: He pursues his idiosyncratic passions with intensity, and doesn't particularly care how he appears or what people think about how he operates.

The mavericks are the smallest of the five segments, representing 13 percent of the wealthy, but they are highly distinct in their motivations and perceptions of value. They enjoy average incomes of over $3 million each year (highest of any group) with assets of $38 million, and they represent a unique set of independent thinkers who have relied on their own guts and instincts to be successful. Mavericks are often serial entrepreneurs who have found success creating their own businesses, and as primary investors in other companies where they play a critical role in the practices and choices of the organization.

Entrepreneurship is a challenging game with high stakes that mavericks feel confident they can win. The accumulation of wealth is not the ultimate goal; the goal is to have a business vision and execute that vision, while recognizing all the major criteria necessary for success and all the details necessary to achieve them. They play to win, "capitalist style." They take this challenge seriously, as it defines all aspects of who they believe they are. They are far less likely to give money credit for creating happiness, viewing it more as an appreciable by-product and proof point of their competence and efforts. They believe they are lucky to have accomplished what they have, but also firmly believe they have made their own luck. As pure capitalists, they tend to believe that the opportunity for success in America is available to anyone who has the drive to pursue it. This rugged individualism, this "If I can do it, anyone can do it" mentality, often minimizes the contributions of their intelligence, creativity, and business sense that distinguish them from the millions of people who would love to change places with them. Table 8-4 gives an overall picture of typical mavericks.

The entrepreneur, almost by definition, marches to the beat of his or her own drummer. Entrepreneurial success requires pursuing unique ideas in unique ways, and the willingness to move forward when others point out the risks and potential pitfalls of uncharted territory. Mavericks have this quality in spades. They are most likely to report not caring what others think of them and announcing that they judge themselves by their own standards. Interestingly, they are least likely to agree with statements like, "I am very good at most everything I do"—not because they believe themselves untalented, but because they are willing to pursue new interests and ventures, regardless of any past relevant experience or success.

Table 8-4 **Characteristics of mavericks**

Mavericks Are Not Likely To . . .	Mavericks Are Very Likely To . . .
Take the safe path	Explore the road not taken
Feel traditional luxury products and brands are a waste of money	Spend heavily and without reservation on their passions
Shop for sport	Shop with a purpose
Be well-known philanthropists	Be serial entrepreneurs and rugged individualists
Feel they are excellent at everything they do	Take on challenges that intrigue them, even outside their traditional comfort zones

As we have seen, mavericks play by their own rules and often have idiosyncratic lifestyles. We have tried to paint a portrait of a typical maverick, but that is harder to accomplish for this segment than for any of the others. On many of our measures, mavericks show more variability or bimodal distributions, making them more difficult to describe with a simple statement such as, "Mavericks tend to be X."

Consider vacations. Over half of the mavericks surveyed have taken three personal trips or fewer in the past year—that's the highest percentage of infrequent travelers in any segment. But nearly 15 percent have taken ten or more vacations—that's the highest percentage of frequent travelers in any segment. The same pattern emerges for business travel. Twenty-nine percent of mavericks didn't take a business trip in the past year, yet 31 percent took twenty or more—both figures are the highest among the segments.

This same pattern occurs for basic demographics as well. On average, mavericks tend to be in their early to mid-fifties, with a $3.3 million annual pretax income and a $3.4 million home. But their responses on all of these measures show considerable variability and dispersion; in short, being a maverick is about a mind-set and a lifestyle that is only loosely related to a particular demographic profile. This intra-segment diversity of opinion and interest is apparent in other ways, as well. They are among the heaviest readers of *Architectural Digest, Smithsonian,* the *Wall Street Journal,* and *Condé Nast Traveler;* they are also among the heaviest readers of *Entertainment Weekly* and *People* magazine. They are least likely to do home entertaining, but are most likely to say that the kitchen is the favorite room in their house; they are the heaviest readers of *Bon Appétit* and *Gourmet* magazines. They are the most likely to travel to France or England, but the least likely to travel to the Caribbean and many other destinations. Simply put, they are not easily pigeonholed.

The maverick approach to the marketplace is shaped by another unique combination of two attitudes. They are highly likely to describe themselves as still being middle class at heart; at the same time, they are demanding and have high standards in the categories that intrigue them. Mavericks do not define themselves by the amount of wealth they have accumulated, and so they do not place great importance on displaying it. In fact, they most adamantly reject the more flamboyant designer brands.

They are generally tied with neighbors for the lowest ownership of traditional luxury brands, and are least likely to read magazines such as the *Robb Report* and *Worth*. Still, they have high expectations, preferring to stick with the brands they feel have substance, have been reliable, and can be trusted over time. Flashy brands that do not offer real meaningful substance behind their artistic expressions are seen as frivolous and wasteful, and those who choose these brands are perceived as lacking substance and integrity. Mavericks can take great trips, own beautiful properties, drive great cars, and never feel they have to apologize for their choices. They bring a practicality to these choices that justifies their purchases in value, even if the value equation is well beyond the average American. This is, in part, because they answer to their own standards, but also because they perceive themselves to be conservative in their spending habits.

Relative to other wealthy segments, they do tend to spend less in a variety of outlets and categories: department stores, clothing, collectables, home renovation, and so on. They will spend where they have interest and perceive value—indeed, among our groups, they are least focused on getting a good deal—but they have a tremendous disdain for waste, pretension, and shallowness. In a retail context, they don't look for an exclusive or luxurious sales environment, nor do they want to be made to feel like they are the most important customer in the store. Instead, they want sales staff who are knowledgeable, are down to earth, and treat them like "any other person off the street."

Mavericks are living in the moment, and are inherently self-focused; as a result, they tend to be less worried about the legacy of their money. In a sense, their estate plans are more often in their minds than on paper. While they are relatively likely to say they *envision* passing their companies to their children, they are among the least likely to have actually communicated any kind of plan for what would happen in the event of their injury or death. They are so psychologically entwined with their businesses and their ambitions they often find it difficult to think in concrete terms about any kind of exit or succession plan. Moreover, their feeling of "If I can do it, anybody can do it" allows them a confidence that their children could (and probably should) do the same thing.

The capitalistic mind-set of mavericks often extends to their thinking about charities as well. Most do not like charity events, and as a group they are not overly motivated to give to charities. Mavericks tend to be far more cynical about the value of charitable causes, having seen too many handouts that did not result in lasting change, or that might even reinforce a deeper dependency among recipients. Mavericks believe charities should be designed to eliminate their risky dependence on outside funding, which is generally not the case for most philanthropic organizations. Other factors dissuade them from charities as well. They believe that most individuals can rise up if they choose to (just as they have done), and that market forces will ultimately guide proper decision making when the economics are right.

Mavericks do engage charities, but as always, they do so in their own way. They believe in giving anonymously, for instance. They prefer to give money rather than time, believing their time is better spent generating more wealth for future needs than being in the trenches themselves. And they are particularly intrigued by the emerging venture-philanthropy approach to charity—one that applies business savvy and for-profit models to charitable endeavors—that we detail in Chapter 11.

Mavericks are also less apt to align themselves with organized politics, being twice as likely as those in any other segment to define themselves as political independents (37 percent). Nor do they ascribe a great deal of enthusiasm for religion. They are far too pragmatic and self-reliant to be overly invested in the products of faith beyond their control. They believe that if they live a reasonably good life here, then heaven should take care of itself when and if that day comes. Of course, heaven does not come easily, and the entrepreneurial lifestyle is not without challenges and temptations. Over 60 percent of mavericks feel their business pursuits have come at the expense of their family life, and one in four feels they have compromised their values for money; both of these figures are higher than for any other segment.

Directors

"Money is serious business."

Neighbors may camouflage their wealth, wrestlers may worry that it will destroy them, mavericks have vowed to not let it reflect their moral values, and, as we shall see, patrons have come to accept it. By comparison, directors, who at 30 percent of the wealthy are the largest segment of that population, place far greater importance on the attainment and retention of wealth than do those in any other segment.

Directors have come to see wealth as essential to living a good life and, as a result, view money as a critical resource to handle responsibly (by both the immediate family and future generations) so that the clan will be able to enjoy the high standard of living necessary to attain happiness and fulfillment. Nearly all of them want their heirs to be stewards of family wealth, and 87 percent have established trusts in those interests. Indeed, no other segment finds money as important as directors, and they cannot imagine life any longer without it.

Because money plays a greater role for this segment relative to any other group and perhaps because they have not yet had the years of experience of patrons, directors are most aggressive about defending their wealth and building on it. Over 80 percent still define themselves as being on the front lines of their businesses, well ahead of any other group. This steadfast Republican segment (73 percent) feels that they have earned every penny they have and that the government is usually excessive and wasteful in attempting to tax it away from them. Directors pride themselves on their competence and confidence in all aspects of life, including family, business, and finances. Indeed, two-thirds feel (accurately) that the economy would suffer if people like them stopped spending. Table 8-5 gives an overall picture of typical directors.

With their total assets just ahead of the mavericks, directors are the most financially successful of the segments, with $40 million in worth, on average. They have the most sophisticated financial portfolios of the five groups, with more investments in commercial real

Table 8-5 **Characteristics of directors**

Directors Are Not Likely To . . .	Directors Are Very Likely To . . .
Feel insecure about their financial or social standing	Spend extensively in every category, yet have a confident and classically conservative approach to investing
Feel luxury goods are a waste of money	Be the last of the traditional luxury shoppers, providing keystone margins
Believe that money has made their lives more complicated	Associate money with happiness, and feel they deserve everything they have
Be Democrats	Resemble the stereotypes of inherited wealth

estate, oil and gas, commodities, and currencies. Directors also clearly have the highest spending patterns associated with the good life they are creating. One-third own a boat, 60 percent have a second home, and over half have three or more cars (typically a new Mercedes, but many also drive Cadillacs). They far outspend others in and around the home, from outdoor landscaping to home furnishings.

They are the most avid and highest-spending collectors in virtually every category, from fine wine to vintage cars and jewelry. They tie or exceed wrestlers in terms of having high-tech toys such as high-end televisions, in-home theaters, and high-capacity digital video recorders. One-third have satellite radio, the highest of any segment. They are among the highest readers of the magazines one might stereotypically associate with the wealthy: *Cigar Aficionado, Forbes, Fortune, Travel + Leisure, Departures, Food & Wine, Gourmet,* the *Robb Report, Vanity Fair,* and *Worth.* They also read up on country club sports with *Golf Digest* and *Tennis* magazines. (Interestingly, they report that the library or office is their favorite room in the house.)

They are also the heaviest business travelers, often flying first class, and nearly one-quarter flying on private jets. They tie or surpass patrons in ownership of virtually all luxury brands, and they have "traditional" expectations, from a luxury retail experience, to an exclusive luxurious environment, to salespeople who make them feel like the most important customers they have. They are also second only to patrons in terms of their enthusiasm—monetary and emotional—for charity and philanthropy.

In short, directors are the men and women who lead companies, serve on corporate boards, maintain powerful networks, and build family dynasties. Although they are just as likely as the other segments to have created their wealth through entrepreneurial means, this segment most reflects the mind-set and lifestyle of inherited wealth.

George Russell was a director, and in that sense, he sometimes seemed to be at the center of the world. Everything and everyone revolved around him. He expected people to come to him, not the other way around. He had a sprawling network of friends, associates, partners, helpers, and advisers. He was so thoroughly woven into his community that it was virtually impossible to make a move without somehow bumping into him.

Many of his nonprofit endeavors were focused on promoting global business cooperation, to the benefit of both the world and his organization. His Russell 20-20 was a learning-focused nonprofit association of institutional investors, and he created a series of reports to foster communication between public and private sector financial leaders throughout the world. He served on the board of the Woods Hole Oceanographic Institute and was chairman emeritus of the Museum of Glass: International Center for Contemporary Art. He was cochairman of the EastWest Institute, and brought to it the specific focus of educating Americans about the Islamic faith. As chairman of the National Bureau of Asian Research, he sought to educate Americans about the potential of globalization to reduce poverty and to bring the haves and have-nots closer together throughout the world. He was honorary chair of the Business Humanitarian Forum. He cofounded the Kendall-Russell Centre for Corporative Competitiveness in Russia. The list goes on.

In retrospect, it seems that Russell was destined to be a director. He was born in Tacoma, Washington, attended public elementary school, and then traveled east by train to Phillips Exeter Academy in Exeter, New Hampshire, where he spent his high school years. He did his undergraduate work at Stanford University in California, and then came back to New England to attend Harvard Business School. His business training was interrupted by two years in the army, after which he completed his MBA at Harvard. After school, he joined his grandfather's small brokerage firm with the goal, not of making money, but rather of building a business.

Within six months of joining up, George's grandfather died and George began setting the firm on a new path—what appeared to him as the next logical step. He steered the company through decades of tremendous growth, pioneering now-lucrative fields such as pension fund consulting and asset management. (The well-known Russell 2000 Index—the Dow Jones Industrial Average of small companies—was created by his firm.) Starting in 1974, the company experienced rapid expansion and has averaged 24 percent annual growth every year since.

Russell had a number of liquidity events along the way, but his big one came in 1999, when the company—which was routinely listed as one of the best companies in America to work for—was sold to Northwestern Mutual Life for approximately $1 billion. It continues to operate under the Frank Russell Company name and serves more than 1,100 clients in some forty countries with assets exceeding $2.4 trillion. Russell himself is recognized as one of the four most influential people in the world of institutional investing (Warren Buffett is one of the others) and received many honors, awards, and honorary degrees.

When directors describe their lives, it can all sound pretty easy and inevitable. But it took Russell forty years to reach his big payday. And, like most directors, Russell always declined to talk much about the failures, the deals that went wrong, the opportunities that were missed, and the times he was not able to create good luck for himself.

Patrons

"The best thing I do is give—and it's the most fun, too."

There comes a time in life for many wealthy individuals when the sense of accomplishment attained through business endeavors turns less novel, less challenging, and less inspirational. There comes a point when they say, "I've made it. I am successful. It is time to focus on giving back. I want to make a difference." This is the defining mind-set of patrons.

Fifteen percent of today's wealthy population are patrons, and they are the most mature of the five groups at an average age of sixty years, with the majority of them having held their wealth for ten years or longer. Like the other segments, they are predominantly entrepreneurs, although roughly one in ten inherited most of his or her wealth. Two-thirds are empty nesters, whereas among the other segments, about half have children under eighteen years old at home. Financially, with an average net worth of $25 million and pretax income of nearly $2 million, they tend to fall between the "minimally wealthy" neighbors and wrestlers on the one end, and the higher-end mavericks and directors on the other.

But demographics and bank accounts are less defining of this segment than their passion for charity. Philanthropy is the focus of their lives, not only in terms of how they use their money but also in how they invest their time and emotional energy. Three-fourths serve on nonprofit boards. They are pioneers in venture philanthropy (which we'll detail in Chapter 11). They seed pro-social and pro-environmental start-up companies. One in four has his or her own charitable foundation, and another one-third intend to start one. They anticipate dedicating 30 percent of their estate to charities (more than any other segment), and one-quarter intend to distribute half or more of their $20+ million in assets to charities at the time of their death. Seventy percent indicate that building assets for phil-anthropic goals is a major life goal. On every attitudinal measure related to contribution and charity, patrons outscore every other seg-ment by a wide margin. Table 8-6 gives an overall picture of typical patrons.

In terms of Maslow's hierarchy of needs, the freedom that pa-trons feel to focus on making contributions is, in a sense, a luxury enabled by their having largely addressed their own financial and psychological needs. Making the world a better and more beautiful place is a noble goal, but a difficult focus for wrestlers (for example) as they struggle with their own real and perceived challenges. Pa-

Table 8-6 **Characteristics of patrons**

Patrons Are Not Likely To . . .	Patrons Are Very Likely To . . .
Be anxious about their financial standing	Devote considerable time and money to charitable activities
Feel stressed and out-of-control	Describe themselves as very happy, content, and grateful
Describe themselves as having simple needs	Perceive value in sophisticated luxury items, but not define themselves by them
Feel isolated and targeted because of their money	Feel socially connected to family, friends, and networks of social influence

trons, in contrast, are distinct in the comfort they feel in so many areas of their lives.

For example, patrons are more likely than wealthier mavericks and directors to be free of worry about protecting their wealth, highlighting how contentment is more a state of mind than a state of one's bank account. Patrons are most likely to have well-thought-out, well-communicated exit and succession strategies for their business. They are the least likely to fear family squabbling over their inheritance, and least likely to feel that their dedication to business pursuits has come at the expense of their family life. On a personal level, they are least likely to say that money has complicated their lives, or that they can never find enough time, or that they need to simplify and streamline. In a sense, they've got it all figured out.

This sense of control and contentment emerges partly because charity is the defining and grounding element in their lives, rather than money, possessions, or success. They are comfortable with their wealth, but it doesn't define them. Most are adept with technology, but their gadgets don't define them, either. They like nice cars, most typically driving a new Mercedes or Lexus, but they don't derive their identity from what they drive. They are least likely to say that they have compromised their values for money. They have enjoyed money long enough that they have been able to forget some of the toll it required to accumulate it, they are far less fearful of the impact it may have on their family, and they have lost the anxiety of being judged by others. They're not even mad at the government for how much of their income goes to taxes. They no longer feel a need for these concerns. They have arrived.

Patrons are also grounded by their connections with friends, family, and social networks. Money generally leads wrestlers to feel isolated and targeted. Neighbors stay committed to their mainstream friendship networks. Mavericks and directors are in social transition while they develop new personal and business networks among the other affluent they meet. Patrons have largely completed these transitions, and have developed wealthy social networks formed with other do-gooders. Money and charity have combined to be powerful connecting factors in their lives.

They truly enjoy being part of a charitable social network. More than 80 percent enjoy charitable events; nearly all of them feel charitable organizations use their money effectively. Only 16 percent prefer to support philanthropies anonymously, in part because they like the social recognition, but also because they like the inherent social connections. They seek to include their children in their charitable networks; patrons are most likely to have encouraged their high-school-age kids to participate in community service activities, and are least likely to have encouraged them to get jobs. Patrons are, simply put, social people; two-thirds entertain friends at home several times a month or more, far outpacing any other segment.

Patrons invest in causes and campaigns they personally believe in and that they hope will bring about positive change for society. Because of their social connections, two-thirds of them feel they can sway the political agenda more than others, but only one-quarter are doing so for business purposes. Again, their pro-social mind-set shines through: They recognize that money brings the power for change, and they feel a responsibility and desire to do what they can. This mind-set of taking responsibility to help others, as opposed to a "Let people pull themselves up by their bootstraps" rugged individualism, shapes their political attitudes as well. This is the only segment of the wealthy in which Democrats (42 percent) outnumber Republicans (33 percent), and they are most likely to be concerned about societal issues such as federal budget deficits and the growing gap between the rich and the poor.

The nobility of the patrons shouldn't be confused with self-denial or an ascetic lifestyle. While patrons may be reluctant to ascribe money as a source of happiness, and like to be charitable, they clearly use it freely to engage in their own pleasures. They are least likely to describe themselves as conservative in spending money. Indeed, they spend over $60,000 each year on the six vacations they take ($25,000 higher than the next closest segment). Their houses are large and comfortable, typically worth over $3 million. Nearly eight in ten have vacation properties. Nine in ten own commercial real estate. The lines of what money buys and who they are have become blurred so that they now simply embrace this lifestyle as a state of being rather than something that money buys.

Generous is obviously an apt term for describing patrons, as is *content*. Yet another is *sophisticated*. They are least likely to describe themselves as having "simple needs." Although 61 percent still feel middle class at heart, this is the lowest percentage of any segment; and in many respects, their connection with their mainstream upbringing is diminishing. They are about average in terms of how much time they spend reading magazines, but their tastes skew toward relatively sophisticated lifestyle and literary magazines, including *Architectural Digest, The Atlantic Monthly, The Economist, Gourmet, Martha Stewart Living, The New Yorker,* and *Town & Country*. Two-thirds regularly read the *New York Times*—by far the highest of any segment. They are regular readers of business periodicals such as *Forbes* and *Fortune*, but have the lowest readership of financial how-to magazines such as *Kiplinger's* or *Smart Money*. This sophistication extends to how they shop and engage the marketplace more generally. Patrons are the only segment more likely to cite New York City as their favorite shopping place over their hometown.

In a retail context, patrons are least likely to desire a salesperson who makes a personal connection with them, and most likely to want an expert in sophisticatering who can explain the sublime distinctions that help determine an item's exceptional value. Confident in their own style, patrons don't look to brands in an effort to help strengthen their identity; rather, they look for products that match their own taste and aesthetic. In terms of awareness and ownership of luxury brands, patrons are generally at par, or nearly so, with directors. Both segments express the highest affinity for traditional luxury brands, including Burberry, Cartier, Chanel, DeBeers, Giorgio Armani, Louis Vuitton, Tiffany, Ferragamo, and Hermès. Of all the segments, patrons are the most likely to collect rare books, fine art, and antiques (although they rank lowest for cigars). Patrons are particularly passionate about the arts; they describe themselves as curious individuals always seeking to learn more about the human condition, as well as the objects, experiences, and opportunities that exist to explain it.

In light of recent wealth formulation in America, we can only expect the patron portion of the wealthy population to grow significantly in the years ahead, as money in America matures and causes the wealthy to be more relaxed about what they can give without risk. This trend has gained great visibility with the works of people like Ted Turner, Bill and Melinda Gates, Gordon Moore, George Soros, and Warren Buffett. But becoming a patron is generally a process—it is a state achieved after some experience with wealth. Recall the story of Jim McCann, who grew up in the middle class and retains the values he learned as kid and that he espoused to the boys at St. John's Home. Jim entered the arc of maturation as a neighbor, but with ten years of wealth behind him, he became a full-fledged patron. Although still on the front lines of the flower business, he spends much of his time working with other organizations and distributing his wealth. Jim serves on several corporate boards, including those of Lottomatica, GTECH Corporation, and Willis Group Holdings. He also contributes time and energy to education and to health care as a trustee for Winthrop University Hospital, a teaching hospital on Long Island.

Summing Up: Insights into Action

Beyond insights, there are a range of practical applications for this segmented approach to understanding the wealthy population. It is, for example, a useful framework for understanding the appeal and potential reach of luxury brands. Any given brand tends to have greater or lesser presence among each of these segments, and there is a disproportionate opportunity to expand their presence among each. Some brands are capable of holding their appeal across all of the segments, typically because they are grounded in sound value propositions based on inherent quality and integrity. Others have a narrower, more concentrated opportunity.

Some classic brands have become associated with emotional imagery and higher prices that combine to focus their appeal among directors and patrons. Others have a more socially oriented high-status appeal that can be leveraged with an unambiguous "I've made it" message to wrestlers. More subtle messaging to promote a brand of solid quality and value would likely appeal to neighbors.

Sales training is another valuable application. Obviously salespeople in any category, from retail apparel to financial services, can more effectively connect with well-to-do prospects if they have an accurate understanding of the mind-sets and attitudes of wealthy individuals in general. But in our training efforts, we have found that the greatest leap in sales performance comes with a segmented approach to selling. Much of our training involves helping salespeople quickly and unobtrusively assess which segment a prospect most likely belongs to. Then we help them fine-tune every aspect of sales approach accordingly, from building rapport to countering objections to most persuasively describing the benefits of what they offer. One of our financial service clients has witnessed an average increase in revenue of *several million dollars* within one week of its sales teams being trained in the nature of wealth today, as well as in the art and science of segmented selling to the wealthy.

CHAPTER NINE

Globizens

Global Citizens and the Waning of Nationalism

"I AM NOT AN ATHENIAN OR A GREEK,
BUT A CITIZEN OF THE WORLD."

—Socrates

EVERYONE ALIVE TODAY has always known the world to have one fundamental geopolitical building block: the nation-state. In theory, at least, a nation-state is an autonomous, sovereign territory whose residents share a common language, culture, and values. Of course, in reality, nation-states have diverse populations, countries fight over borders, ethnic minorities struggle for their own nations, and so on. But nevertheless, it is a way of dividing up the world that is so central to modern life that most people have rarely considered it could be any other way.

In fact, historically speaking, the nation-state is a relatively recent invention. On islands such as England, or in areas with strong geographical boundaries, such as Portugal, something resembling the modern nation-state emerged nearly a millennium ago. But for most of Europe, the nation-state didn't evolve as a dominant force until the mid-nineteenth century. Germany and Italy, for example, didn't emerge as nation-states until the 1870s. Previously, those areas consisted of very small states or territories, often ruled by monarchies, and had no defining language because they shared the culture and language of neighboring principalities (some of these "micro-states" survive to the present day, such as French-speaking Monaco and German-speaking Liechtenstein). Much of the world outside Europe was colonized as part of large multiethnic empires such as the British Empire, leaving local residents with little self-determination. The nation-state arrived in these parts of the world much later, and often only after considerable conflict.

Today the nation-state is ensconced throughout the world, and in our minds. But change is coming. The nation-state is slowly, silently fading. In many ways, our world is splintering, and broad social structures defined by geography are quietly being replaced by self-forming micro-cultures defined more by lifestyles, values, and interests. Throughout the world, the wealthy are coalescing into one such global micro-community, with the world's richest, most powerful people increasingly connected with one another, yet less and less connected with the other residents of their own countries. Technology certainly plays an enabling role, but for the most part this isn't one of those blogging/IM'ing/MySpace communities. It is a real and virtual community driven by common experiences, shared lifestyles, collective aspirations, business partnerships, and investment opportunities. The term "global wealth oligarchy" may sound a little far-reaching, but it is accurate. We prefer to think of it as the era of globizens—global citizens.

Globizens and the International Wealth Explosion

Our studies of wealth have focused primarily on residents of the United States, but the tremendous concentration of wealth in the hands of a few is a global phenomenon. There are now nearly 10 million millionaires around the globe, and their population is growing by over 8 percent annually, with the strongest percentage gains in Africa, the Middle East, and Latin America. (Figure 9-1). Put into context, the global 8 percent growth rate of the millionaire population is seven times higher than the growth rate for the global population as a whole, which is approximately 1.1 percent today, and which

Figure 9-1 Growth rates of millionaires by continent.

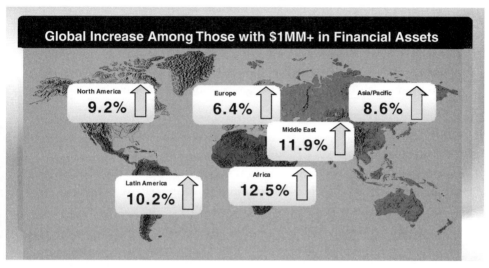

SOURCE OF DATA: Merrill Lynch Capgemini World Wealth Report 2007.

peaked at a "mere" 2 percent during the height of the population explosion in the 1960s. In fact, the 8 percent growth rate of millionaires is a higher growth rate than that of any single country in the world. But even that pales in comparison to the nearly 20 percent growth rate among billionaires. In 2008, *Forbes* identified 1,125 billionaires throughout the world, up from 946 just one year before.

Throughout the world, the new financial elite are remarkably similar. For example:

- Regardless of their culture of origin, they tend to be self-made entrepreneurs who value hard work, persistence, and relationships.
- Regardless of their company size or category, their businesses are multinational.
- Regardless of their language of origin, they typically speak English, which has become the international language of business as well as the preferred second language in many countries.
- Regardless of their country of residence, they travel widely, and often have residences in other countries.

- Regardless of their passions and interests, they aspire to own the same stuff and the same brands.

The result? Increasingly, wealthy people in the United States have less and less in common with the "typical" American, and more in common with their wealthy brethren from other countries.

The Shared Mind-Set of the World's Wealthiest People

We see the emergence of globizens and the "homogenization" of the world's wealthy class when we examine the uppermost echelon of financial achievement. For example, if we look at the wealthiest few individuals from each country around the world, we see surprising similarities in terms of their backgrounds, mind-sets, and sources of wealth.

In the United States, the stories of the two wealthiest—Bill Gates and Warren Buffett—are likely familiar to most readers. Bill Gates was hardly a child of poverty—his father was a successful attorney and his mother was on the board of directors of United Way. There have been rumors that his grandfather left him a million-dollar trust fund, but those have been widely denied. Regardless of the truth or falsehood of these rumors, it is clear that he generated the vast majority of his wealth through his own entrepreneurial efforts. He was only fourteen when he started his first business (with colleague Paul Allen, himself number forty-one on the worldwide list) and generated $20,000, a figure that declined dramatically when their client learned their true ages. He later briefly attended Harvard, but dropped out and went on to start Microsoft on a relative shoestring. Warren Buffett's story is similar. He was not a child of poverty either, as his father was a stockbroker and member of the U.S. House of Representatives. Nor was he an aristocrat. As a youngster, he worked in his father's stockbrokerage, and he had various part-time jobs such as paper routes and installing pinball machines. His first business was financed like most start-ups today—with money from family and friends—and he ran it out of his bedroom. He maintains a relatively low-key lifestyle, still has the Omaha house he bought in 1958, which is valued at less than $1 million.

The next richest American, Sheldon Adelson, does not have the widespread name recognition of Gates or Buffett, although he has about half of their wealth, which places him twelfth globally on the *Forbes* list. His upbringing was more working class—his parents were Ukrainian immigrants, and he grew up in Boston's tough Dorchester neighborhood. The son of a cab driver, he borrowed $200 from his uncle when he was just twelve to finance his newspaper delivery route and later dropped out of college to become a court reporter. Today he owns the Venetian Las Vegas luxury hotel, as well as numerous other properties throughout the world. In 1995 he sold his successful trade show business, featuring the high-tech showcase COMDEX, for $860 million. Another college dropout, Oracle founder Larry Ellison, is just behind Adelson with a total net worth of approximately $25 billion.

The commonalities among America's wealthiest people—self-made wealth, entrepreneurship, modest backgrounds—are also prevalent among the wealthiest individuals from other countries as well. Mexico's richest person, second overall in the world behind Buffett, is Carlos Slim Helu. His father was a Lebanese immigrant who created a successful general store in downtown Mexico City. But that success was nothing compared to what Carlos achieved on his own. Like Buffett, he started as a stockbroker but found he had more aptitude for buying and selling companies. He parleyed his initial successes into more and more acquisitions, particularly in telecommunications. Today his companies control over 90 percent of the landlines in Mexico and nearly three-fourths of the cell phones. Through the gravitational pull of wealth (and, some would say, unfairly government-supported monopolies), his net worth is estimated to have risen from $20 billion to $60 billion in just two years. Still, he's known for his thrifty lifestyle, doesn't use a computer, and is proud of the fact that he owns no homes outside of Mexico. *The Wall Street Journal* quoted author and friend Alvin Toffler as saying of Slim: "If you didn't know he was the richest guy in the world, you'd just think he was a likable and intelligent guy."

India now boasts four of the ten richest people in the world, up from just one in 2007, led by steel magnate Lakshmi Mittal (number four globally with an estimated net worth of $45 billion). He was born to a relatively modest family, and his father made considerable wealth in the steel business. But the wealth from his father's business success paled in comparison to that he created by expanding the company internationally, and through occasionally contentious and controversial mergers and acquisitions. Mittal is followed closely by the estranged Ambani brothers—Anil and Mukesh—who, despite their conflicts, have managed to multiply their father's fortune many times by growing their telecommunications and energy businesses. KP Singh ranks number eight globally, and like his Indian colleagues on the list, has exponentially grown his father's fortune, in his case one made through real estate. Singh and the Ambani brothers all saw their net worth increase by about $20 billion from 2007 to 2008.

Europe's richest person, IKEA founder and billionaire number seven, Ingvar Kamprad, is known for his thrifty lifestyle. Growing up on a farm in rural Sweden, he sold goods to his neighbors on his bicycle, including matches, pens, Christmas decorations, and even fish. His father helped him finance the company that would become IKEA, and today he is known for driving an old Volvo, flying economy, and eating inexpensively at the IKEA cafeteria. Certainly he is not without the comforts that $30+ billion affords, and his frugal image is in part cultivated to reinforce the Spartan culture of his company, but by all accounts, the down-to-earth attitude he learned on the farm remains sincerely and securely intact.

Karl Albrecht, Germany's richest person, boasts a similar rags-to-riches story as he worked with his brother to turn their mother's corner grocery store into a multibillion-dollar retail empire. He epitomizes stealth wealth to such an extent that little is known about him. In that sense, he is much like Spain's richest man, Amancio Ortega, who refuses to give interviews (even pictures of him are rare). The son of a railway worker who started by making clothes in his living room with his then-wife, Ortega's retail empire today includes 3,000 Zara apparel stores around the world.

France's richest person, billionaire number thirteen Bernard Arnault, inherited significant wealth, primarily in the form of his father's construction company. But his wealth grew exponentially—from $26 million to $26 *billion*—when he leveraged that construction company into a string of acquisitions that included some of the top luxury brands in the world, including Christian Dior, Louis Vuitton, Dom Pérignon, Fendi, and Tag Heuer.

Outside of Western Europe, even more dramatic rags-to-riches stories are prevalent. Asia's richest man, Hong Kong's conglomerate magnate Li Ka-shing, was a refugee's son and poor immigrant who got his start selling plastic flowers, and didn't graduate from high school, working instead to support his parents. His $26.5 billion ranks him eleventh globally, where he is bracketed by a pair of self-made Russians: former metals trader Oleg Deripaska and former orphan-turned-college-dropout-turned oil baron Roman Abramovich.

Shared Mind-Sets + More Interaction = Closer Relationships

Since the beginning of this book we've explored how the genesis of wealth today—from a middle-class upbringing to financial comfort through entrepreneurship—shapes everything from self-concepts to parenting styles to brand choices. As a result, when wealthy individuals from different cultures interact, they have a great deal in common, both personally and professionally. And they are interacting more often, virtually, via e-mail, and in person. About one in five wealthy people owns a second home, including over 40 percent of directors and patrons and over 50 percent of mavericks; among those with multiple homes, nearly one quarter own homes outside the United States, with two to three times that figure seriously considering a home purchase abroad.

Of course, home ownership is an extreme level of global citizenship. International travel itself helps cement the wealthy microcommunity, and it is commonplace. Roughly 90 percent have traveled internationally in the past year, and virtually all plan to travel abroad again in the next two years (Table 9-1).

Table 9-1 **Top 15 international destinations the wealthy are likely to visit in the next 2 years (% of those surveyed)**

Italy	38
Caribbean	36
United Kingdom	34
France	29
Mexico	27
Canada	21
Germany	19
Australia	17
Spain	16
South America	15
Ireland	14
China	14
Alaska	14
Greece	13
Japan	12

Every Business Is Multinational

Certainly, shared experiences and collective mind-sets are combining with international travel and home ownership to help cement the global wealth micro-community. But for today's entrepreneurs, the strongest bond is business, which is a truly global game.

It now goes without saying that the Internet has enabled every company to tap global markets. Beyond that, virtually all major companies are now multinationals, and it has become increasingly difficult to even say where a company is "located." But these days, many smaller businesses and even start-ups have some global scope. Manufacturing in China, software programming in India, call centers in the Philippines and Argentina—all are within the reach of even modestly sized businesses. No longer a luxury, leveraging the efficiencies of the flat world has essentially become a business necessity. The United Nations estimates there are over 60,000 multinational corporations, a figure that has doubled over the past two decades, while the average size of multinationals has dropped dramatically.[1]

Globalization isn't just about moving work to where it can be done at the lowest cost; increasingly, it is about getting the best people, bigger teams, and leveraging time-zone differences to enable work to continue 24/7. And it is often about growth opportunities. Israeli high-tech start-ups, for example, are often born global, or go global very quickly, because the markets in their home country are small. Indeed, this model is sometimes called "Israeli Internationalization," and it is increasingly being applied in other small countries.[2] Indeed, whereas historically companies started locally and grew globally, today some of the hottest buzzwords in entrepreneurial circles are *global start-ups, born global,* and *micro-multinationals.*

The bottom line for our purposes is that today's wealthy are far more likely to have an intricate network of international connections, relative to the generations of wealthy individuals who came before them. We've seen how their career paths as entrepreneurs were likely to be international in some form; with two-thirds still actively on the front lines of their businesses, those global connections with partners and vendors are likely continuing. Moreover, as fully formed members of the wealth class, these people have international business connections that are strengthened in two additional ways. First, many are involved in seeding start-ups, either through private equity funds or more directly through angel investing, and such investments increasingly mean evaluating multinational teams of executives.

Second, the wealthy are heavily involved as members of corporate boards, with 40 percent serving on at least one corporate board of directors, and most of that 40 percent serving on more than one board. Like start-ups, the boards of major corporations are becoming increasingly international in scope. For example, two-thirds of the thirty companies constituting the Dow Jones Industrial Average have at least one international board member; over 20 percent of the board members are non-Americans at Dow component companies Alcoa, Citigroup, General Electric, IBM, and Walt Disney.[3] International board membership is often even stronger outside of the United States, with companies in developing countries increasingly looking for board members from outside of their home country, as this fosters connections that fuel business growth, and makes potential investors more confident that the company is stable and well managed.[4]

All of these global business relationships deepen the ethic of global citizenship. Doing business, whether within or across borders, fosters relationships between businesses and business owners. They work together. They solve problems and grow closer. They ask each other for references and referrals, further expanding networks. They work together to find mutual growth opportunities, and often to co-sponsor new ventures. They share investment ideas, from publicly traded stocks to start-ups worthy of an equity stake. We've seen how the consuming nature of entrepreneurial ventures creates only thin lines between their business and personal lives, and it is inevitable that the wealthy end up talking about where they live and what they buy, and their aspirations for their kids. In short, they start building a community. In the process, they begin to realize that they often have more in common with their international counterparts—who share the challenges of entrepreneurship and wealth—than with their less well-to-do counterparts in the country in which they live.

The Global Homogenization of Stuff

The global micro-culture of wealth is held together by shared experiences, shared attitudes, business connections, and also by an increasingly common material culture. In short, throughout the world the wealthy buy, and aspire to buy, the same brands and products.

Actually, this phenomenon is not limited to the wealthy. One of the ironies of our splintering world is that while our communities become smaller and more geographically dispersed, the world is increasingly connected by a common material culture. American brands have global reach, and for the most part, are aspired to throughout most of the world: Microsoft, Coca-Cola, American Express, Apple, Disney, McDonald's, Starbucks, Google, Citicorp, General Electric, and so on. The same is increasingly true for top international brands, many of which have shown even stronger growth rates than their U.S. counterparts in recent years: Nokia, Sony, Virgin, Mercedes, BMW, Toyota, and the like.

Across the world, luxury brands have a similar cohesive effect among the financial elite, creating shared purchasing patterns and a shared aesthetic. Regardless of what country one lives in, *Lexus* has become synonymous with engineering perfection, *Chanel* is synonymous with elegance, and so on. In business-focused interactions, a shared sense of brand meaning and a mutual appreciation of quality help create a common frame of reference and sense of confidence. Moreover, displaying universally understood symbols of quality helps communicate intelligence, which is valued in both business dealings and consumer market purchases. International studies of higher-end consumers have shown remarkably homogeneous attitudes toward luxury products and brands, with the wealthy considering the products to be less about price and status and more about experiences, self-expression, time-savings, and true quality.[5] The pull of these brands is powerful, with only 23 percent of consumers globally preferring local designers over international luxury brands.[6]

However, although luxury brands have truly global identities, currencies do not. Indeed, currencies are a strong cohesive economic force that helps define a nation and differentiate it from other nations. In a world of wealthy globizens and a weakening U.S. dollar, some people are starting to consider the choice of currency to be a test of patriotism and national loyalty. Consider the recent uproar over supermodel Gisele Bündchen. She made headlines when it was announced that her contract to promote Pantene, a product of Cincinnati-based Procter & Gamble, called for her to be paid in euros instead of dollars.

While covering this story, *The Economist* used the headline "Who Says Supermodels Are Dumb?" But many had a very different reaction, considering it an unpatriotic snub of her adopted home. (She spends much of her time in New York City, although she is from Brazil, where her family has lived for six generations.) Outside of the media spotlight, the entrepreneurial wealthy are increasingly globalizing their assets and spreading their money into different currencies. Forget "Made in America"—the new patriotism test will be "Paid in America." It's one that many globizens will find unfair and irrelevant to their lifestyles, and will no doubt be a source of social

Figure 9-2 Dynamics of the globizen phenomenon.

conflict between the haves and the have-nots. Figure 9-2 summarizes the characteristics of the globizen phenomenon.

Notes

1. Michael Copeland, "The Mighty Micro-Multinational," *Business 2.0*, July 28, 2006, http://money.cnn.com/magazines/business2/busi ness2_archive/2006/07/01/8380 230/index.htm (accessed April 16, 2008).

2. Globalization Survey, sponsored by the Alpha Summit Europe 2005, http://www.munichnetwork.com/SITE/UPLOAD/DOCU MENT/ASE_Mgmt-Sum mary_lowres.pdf (accessed April 16, 2008).

3. William J. Holstein, "A Global Casting Call for Corporate Boards," *The New York Times,* November 19, 2006, http://

www.nytimes.com/2006/11/19/jobs/19advi.html?_r = 1&fta = y&
oref = slogin (accessed April 16, 2008).

4. For example, the expression of this trend among Russian companies is explored in the report "Independent Foreigners on the
Board of Directors of a Russian Company"; see http://www.heid
rick.com/NR/rdonlyres/E9E8DC88-8DEF-4678-A578-C77D52
80C049/0/HS_RussiaBoardReport_English.pdf

5. "Luxury Consumers Around the World Are Very Similar: Value
Is Placed on Freedom to Experience Rather Than Possessions,"
Restaurant News Resource, March 14, 2008, based on research
conducted by The Conference Board, *The Global Luxury Market:
Exploring the Mindset of Luxury Consumers in Seven Countries;*
see   http://www.restaurantnewsresource.com/modules.php?op =
modload&name = trends&file = detail&sid = 28500 (accessed April
16, 2008).

6. "Gucci Reigns as the World's Most Coveted Luxury Brand," *Inside
Retailing Online*, February 28, 2008, http://www.insideretailing
.com.au/articles-page.aspx?articleType = ArticleView&articleId
= 2376 (accessed April 16, 2008).

CHAPTER TEN

Wealtherkind

The Children of Entrepreneurial Wealth

"Recommend virtue to your children; it alone, not money, can make them happy. I speak from experience."

—Ludwig van Beethoven

"May all your children have wealthy parents."

—Irish toast

ALL PARENTS WANT the best for their kids. They all worry about their kids. The nature of parental concerns and aspirations, however, differs across time, place, and, yes, wealth. Parents living in poverty worry that they won't be able to provide their kids with the basics of food, shelter, security, and a good education. Wealthy parents have a different set of worries, primarily the concern that the money they worked so hard to achieve, which has provided them with such comfort, will turn around to be the eventual undoing of their children.

Unlike the cautions and concerns that apprentices have for themselves during their first five years of wealth, these concerns for their children tend to remain strong and pervasive over time. Over half of the wealthy are concerned specifically about their children's work ethic because the children have grown up with money. This figure rises as wealth increases, but it doesn't change regardless of how long the parents have been wealthy.

The unfortunate reality is that affluent and wealthy parents have

169

plenty to worry about. A growing body of academic research has found that, starting in junior high school, kids from higher-income households have increasing and higher-than-average rates of depression, anxiety, drug use, alcohol use, rule breaking, eating disorders, and general unhappiness.[1]

Our data lend insight into the complex psychological dynamics of today's teens. Our 2007 Affluent Teen Survey found that affluent kids are, in many respects, high achievers. They are more likely than their less affluent peers to describe themselves as hard workers and leaders (Table 10-1). They are also more likely to exhibit athletic excellence, garner academic awards, and display extracurricular leadership. The psychology of achievement, however, is complex. Personal accomplishments can certainly build a sense of confidence and be a source of pride for themselves and their parents. Interestingly, that's not necessarily what happens for affluent teens.

A huge body of research has shown that accomplishments have these and other positive benefits *if* they are intrinsically motivated—that is, when they are pursued in accordance with the child's own interests and values.[2] Intrinsically motivated endeavors are pursued with greater excitement and passion. They are associated with more creativity and determination and with rebounding from setbacks rather than giving up as a result of them. And perhaps most important, intrinsic motivation is associated with positive outcomes such

Table 10-1 **Self-reported achievements of teens (by household income; % of responses)**

	<$50k	$50k–$75k	$75k–$150k	$150k +
I work harder than most people	48	56	49	66%
I am a leader among my peers	49	56	58	63
I have won a scholastic award	35	39	40	49
I have won an award for athletics	23	32	30	44
I play a musical instrument	25	38	39	44
I have been elected to a school office	11	11	15	21
I am the captain of a sports team	6	9	7	15

as higher performance, more energy, enhanced self-esteem, and overall emotional well-being.

Unfortunately, kids today often feel driven to accomplish more, not because of their own innate interests, but because of real or perceived pressure from parents or peers. Extrinsic motivation, such as the desire to please parents whose love and pride are perceived as conditional on continued achievements, is associated with the opposite psychological patterns: lower interest, less energy, minimal creativity, hampered self-esteem, and less happiness.

Stress, pressure, and extrinsic motivation are growing concerns among kids of all socioeconomic backgrounds, not just upscale ones, and often these concerns stem from what we call "domino thinking." Kids of all ages, particularly teens, often view their future accomplishments like dominos, carefully aligned and waiting to fall, with each one contingent on the one before it: tomorrow's geography test, next month's final exam, next year's entrance into advanced placement courses, SATs the year after that, followed by admission to a top college, stellar performance there, a great job, career success, financial success, and so on.

If each accomplishment is contingent on the one before it, well, that sure puts a lot of pressure on tomorrow's geography test. Four-fifths of kids today say it is "essential for their success" that they get into a good college, and three-fourths believe they will make "a lot of money some day."

Again, many studies have shown that people with a compelling vision of what they want from life not only achieve more but also are psychologically and physically healthier than others.[3] But domino thinking puts a negative spin on otherwise positive visions of the future. Some respond to the pressures of domino thinking by working harder, sometimes losing the passion, enthusiasm, and creativity that typically accompany intrinsic motivation. Others fold under the pressure of domino thinking, choosing to "opt out" by underachieving, breaking rules, self-medicating with substance abuse, or any number of other counterproductive behavioral patterns.

Kids of many backgrounds today feel the pressures of high expectations and domino thinking, but affluent kids have the added burden of living up to their parents' achievement. They may not know exactly how much their parents are worth, but clearly they are aware of their financial comfort and their parents' accomplishments.

Raising kids in an era of domino thinking is challenging for parents of any socioeconomic status. For wealthy parents, it is a difficult balancing act of encouraging achievement while minimizing pressure, of using their financial means for the benefit of the whole family while fostering the work ethic, modesty, and middle-class values to which they attribute their own success. Indeed, it is a balancing act largely unknown to previous generations of the well-to-do.

The Carnegies, Rockefellers, and other scions of inherited money, raised their kids amid obvious and unconcealable wealth. Unlike today's wealthy, they had generations of experience in raising kids amid abundance. Through boarding schools and family philanthropic endeavors, they had structural supports in training their kids in the fine art of managing wealth and living without financial worry.

For today's entrepreneurial wealthy, raising balanced kids and teaching them about money are learning processes they've had to figure out on their own, just like other aspects of living with abundance. Most arrive at strategies for training their kids in wealth with some combination of these four key strategies:

1. Preaching, and living, their values
2. Using shopping as a training and bonding tool
3. Taking a team approach to planning and spending
4. Using philanthropy for moral and business development

Preaching, and Living, Their Values

The transmission of middle-class values to their children is extremely important to today's wealthy. We saw in earlier chapters that today's wealthy generally didn't set out to make a lot of money; instead, they worked hard, pursued a passion, and had success in doing so. It is this mind-set they try to instill in their own children. Indeed, when we explicitly ask them about what advice they have for the next generation, it is the middle-class values to which they attribute their own success that dominate the list:

1. Work hard.
2. Do something you enjoy.
3. Have a plan (but stay flexible).
4. Have integrity.
5. Obtain education and keep learning.

Here's a small sampling of their advice in their own words:

"You got to be interested in your work. It's got to be something you enjoy. I tell people, 'You know, if you're not enjoying your work, life is too short. Go find something that you enjoy, and don't sit here and bitch.'"

"Never, ever, ever put your goals ahead of your principles. If you remain true to your principles, people will come around to your way. Your colleagues will see that, well, we may not agree with you the first time or two because you didn't accomplish something in twenty-four hours that they wanted to see . . . but, ultimately, it was done the right way."

"These people who have a plan for their life—I think that's the biggest mistake you can make. Because I had people who came to work for me with their plan: by this time they were going to be this, this and this. You ought to plan to do something and so on, but you shouldn't put those goals [ahead of everything]. . . . You're happiest if you play it as it comes, and maximize what you're doing at the time. And do the very best job at whatever you're given to do. The rest will take care of itself."

"It would be the quality of life, not the quantity of life. That's it. That's the whole speech. We don't have to make millions and millions of dollars to be happy. As a matter of fact, some people that make millions and millions of dollars are miserable. You seek the relationships that are closest and most personal to you, and that's your family and friends."

"Plastics. . . . On a more serious note, keep your life balanced. Make sure there's always time for body, mind, and the spirit. All work makes a dull Jack. Makes a lot of Jack, but makes a dull Jack. All play makes a poor Jack."

"It's not all about the money. It's about how you live. It's about you as a person, not about what you have."

"Sample a lot of different things. This generation is so much more focused on a path. You go to school, you get this. You get this first job, you get that, all on this very regimented path. And yet you look at the successful people that you and I know and get to meet . . . [their success came from] mistakes, accidents, because they happened to be there, they saw this, they thought that might work. And so my encouragement is: Look at your life as a résumé and constantly be résuméing in terms of exposures and experiences. A résumé is now a verb, and not a noun."

When it comes to instilling values in their children, the wealthy walk the walk, not just talk the talk. Their respect for work and self-sufficiency is seen in the fact that 80 percent of today's wealthy feel strongly that their kids should get a job during their high school years, and by the time they reach high school, about 70 percent have in fact held a job. The kids also seem to be learning the middle-class value of saving, as they report saving about one-third of all the money they earn from their jobs. There is still, however, much to be learned about pursuing one's passions and finding one's bliss—less than one-third of affluent teens describe themselves as "passionate" about their job.

Affluent teens have certainly heard the message about how to create wealth, although they are not alone. Indeed, regardless of parental income, teens today have a relatively consistent—and accurate—view of the sources of wealth. Hard work and determination top the list, followed by education and expertise; compromising principles falls at the bottom of list (Table 10-2).

Only about one in four believes wealth is typically attributed to inheritance, in stark contrast to the opinions of most adults. Relative to other teens, affluent teens are somewhat, but not dramatically, more likely to associate wealth with inventiveness, great instincts, and having a good business background. The general consistency in teen views of the sources of wealth suggest that these opinions come, not so much from parenting per se, but from media and cultural forces. Adults today grew up with names like Carnegie and Rockefeller being cultural icons associated with wealth. For kids today, these names and associated images are much less familiar and hold much less meaning; names of entrepreneurs like Bill Gates, Steve Jobs, and Richard Branson are much more personally relevant.

Table 10-2 **Affluent teens' views of how wealth is created (% of those surveyed)**

	$150k +
Hard work/determination	68
Having a good education	61
Skill/Expertise in one's field	57
Being inventive	43
Great instincts	41
Good business background	40
Treating others with respect	40
Being smarter than others	36
Having strong social networks	34
Having great sales skills	31
Being a good judge of character	31
Coming from money	28
Being willing to take chances and risk it all	26
Good luck	23
Access to inside information	18
Being willing to sacrifice principles	11

Clearly, affluent teens have come to appreciate the value of hard work and how it combines with education to play a key role in financial success. But in many respects, when it comes to instilling a broader-based middle-class mind-set, wealthy parents have their work cut out for them. "Middle class" has positive connotations for parents—it implies humility, modesty, and pride in the feeling that their values have not been compromised by their money. But whether their kids are ambitious, or feel a sense of entitlement, the phrase "middle class" tends to be something that many of them aspire to move beyond. Although 56 percent of affluent kids describe themselves as middle class at heart, this is lower than any other income group (although obviously some of this is to be expected as some of these groups are in fact middle class; Table 10-3). But the point is that the other 44 percent simply don't resonate to the phrase "middle class." This shift away from the middle-class mind-set in the next generation of the wealthy is apparent in some of their brand preferences. Affluent teens are slightly but consistently more likely than their less affluent peers to prefer brands that communicate success or that convey a feeling of privilege.

Shopping as a Training and Bonding Tool

Instilling a middle-class mind-set is certainly a challenge, particularly amid a culture that values achievement and a household that—often

Table 10-3 **Youth who see themselves as ''middle class at heart'' using ''brand as badge'' (% by income groups)**

	<$50k	$50k–$75k	$75k–$150k	$150k +
I would describe myself as middle class at heart	59	67	77	56
I like brands that . . .				
• Communicate to others that I'm successful	51	51	55	62
• Make me feel like I'm a trendsetter	53	59	57	62
• Make me feel privileged	55	53	51	58

unintentionally—exudes messages of accomplishment. Teaching the wise use and spending of money is a different kind of challenge. For most wealthy parents, tackling this challenge implicitly involves invoking the ironic quip: "When the going gets tough, the tough go shopping." Shopping among the wealthy often becomes a family activity; in a sense, it's a training ground on which kids are taught the strategic value of money and the tactics of smart shopping. As they get older, it is how the fine art of discerning sublime qualities of luxury is taught. Over time, the opinion of the kids in matters of shopping comes to be respected, and even sought out, particularly in categories related to technology.

Of course, simply by virtue of their financial status, affluent teens have more opportunities to spend and shop. In a typical holiday season, for example, affluent teens report spending approximately $375 on holiday gifts for friends and family—twice what the average teen spends. In the past year, 60 percent of affluent teens shopped online, compared to less than half of their less-affluent counterparts. They spent an average $275 online, which is roughly quadruple that of teens in lower economic strata.

Affluent teens not only shop more and spend more, but their shopping is qualitatively different as well. For example, they have a greater opportunity to own and purchase luxury brands, particularly in terms of electronics, apparel, and jewelry (Table 10-4). Still, luxury ownership is significantly less than one might expect.

Table 10-4 **Percentages of youth who own luxury or high-end brands in each category (by income groups)**

	<$50k	$50k–$75k	$75k–$150k	$150k +
Electronics	40	46	47	55
Shoes	39	43	39	31
Fashion apparel	28	34	32	35
Purses/wallets/accessories	20	18	24	31
Cosmetics and perfumes	14	19	22	23
Jewelry	14	15	15	21
Watches	13	12	16	24

But the most interesting dynamic among affluent teens is the "quality seeking meets smart shopping" mind-set so prevalent among their parents. Among both wealthy parents and teens, brand affinity is driven by the same basic elements: quality, design, craftsmanship, and technology (Table 10-5). These are often the sublime qualities

Table 10-5 **Shopping mind-set of the wealthy (% of those surveyed, by income group)**

	<$50k	$50k–$75k	$75k–$150k	$150k +
Quality-focused: I like brands that . . .				
Have a reputation for the best quality	71	74	75	78
Reflect high craftsmanship	58	66	67	71
Have a reputation for design	60	64	66	69
Have a reputation for technology	54	62	59	65
Research-driven				
From independent consumer product reports	32	37	37	46
Information found in informative/blog/social sites on the Internet	29	37	40	42
Internet-liberated				
I research the items on the web I am going to buy to make sure that I am not taken advantage of	39	46	48	54
The Internet has liberated my shopping	28	36	42	49
Less price-sensitive				
I usually wait for something to go on sale before I buy	59	61	59	49
I prefer to shop in stores with a reputation for great pricing	65	75	70	59

that differentiate true luxury, but they are also the hallmarks of excellence in more mundane products (and at lower price points).

Coupled with the hunt for excellence in products is the quest for excellence in the process of shopping. Affluent teens are significantly more likely than others to do research-driven shopping though Internet searches, *Consumer Reports*-type publications, and so on. Certainly the Internet plays a key role in this savvy shopping mind-set, with half of affluent teens reporting that the Internet has "liberated" their shopping, and a similar number using the Internet to specifically avoid being taken advantage of.

When we examine purchasing preferences, we see further subtle signs of the middle-class mind-set slipping away within the first generation. Affluent teens are significantly less focused on sales and on finding stores with reputations for low prices. When asked about their favorite stores, we find all groups of teenagers to be equally enthusiastic about shopping electronics retailers such as Best Buy and Circuit City, and at upscale-style-at-low-price retailers such as Target (see Table 10-6). But significant, and telling, differences emerge as we look deeper into store preferences. Affluent teens are much less likely to shop at lower-priced mass merchants such as Wal-Mart, J.C. Penney, Sears, and Kmart. (Costco, a favorite of wealthy adults with a unique value proposition, is an exception.) And they show a distinct preference for higher-end department stores (Neiman Marcus, Saks), specialty retailers (Abercrombie & Fitch, American Outfitters), and luxury brands (Cartier, Tiffany).

A Team Approach to Planning and Spending

Over time, the wealthy family increasingly takes on the appearance of a business. Household budgets grow, and they move from "in the head" to "in a spreadsheet." Individuals become less likely to clean the house or mow the lawn, or to pay the bills or make the investments; they become more likely to manage the people doing those tasks. In this sense, shopping and spending constitute the frontline training program for teaching kids about how to shop, the value of money, and living with abundance. There is a second line to this

Table 10-6 **Favorite stores of teenagers
(by income group)**

	<$50k	$50k–$75k	$75k–$150k	$150K+	Gap*: $150K + % minus <$50K %
Best Buy	65	71	65	73	8
Barnes & Noble	45	57	63	67	22
Target	63	72	70	62	−1
Borders	30	48	52	60	30
Abercrombie & Fitch	23	26	40	60	37
Old Navy	56	66	60	57	1
Circuit City	47	60	52	51	4
American Eagle	33	42	50	51	18
Aeropostale	31	36	47	51	20
Sports Authority	22	40	45	50	28
Wal-Mart	73	67	59	43	−30
Banana Republic	17	25	29	40	23
Nordstrom	12	13	24	39	27
J.C. Penney	58	54	47	38	−20
Sephora	8	11	21	37	29
J. Crew	12	12	24	35	23
Bloomingdale's	8	9	15	30	22
Neiman Marcus	7	9	15	29	22
Saks Fifth Avenue	6	13	19	26	20
Kmart	47	34	26	24	−23
Sears	39	46	38	23	−16
Tiffany	7	10	19	23	16
Cartier	6	4	8	22	16

*A high gap reflects a higher preference of affluent teens for these outlets relative to that of less affluent teens. Low gap scores reflect consistent interest across income groups.

training program—an advanced course, if you will, that follows Spending 101. It involves a team approach to making not just big-ticket purchases, but even significant financial and family decisions.

At its most basic level, this team approach to decision making begins with greater collaboration between parent and child on purchases. And we're not just talking about what sweater to buy at the Gap or which coffeepot to buy from Target. We're talking about where to go on vacation, what cars to buy, what computers to purchase, and more. Nearly two-thirds of wealthy parents tell us that their children's preferences are at least somewhat important in making big-ticket purchase decisions, such as cars, computers, and televisions. About half are influenced by their kids' preferences when it comes to interior decorating within the house, and major household purchases such as appliances and furniture. One-third even consult their kids on their purchases of clothes—not just for the kids but also for themselves.

Planning and taking vacations are particularly important processes, and they are particularly collaborative ones. Kids have at least some impact on 95 percent of the choices for vacation destinations and have a major impact nearly two-thirds of the time. But what happens on those vacations is even more important, because it is there that many of the bigger family decisions get made.

Consider it another parallel between how wealthy families are run and how businesses are managed. Corporations have executive retreats and off-site meetings when the managers get away from distractions and chart a new long-term course. Wealthy families often do the same. Over half of the wealthy tell us that their family vacations are key opportunities to reflect on their priorities, make decisions about their lives, and even make significant financial decisions.

Vacations become, in a sense, the time when family capital spending is discussed and planned. And vacations are often among the first places that financial planning, at least at a conceptual level, gets introduced to kids. Three-fourths of wealthy parents have taken specific steps to educate their kids about financial decision making. A few choose to outsource the process, and in recent years, a cottage industry has developed among consultants offering financial education seminars to children of the wealthy. But whether financial education is conducted "in-house" by parents, or is outsourced to consultants, it generally remains a process that unfolds slowly, over time, and often with only abstract references to their own wealth.

For example, only 27 percent of apprentices have told their kids how much the family is worth. Among masters, with fifteen or more years of experience with wealth, 49 percent have done so. Obviously that is a nearly twofold increase across the arc of maturation, but still, this 49 percent figure is remarkable: it means that roughly half of masters still haven't completely opened up to the kids. Clearly their concerns about the destructive aspects of wealth persist.

Wealthy parents find a variety of techniques for easing their children into responsible money management. Some give them small amounts of money to invest in online brokerage accounts; others offer matching funds for investments or other purposes. Regardless of the specific technique used, the same underlying principle of strengthening their children and maintaining motivation despite abundance is clear. One of our respondents, a winery owner, used the metaphor of a vine to convey this philosophy:

> [Tending] a vine is . . . [like] raising children—in other words, the [children are the] grapes [and the vine is the mother]. If you give the vines unlimited water and nourishment, they grow too leafy, creating too much shade, and they end up being very flabby grapes. I mean, they're just very, very well protected. And there's no character in those grapes. . . . In the vineyard, we may actually take away some nutrients so that the mother is more concerned about the future of her children than she is of herself. And she puts as much energy into those children as biologically possible. Thus, [we] create a more robust, more dynamic flavored grape, making it a better and more dynamic wine.

Using Philanthropy for Moral and Business Development

Another child-rearing tool that today's wealthy use is actually a time-honored technique pioneered by the families of inherited wealth: getting the kids actively involved in community and charity activities. Clearly, "giving back" is on the minds of affluent teens—by word, deed, and donation, affluent teens show a significant interest in helping the less fortunate (Table 10-7).

Table 10-7 **Altruistic actions and attitudes of teenagers (by income groups)**

	<$50K	$50k–$75k	$75k–$150k	$150+
I have donated my own money to a charity	28	37	38	48
I have volunteered for a local charity	26	37	32	45
I belong to a club that does good deeds in the community	20	18	27	31
I would be willing to pay a premium for brands that support charitable causes	43	45	45	51

Today's wealthy are going to great lengths to instill altruistic attitudes among their kids to ameliorate the potential negative effects of growing up amid abundance. But as we shall see, today's wealthy bring a uniquely entrepreneurial flair to their philanthropic endeavors, and fostering entrepreneurial values in their kids is equally important. One of our respondents summed it up well when we asked about his unfulfilled goals in life: "One of my goals is to get my kids into a situation where they are both entrepreneurial and philanthropic at the same time. I'm working with them to find something that they have an interest in, that they can start something philanthropic, and have some ownership of." This unique intersection of business and philanthropy has the potential to reshape not only their children's lives and their identities, but also the nature of society itself.

Notes

1. Suniya S. Luthar and Chris Sexton, "The High Price of Affluence," in *Advances in Child Development*, ed. R. Kail (San Diego, Calif.: Academic Press, 2005). See also Madeline Levine, *The Price of Privilege: How Parental Pressure and Material Advantage Are Creating a Generation of Disconnected and Unhappy Kids* (New York: Harper Collins, 2006).
2. For a review of the intrinsic motivation research, see Edward L.

Deci and Richard M. Ryan, eds., *Handbook of Self-Determination Research* (Rochester, NY: University of Rochester Press, 2002).

3. For a review, see Stephen J. Kraus, *Psychological Foundations of Success: A Harvard-Trained Scientist Separates the Science of Success from Self-Help Snake Oil* (San Francisco, Calif.: Change Planet Press, 2002).

CHAPTER ELEVEN

The Third Age

Reinventment and Philanthrobusiness

"SURPLUS WEALTH IS A SACRED TRUST WHICH ITS POSSESSOR IS
BOUND TO ADMINISTER IN HIS LIFETIME FOR THE GOOD
OF THE COMMUNITY."

—Andrew Carnegie

RETIREMENT IS, IN many respects, becoming an antiquated concept in our society. Like so many social trends over the past half century, the waning of the traditional notion of retirement is driven by the maturing of the baby boom generation. Seventy-eight million boomers were born between 1946 and 1964, creating a demographic "pig in the python" that reshapes everything from pop culture to social institutions as they pass from one life stage to the next. Up next are the golden years, which will be reshaped by boomers in what has been called the "silver tsunami."

The first baby boomers qualified for AARP membership over ten years ago. On October 15, 2007, "first boomer" Kathleen Casey-Kirschling, who was born one second after midnight on January 1, 1946, became the first baby boomer to apply for Social Security.[1] Over 10,000 a day are expected to follow suit over the next two decades. Although the aging of the baby boomers is inevitable, the unique approach they will undoubtedly bring to senior citizenship is

185

still evolving. Indeed, an increasing number of baby boomers appear to be poised to choose "reinvenment" over retirement.

Boomers have always been a generation adept at reinventing themselves, as evidenced by their evolution from flower-power hippie children of the 1960s to yuppie owners of SUVs adorned with "baby on board" signs in the 1980s. And despite their aging, they have been able to maintain much of the youthful, semi-rebellious self-image that characterized their upbringing. These factors are combined as boomers are increasingly putting their own stamp on retirement and giving it a youthful, energized face-lift. For example, nearly two-thirds expect to travel widely in retirement, with substantial numbers expecting to travel overseas.[2] The philosophy of youthful reinvention is apparent in attitudes toward work as well. Additional studies suggest that half to two-thirds of boomers expect to work into the traditional retirement years; of those, half anticipate starting a second career.

Marketers have taken notice. Essentially gone from today's advertising lexicon are age-related, and hence boomer-unfriendly, terms such as "senior citizens." Even staid topics such as retirement planning are getting an aspirational, boomer-focused makeover. (Consider the Ameriprise campaign featuring an aging but still edgy Dennis Hopper preaching "the thing about dreams is . . . they don't retire" with his usual intensity, all of which can barely be heard over the strains of the 60s rock anthem, "Gimme Some Lovin'.")

Of course, for most baby boomers, financial necessity plays a considerable role in their "decisions" to reinvent themselves during their golden years. Three-fourths don't feel financially prepared for retirement, and those who plan to continue working are typically more likely to cite financial need rather than passion for work as the main reason. Here, of course, is where the paths of today's wealthy diverge from those of most baby boomers. Unconstrained by financial needs, today's wealthy are charting a course into the next stage of their lives that is emboldened by their financial freedom. In a sense, the wealthy's approach is an illustration of what most boomers would want, if they had the time and money to make it happen.

Perhaps the phrase "the third age" is more appropriate than ever. The first age is that of childhood, characterized by dependence, with the major challenge being socialization. The second age brings an adult focus on career and family—in a sense, borrowing Freud's formulation that work and love are the two major challenges of adult life. The third age is one of independence and self-focus, after obligations to family and commitments to work have diminished. It is not the passive conception of later life implicit in phrases such as "senior citizenship" or "the golden years." Instead, the third age is a time of growth, self-actualization, liberation, even triumph. It is a time for pursuing one's own passions instead of attending to the needs of others.

The third age is a particularly apropos phrase for describing the wealthy because, in many cases, they have reached a crossroads in their lives where they don't have to work, but they are far ahead of schedule chronologically. Indeed, we've talked about how boomers are reshaping retirement trends because, in the population at large, chronological age determines when one "should" retire. But the wealthy are freed from financial constraints and can pursue their third age at any time; for them, "retirement age" simply isn't a relevant concept. Indeed, although nearly 60 percent of the wealthy are boomers, over one-third are Generation Xers, and they are ready for their third age many years before the traditional age of retirement.

Working by Choice, and Parallel Passion Pursuit

Whereas boomer reinvention in the general population is driven largely by financial necessity, wealthy reinvention is driven more by the desire to continue pursuing one's passions. Recall that most wealthy people did not start off with a tremendous financial ambition to be rich; instead, wealth came as a by-product of pursuing an entrepreneurial endeavor that was personally meaningful. As a result, they tend to stay with their jobs long after the financial need for a paycheck has passed. Among the wealthy, over 60 percent retain an active senior leadership position in a business venture, whether as a founder or a senior executive. Many of the rest act as consultants or advisers to their previous firms. Fewer than 10 percent describe themselves as retired or otherwise "out of the game."

Even among the ultrawealthy, these figures remain essentially unchanged. Think of it as *parallel passion pursuit*. As with spending, and so many other aspects of living with abundance, the "spoils" of wealth are added on top of existing behavioral patterns, rather than replacing them. They don't give up work to pursue other passions; they pursue other passions while continuing to work. Many might be best described with the term "half-tired"—not fully retired, but finding ways to keep a hand in their business while enjoying considerable leisure time. As one of our respondents explained it:

> The ability to bring on top executives for a large-sized business gives me the luxury of essentially not working. I'm kind of halfway between president and chairman. You know, I'll take the summer off and go to Europe with the kids, and it's not an unexpected thing, because I do it pretty much every summer. And there's a team there that knows how to run it, knows what level of things I need to be involved in. I've got [a colleague] coming in twice a month to look things over for me, help me out. He's retired; he doesn't want to stay home all day, so it's a good thing for him, it's a good thing for me.

In total, over 90 percent of the wealthy feel they still have *something* to accomplish, although their unfulfilled goals are fragmented and highly individual (Table 11-1). One in four says they have significant business goals yet to attain; conversely, three-fourths do not feel that way.

Giving Back

When we asked the wealthy what they want their personal legacies to be, many had simply not given much thought to the subject. For some, the thought of death did not fit with their youthful and generally optimistic nature. Others are so focused on the here and now that they hadn't considered the topic. This response was typical:

> My legacy? [laughter] Oh wow! Well, you know, not too many people ask a forty-three-year-old that question. A forty-three-year-old doesn't often think about that. But, if you

Table 11-1 **Goals the wealthy have yet to attain (% of responses)**

Business goals	25
Philanthropy/charity	17
See kids/grandkids grow up/succeed	13
Travel	13
Retire	8
Accumulate more wealth	8
Achieve true happiness/contentment/peace	8
Grow strengthen family/personal relationships	5
Something creative/arts/music	5
Good health	4

were to write an epitaph on my tombstone, what the hell would it be? . . . Basically as far as leaving a legacy behind, to quote you specifically, I would like to leave behind that we started something here [at his company]; we've touched many, many people's lives for a very positive experience. And they each had—I can't say fun, but yet, it is fun. They enjoyed being here. They enjoyed even knowing me. And that's . . . yeah . . . I'm going to have to go home and ponder that question, because it's one of those things that all the success books tell you to look at, and to really ask yourself what you want somebody to think about. At forty-three you don't think about death, but you should.

When pressed about their legacies, virtually none mentioned their art collections or the exotic material elements of their fortunes. Only a few mentioned their businesses, and those that did, as with the respondent we quoted above, focused more on the relationships that came out of their business than the financials accomplished. Ultimately, most focused on family, children, and good works. Many hoped to be remembered for changing the world for the better in some way.

As wealth and the third age have dawned much earlier for today's wealthy, so too have thoughts about how to distribute their wealth philanthropically. Certainly the attitudes underlying philanthropy are widespread, as our findings show:

- 95 *percent agree*: "With money comes a responsibility to help and support others who are less fortunate."
- 83 *percent agree*: "Because I am wealthy, I have an obligation to help my community."
- 50 *percent agree*: "Building assets to be used for philanthropic purposes is a major financial goal."

The wealthy match these attitudes with philanthropic actions. For example, 98 percent donate money to charity. On an annual basis, the typical wealthy individual donates approximately $64,000, a figure that triples among the ultrawealthy. Of course, some donate much more, with about 1 percent of our respondents donating over $1 million each year. In most cases, their charitable contributions range from 5 to 10 percent of their discretionary income (historically, the average American donates about 2 percent).[3] Interestingly, the wealthy are roughly split between those who prefer to donate anonymously and those who do so more publicly.

Giving is a highly individual process, and no single charity or charitable focus dominates the list of popular outlets for giving (Table 11-2). Roughly half give a significant amount of money each year to their church, temple, or synagogue, and religious charities garner one-fourth of the dollar volume of donations. Education, health, and poverty-related charities are the next most popular options.

Transformational Giving

Based on the numbers described above, the wealthy donate roughly $70 billion annually to charity, a figure that rises to over $200 billion if we include the affluent as well. But these amounts pale in comparison to the massive "payday" that awaits America's charities just over the horizon, as today's wealthy prepare to shed their wealth at the end of their lives. Once again, the entrepreneurial wealthy are on the verge of completely rewriting the rules, this time in the nonprofit world.

Table 11-2 **Percentage of charitable contributions by category**

Church/religion	25
Education	17
Health/medical	14
Homeless/poor	14
Other	8
Arts	5
Animal-related	5
International-relief	5
Environment	4
Political	2

Our respondents estimate that approximately one-fourth of their financial estate will go to taxes; of the rest, they project that approximately three-fourths will go to their kids, and nearly one-fourth will go to charity. In total, this represents between $5 *and* $6 *trillion* in new money flowing into charitable outlets over the next twenty to thirty years.

In many respects, even these figures may be conservative. The biggest and most sophisticated donors tend to have been wealthy the longest, and as young wealthy families mature, they are likely to increase their sensitivity to the need to "give back." In addition, the gravitational effect of wealth will likely continue, meaning that today's apprentices may be worth substantially more by the time their estates come into play. Perhaps most important, the concern that money may "ruin" the kids is causing many of today's financial elite to limit how much money they pass on to their children.

Indeed, twenty years ago Warren Buffett said that "a very rich person should leave his kids enough to do anything but not enough to do nothing."[4] That remains his philosophy today. For years, Buffett was criticized by some for holding on to his wealth so long. He countered that his massive holdings allowed him to use the gravitational effect of wealth to get a bigger rate of return on his vast sums, and therefore donate more to charity later. In 2006, he decided to give away 85 percent of his wealth during his lifetime to five charities, after long suggesting that his billions would be used for philanthropy after his passing. Of course, the remaining 15 percent of his fortune is still over $7 billion, so his kids won't exactly be living in poverty (plus the fact that three of the foundations receiving his money are run by his children; the bulk goes to the Bill and Melinda Gates Foundation). Still, you get the idea. Buffett believes that when kids grow up with all the advantages of wealth, substantial inheritances aren't good for them, or for society at large. "[I]t's neither right nor rational to be flooding them with money. In effect, they've had a gigantic head start in a society that aspires to be a meritocracy. Dynastic mega-wealth would further tilt the playing field that we ought to be trying instead to level."[5]

Buffett's philosophy is shared by many of the millionaires who fall far short of his billions, and the net effect may be trillions more for charity in the coming generation. This approach is very different from that espoused by the wealthy of the industrial era, who certainly contributed to charity and created nonprofit foundations, but whose trusts also focused on providing wealth for dozens (now sometimes hundreds) of family members in generations to come.

Today's wealthy will transform giving, not only by the magnitude of their offerings but by the organizations they give to as well. They share their wealth not only because they want to spruce up their image or gain political points but also because they truly believe in a cause or activity. Ninety percent say they are "passionate about the causes they give to." Passion, by its nature, is specific and idiosyncratic. Passion is value driven. And passion is about making a difference, not writing a check. So expect that, in relative terms, the coming tidal wave of philanthropic donations will be less focused on traditional charities with broad interests, such as United Way, and more toward massive donations to causes that are run with a business-like efficiency and targeted toward a very specific goal for social remediation and change.

It is the combination—big gifts to targeted causes—that can truly transform charitable institutions, and philanthropy itself. For example, in 2005, the Yale School of Music received an anonymous bequest of $100 million.[6] This gift was on an order of magnitude greater than any the school had ever received; in fact, it was so large that the school literally didn't know what to do with it all. Yale began by allowing all music students to attend tuition-free (normally over $23,000 a year), vastly expanding the accessibility and meritocratic nature of the school; after that, it had to undertake a study to explore additional options for wisely using the money.

Thomas Duffy, acting dean of the school, summed up the impact: "This is so transformational. This gift means we can embrace our goals in a matter of years instead of decades."[7] Transformational giving, like any passion project, is also potentially controversial. After the anonymous donation, the *Yale Daily News* published a series of letters to the editor in which some questioned the value of such a large gift to a music school when so many other worthwhile charities might have benefited as well.[8] Others, such as *New York Times* music reviewer Anthony Tommasini, felt very differently, asking rhetorically, "How many of us associate transforming moments of our lives with transforming artistic experiences? Nothing in my youth was more overwhelming than hearing Leontyne Price as Aida at the Metropolitan Opera when I was fifteen, or hearing Stravinsky conduct his 'Symphony of Psalms' with the New York Philharmonic just before I headed off to college."[9]

The list of transformational gifts is growing longer, and although this trend is pioneered by today's self-made wealthy, it is certainly not limited to them. In 2002, Ruth Lilly, great-granddaughter of pharmaceuticals tycoon Eli Lilly, bestowed a $100 million gift on *Poetry* magazine. If you've never heard of *Poetry*, you're not alone; although founded in 1912, and having featured works by esteemed poets from Robert Frost to T. S. Eliot, it had fewer than 12,000 subscribers and was run on such a shoestring budget that at one point its total assets were less than $100. Virtually overnight, *Poetry* became not just one of the richest publications of any kind in the world, but by far the largest foundation in the world devoted to poetry. But the implications of this type of giving go far beyond the balance sheet of a single literary journal and have the potential to substantially impact the entire field of literature. As with the Yale bequest, *Poetry* has struggled with the best way to leverage its potentially transformational gift.

A year later, Joan Kroc, widow of McDonald's founder Ray Kroc, raised the transformational giving bar even higher. A frequent (and often anonymous) patron of many charities, her will revealed a series of truly transformational gifts, including $1.6 *billion* for the Salvation Army (roughly half its normal annual budget), and $225 million for National Public Radio (roughly *twice* its normal annual budget). Consider how transformational giving is apparent in the Slate 60, an annual list of the top charitable contributors. In 1996, the average of the sixty largest contributions was approximately $22 million; in 2007, the average had risen nearly ninefold to $193 million. The average of the top five rose over seventeenfold, from $77 million to over $1.3 billion. Indeed, the largest contributions in 1996—$105 million from Samuel and Alice Skeggs (from the family that founded Safeway, Osco, and Long's Drug Stores) and $100 million from financier George Soros—wouldn't even crack the top ten in 2007.

Indeed, since 2006, contributions of over $1 billion have topped the list, with the largest being $43.5 billion from Warren Buffett. (Perhaps surprisingly, the largest donation in 2007 was from "queen of mean" Leona Helmsley, who bequeathed $4 billion to her charitable trust upon her passing away).

From Philanthropy to Philanthrobusiness

Today's wealthy are reshaping the culture of philanthropy in another crucial way as well. They are doing much more than donating money; they are increasingly donating their time, sitting on nonprofit boards, and creating their own charitable foundations. At an even more fundamental level, they are working to replace the traditional, slow-paced, process-focused culture of many nonprofit organizations with the leaner, fast-paced, results-focused entrepreneurial ethic that has served them so well. In a sense, they are leading the paradigm shift from philanthropy to philanthrobusiness.

The entrepreneurial ethic begins with an action-orientation, a sense of personal responsibility, and a personal philosophy one might call rugged individualism. In a charitable context, this means much more than just giving money; it means taking action, and taking responsibility. Eighty-four percent of the wealthy we surveyed feel it is more important to "personally help others in need, instead of looking to the government and companies to lead the way." Thirty-five percent volunteer their own time on a regular basis, compared to 20 percent of the general population; 31 percent regularly attend charity events, compared to 9 percent of the general population.

But today's wealthy are taking it a step further, from "getting involved" to taking charge. It's been called "high-engagement giving," or less charitably (pardon the pun), "control freak philanthropy." Regardless of the label, it typically begins to manifest itself in board membership. Over half of the wealthy, and nearly three-fourths of masters, serve on at least one nonprofit board. Most serve on two or three.

This direct involvement in charities at a leadership level is one of the great unrecognized "facts of American wealth," and it has profound implications. The wealthy are playing a powerful role in defining the charity board agenda. They refine the missions, define the strategies, and oversee the action plans. Moreover, they have a dramatic influence on the selection of officers who manage and distribute the assets and services of nonprofits. The wealthy are, in a sense, both the CEOs and the HR directors of America's charities.

The next step beyond board membership is creating their own nonprofit organizations. Twenty percent have already done so, and an additional 26 percent plan to. These figures are large, but what is truly unique about the nonprofit foundations of today's wealthy is the businesslike approach used in starting and managing them. Aware that charitable organizations, like many businesses, are often very inefficient, today's new breed of foundations emphasize lean organizational structures, few administrative costs, and minimal overhead. They focus on results, tracking quantifiable metrics that assess results achieved per each dollar spent.

Indeed, every aspect of the entrepreneurial economy is being translated into nonprofit equivalents, in part simply by adding the word *social* in front of typical business jargon. "Social venture capitalists" and "venture philanthropists" seek out and invest in "social entrepreneurs" with innovative approaches to making a difference in the lives of others. The goal is "social profits." And like all entrepreneurs, they dream big. The industry mantra is: "Social entrepreneurs are not content just to give a fish or teach how to fish. They will not rest until they have revolutionized the fishing industry."[10]

For all its benefits, social philanthropy has its gray areas and its detractors, of course. Google founders Larry Page and Sergey Brin have pledged to spend approximately $1 billion in social efforts that they believe will ultimately have a bigger impact on the world than Google itself. But in addition to changing lives, Google.org plans to invest in start-up firms and new technologies, which has caused some to question whether conflicts of interest may occur when for-profit business goals conflict with their nonprofit ideals. Google's philanthropic efforts are hardly alone in being the subject of increasing scrutiny, particularly because many charitable endeavors spend just 5 percent of their assets each year—the minimum to avoid paying taxes—while investing the remaining 95 percent.

In 2007, the *Los Angeles Times* explored this conflict as it relates to the Bill and Melinda Gates Foundation.[11] Rightly known for innovation and good deeds throughout the world, the foundation has helped curb the spread of preventable diseases such as polio, measles, and malaria, often tackling public health issues ignored by large pharmaceutical companies because of their lack of profit potential. But at the same time, the foundation has an investing arm—managed separately from its philanthropic efforts—with a fiduciary responsibility to invest wisely and maximize returns. Some have claimed that some of these investments, such as those in major pharmaceutical and petroleum companies, conflict with public health objectives of its philanthropic ventures. The fact is that virtually any portfolio today can be second-guessed as having morally dubious components, and what exactly constitutes "morally dubious" is highly subjective. Moreover, any portfolio that limits itself to investments that are universally hailed as noble and without fault would be so limited as to shirk the legal responsibilities associated with managing a charitable foundation.

These potential conflicts will no doubt lead to continued debate in the years to come, and some charitable causes will seek innovative solutions to resolving them. For example, Nathan Cummings rose from an impoverished childhood to found the company we know today as the Sara Lee Corporation; today the Nathan Cummings Foundation pursues its unambiguous good deeds while also leveraging its nearly half-billion dollar endowment to force the companies it invests in to pursue environmental sustainability and social justice.

Notes

1. "America's First 'Baby Boomer' Files for Social Security," MSNBC .com, October 15, 2007. http://fieldnotes.msnbc.msn.com/ar chive/2007/10/15/412037.aspx (accessed April 14, 2008).

2. Baby boomer research by Pulte Homes, in conjunction with Harris Interactive, 2003 and 2005, www.Pulte.com (accessed April 14, 2008); National Association of Realtors, in conjunction with Harris Interactive, 2006, http://www.realtor.org/press_room/ news_releases/2006/baby_boomer_study_06.html (accessed April 14, 2008).

3. Research conducted by the Giving USA Foundation, cited in "Charitable Donations by Americans Reach Record High," America.gov, June 26, 2007, http://www.america.gov/st/wash file-english/2007/June/20070626152251CJsamohT0.8012354 .html (accessed April 14, 2008).

4. "Warren Buffett Gives Away His Fortune," *Fortune,* June 25, 2006, http://money.cnn.com/2006/06/25/magazines/fortune/char ity1.fortune (accessed April 14, 2008).

5. Richard I. Kirkland Jr., "Should You Leave It All to the Children?" *Fortune,* September 29, 1986, available at http://money .cnn.com/magazines/fortune/fortune_archive/1986/09/29/68098/ index.htm (accessed April 14, 2008).

6. Brian Wise, "At Yale, Paying The Pipers, The Cellists," *New York Times*, November 6, 2005, http://query.nytimes.com/gst/fullpage .html?res = 9C01EFDB143EF935A35752C1A9639C8B63&sec = &spon = (accessed April 14, 2008). This gift was anonymous, so it may have come from inherited, rather than entrepreneurial wealth. Still, it illustrates the growing trend.

7. Ibid.

8. Anthony Tommasini, "Is a Free Tuition in Music Worthwhile?

An Argument For," *New York Times,* November 28, 2005, http://www.nytimes.com/2005/11/28/arts/music/28yale.html?_r = 1&oref = slogin (accessed April 14, 2008).

9. Ibid.
10. www.Ashoka.com (accessed February 28, 2008).
11. Charles Piller, Edmund Sanders, and Robyn Dixon, "Dark Cloud Over Good Works of Gates Foundation," *Los Angeles Times*, January 7, 2007, http://www.latimes.com/news/nationworld/nation/la na-gatesx07jan07,0,4205044,full.story (accessed April 14, 2008).

CHAPTER TWELVE

The Plutonomy

When 5 Percent of the Haves Own More Than the Other 95 Percent Combined

"[I]NCREASING INCOME INEQUALITY IS BAD FOR THE ECONOMY, BAD FOR CRIME RATES, BAD FOR PEOPLE'S WORKING LIVES, BAD FOR INFRASTRUCTURAL DEVELOPMENT, AND BAD FOR HEALTH—IN BOTH THE SHORT AND LONG TERM."

—George Davey Smith, *British Medical Journal*

"OUR INEQUALITY MATERIALIZES OUR UPPER CLASS, VULGARIZES OUR MIDDLE CLASS, BRUTALIZES OUR LOWER CLASS."

—Matthew Arnold

"MANY SOCIAL SCIENTISTS BELIEVE THIS SUDDEN REBIRTH OF ECONOMIC INEQUALITY IS THE BIGGEST NEWS OF THE LAST HALF-CENTURY. . . . THE FUNDAMENTAL BARGAIN, THE CORE OF AMERICA, HAS ALWAYS BEEN THAT WE CAN LIVE WITH BIG GAPS BETWEEN RICH AND POOR AS LONG AS THERE IS ALSO EQUALITY OF OPPORTUNITY. IF THAT IS NO LONGER TRUE, THEN THE CORE BARGAIN IS BEING VIOLATED."

—Robert Putnam, quoted by *The Yard*

WE SAW EARLIER the tremendous financial gains made by the wealthiest 1 percent of Americans. They now own 34 percent of American assets, up from the twentieth-century low of 20 percent at the mid-70s tail of the Great Compression, but down slightly from the dot-com era peak of 38 percent and the twentieth-century high of 44 percent in 1929. But let's now look deeper into the distribution. The next 4 percent of the population controls nearly 25 percent of the assets. In other words, 5 percent of the country—approximately 6 million households—controls 59 percent of the wealth, while the other 107 million households share the other 41 percent.

Take it a step further: The next 5 percent of the population owns 12 percent of the assets; combining this with the top 5 percent highlighted above, means that 10 percent of the country owns nearly three-fourths of the assets. Now let's add in the next 10 percent of the population—the second decile of wealth—that controls just over 13 percent of the assets. Put it all together, and 20 percent of the country owns roughly 85 percent of the assets.

At the other end of the spectrum, 80 percent of the population owns just 15 percent of the wealth in America, with almost all of that being concentrated in upper reaches of that group. Sixty percent of the population owns just 4 percent of the assets, and at the very bottom rung, 40 percent of the country combines to own less than one-quarter of 1 percent of the wealth (see Figure 12-1). At various times, depending on stock prices, Bill Gates himself has had more assets than the 45 million households in the bottom 40 percent of the distribution.

This analysis used overall net worth as a measure of wealth, but the same pattern emerges whether we look at liquid assets, stock ownership, income, or virtually any other metric. Citigroup financial analyst Ajay Kapur and his colleagues coined the term *plutonomy* to describe societies characterized by this kind of massive inequality in the distribution of wealth.[1] In the industrialized world, the United States has the greatest wealth disparity, followed closely by the United Kingdom, Canada, and Australia, all of which have also experienced explosions of wealth among the top 1 percent of their populations during the past two decades. In contrast, much of continental Europe and Japan aren't considered plutonomies by virtue of their more egalitarian wealth distributions and the stability or slight declines among the holdings of their top 1 percent. Kapur attributes plutonomies largely to a collection of factors that are familiar based on our analysis of wealth: technological advances, financial innovation, wealth-friendly tax policies. He also points out the importance of "the rule of law," implying not only societal stability but also strong protections of patents and other intellectual property.

Figure 12-1 Distribution of wealth in the United States.

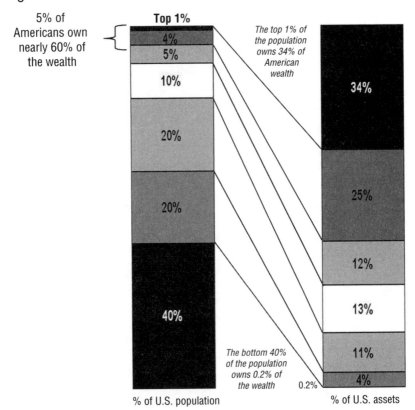

SOURCE: Recent Trends in Household Wealth in the United States: Rising Debt and the Middle Class Squeeze by Edward Wolff. http://www.levy.org/pubs/wp_502.pdf

The Future of the American Plutonomy

Plutonomies have evolved differently throughout history, some ending with the bang of revolution, others fading in a slow whisper. Historians debate whether Marie-Antoinette actually responded to the news that the French population had no bread to eat with the phrase "Let them eat cake"; moreover, if she did say it, perhaps she would have been viewed differently by history if it had been interpreted, as some historians now suggest, as meaning "Let's respond to our flour shortage by letting the average person buy brioches at the same price as bread." But she was guillotined nevertheless, and massive disparities of wealth were certainly key factors in the French

Revolutions of 1789 and 1848. But as Kevin Phillips points out in *Wealth and Democracy*, massive inequality has been a harbinger of significant but more gradual declines among each of the world's most dominant powers since the Renaissance: Spain in the early 1500s, Holland in the early 1600s, and the British Empire of the 1800s.

The future of any plutonomy, along with its social and political implications, depends on a number of factors. First, while the rich have gotten richer, has everybody else gotten richer as well? At the extremes, two scenarios suggest themselves. First, if the economy approximates a zero-sum game, in which the gains of the elite come at the expense of the vast majority, then resentment and class warfare would be more likely. On the other hand, perhaps a rising tide lifts all boats (a phrase John F. Kennedy popularized in responding to criticism that his tax cuts would mainly benefit the wealthy), and the gains of the wealthy elite are symptoms of overall economic growth that results in broad-based gains among all elements of the population. Certainly the economic expansion of the past several decades has been fueled in part by employment growth and technological innovation driven largely by entrepreneurial companies.

Somewhere between these two scenarios is the trickle-down effect, a mildly derisive phrase used to describe the supply-side economic theories generally associated with Ronald Reagan. These theories postulate that the financial gains of the wealthy get spent largely on investments and services that, in turn, create jobs and support small businesses. In New York City, for example, it has been estimated that $200,000 spent on services—everything from drivers and decorators to personal trainers and psychologists—creates roughly five jobs, and that the top 1 percent of earners create over 150,000 service jobs by virtue of their spending.[2]

Assessing which of these scenarios best characterizes the current U.S. plutonomy is a complex economic task. In a plutonomy, statistical averages and the notion of a typical consumer become less meaningful, or even misleading. So, as we look for evidence of financial growth among the less than elite, it is important that we examine it separately among groups of differing financial means. Figure 12-2 traces U.S. Census data on household incomes over the past forty

Figure 12-2 Household income, adjusted for inflation (in 2006 dollars).

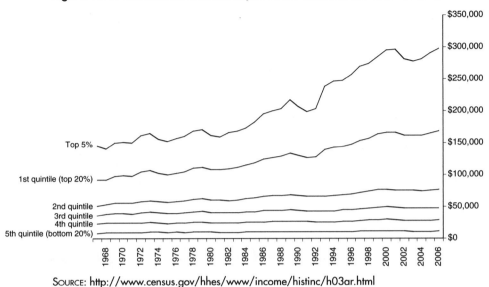

SOURCE: http://www.census.gov/hhes/www/income/histinc/h03ar.html

years, in 2006 dollars after adjusting for inflation. Among those in the bottom 20 percent, household income rose from $8,254 in 1967 to $11,352 in 2006, an increase of 38 percent, or approximately 1 percent per year. For those in the top 5 percent, income rose three times faster, yielding a forty-year increase of 105 percent, from $145,006 to $297,405. The Census department doesn't break out these particular figures for the top 1 percent, but other indicators make it clear that most of the gain of the top 5 percent is likely attributable to gains among the top 1 percent.

Figure 12-3 uses data compiled from a different source (the Congressional Budget Office), a different metric (after-tax income), and a slightly different time period (1979 to 2004), but it presents the same basic conclusion: The financial gains of the top 1 percent are dramatic, nearly tripling over a quarter-century from $314,000 to nearly $868,000. In fact, the income of people in this group increased 20 percent from 2003 to 2004 alone. It took those in the middle 20 percent of the population the full twenty-five years to see a similar increase, up 21 percent from $39,900 to $48,400. Those in the bottom 20 percent were treading water, seeing only an $800

Figure 12-3 Change in average real after-tax income, 1979–2004 (2004 dollars).

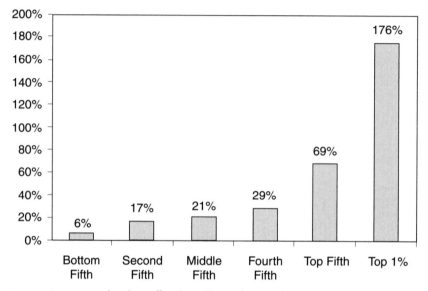

SOURCE: Congressional Budget Office; http://www.cbpp.org/1-23-07inc.htm.

increase in real income over twenty-five years, to $14,700. Depending on the time period chosen, many such analyses suggest that the lowest income groups are actually losing ground; when the Congressional Budget Office compiled figures for 1977 to 1994, for example, they concluded that the lowest 20 percent lost 16 percent in after-tax income, while the next 20 percent up lost 8 percent.

Clearly you could pick and choose the time periods and metrics to suit your point of view, but even then, looking solely at monetary metrics such as income simplifies the complex dynamics in terms of overall financial health and quality of life. Income has risen for many, but today it often takes more hours, more stress, and longer commutes to earn that money. Technology prices drop and purchasing power rises in some categories, while health insurance becomes harder to get, more expensive, and less comprehensive. In fact, several indices of America's overall well-being and social health have shown significant declines over the past several decades.[3]

The bottom line is this: Over the past two to three decades, the wealthy have gotten hugely, massively richer. One could potentially debate whether the lower and middle classes are worse off today than they were then, but it is clear that they haven't even come close to the wealth increases of the financial elite. The overall changes in their lifestyles are, at best, mixed. What, then, is the future of the American plutonomy? If not a revolution, are we at least headed for a really ticked-off electorate?

Class Conflict and Class Warfare

The notions of class conflict and class warfare are as old as humanity itself. Ancient philosophers debated the dynamics of class at a time when wealth was even more radically concentrated than it is today. The glory that was Greece and the grandeur that was Rome, for all their pioneering efforts in democracy that have influenced Western civilization, were both societies built on massive populations of slaves. In ancient times, of course, violent revolution was a far more common occurrence than it is today. In *The Republic*, Plato described how oligarchies often evolve into democracy only after violent revolution: "Any ordinary city, however small, is in fact two cities, one the city of the poor, the other of the rich, at war with one another."[4] Aristotle, always something of a middle-of-the-road kind of guy, waxed poetic in his *Nicomachean Ethics* about the noble qualities of societies in which the middle class was stronger than that above or below it, but he then lamented how rarely those societies developed. Athens, he pointed out, leaned toward democracy (in his view, "rule of the poor") while Sparta was a classic oligarchy—the harmonious balance that Aristotle sought in all aspects of life was particularly elusive in politics.

In contrast to the ancient world, and to France in the eighteenth and nineteenth centuries, class conflict has rarely inflamed a revolutionary fervor in the United States. For all the injustices of the industrial era, for example, political parties that made income equality a central tenet—communists and socialists—were never more than a footnote on the American stage. Their influence peaked at very modest levels during the depths of the Great Depression, with socialist candidate Norman Thomas garnering just 2.2 percent of the vote in 1932—far behind the 57 percent who voted for FDR's substantive but evolutionary approach to change. To a large extent, the American cultural ethos has always tolerated considerable financial inequality, as part of a larger philosophy of free enterprise, rugged individualism, and self-determination. Inequality of finances is seen as a natural by-product of meritocracy and the resulting inequality in ideas, skills, and effort. Even the esteemed biographer of the American spirit, Alexis de Tocqueville, who marveled at so many aspects of the American passion for equality and democracy, also marveled at American materialism and the resulting tolerance for inequality: "I know of no other country where love of money has such a grip on men's hearts or where stronger scorn is expressed for the theory of permanent equality of property."[5]

Inequality in the United States has also tended to result from innovations that did have trickle-down effects, even if the financial gain from those innovations was concentrated at the top. The average American in 1920 didn't see his income rise with that of John Rockefeller or Cornelius Vanderbilt, but he certainly saw tangible changes in his own life and that of his family as a result of railroads, electricity, telephones, radio, automobiles, and the like. In the twenty-first century, the average American has been left behind in the wealth explosion experienced by the entrepreneurial elite, but certainly has experienced personal benefits from cell phones and the Internet. Revolutionary movements in France were precipitated in part because the wealthy elite there came to be associated, not with utilitarian innovations, but with ostentatious and impractical luxury. Louis Vuitton trunks and Hermès bags added value only to the elite few who could afford them.

To the extent that Americans are aware of the financial inequality in society today, they're just not very upset about it. Kevin Phillips summed up this dramatic monetary transformation, and the tepid social response to it: "In just a little over two centuries the United States went from being a society born of revolution and touched by egalitarianism to being the country with the industrial world's biggest fortunes and its largest rich-poor gap. It is a transformation that Americans will have to start thinking about."[6] It is a remarkable—and accurate—choice of words: They *will have to start thinking about* it.

Not rise up, or take to the streets, or create a revolution at the ballot box. Not even *have been thinking about*.

For most Americans, income inequality is an abstract philosophical conundrum that barely registers as troubling, amid the myriad concerns that face them today. In October 2007, Harrison Group conducted a nationally representative survey (of all Americans, not just affluent or wealthy ones), asking which social problems and national issues people were most concerned with; poverty barely cracked the top ten, behind health care, Iraq, terrorism, Internet predators, education, guns in schools, and drugs. Concerns about "the economy" in general at that time ranked sixteenth, and certainly climbed with the recession fears as we moved into 2008. But even then, it was more of a tactical, self-focused concern about one's own job security and mortgage rather than a broader, societal-level concern that "something must be done" to preserve fairness or democracy.

For the most part, financial inequality has barely registered as an issue at the voting booth. The tax reforms of Ronald Reagan and Margaret Thatcher, which among other effects greatly reduced tax rates among the very wealthy, were called by some "class warfare from above," but they were done largely with the blessing of the social classes with which they were supposedly at war. Similarly, George W. Bush's two presidential victories occurred in part because so many people voted against their personal economic interests. More affluent blue-state Democrats voted for candidates who likely would have raised the tax burden on the wealthy, whereas the red states were largely carried by less affluent individuals who would benefit the least from the Bush tax cuts. Social, cultural, and personal factors were stronger predictors of voting preferences than economic self-interest and income equality. As Senator John Edwards ran for president in 2004 and 2008, he spoke eloquently about two Americas:

> One America that does the work, another that reaps the reward. One America that pays the taxes, another America that gets the tax breaks. . . . One America—middle-class America—whose needs Washington has long forgotten, an-

other America—narrow-interest America—whose every wish is Washington's command. One America that is struggling to get by, another America that can buy anything it wants, even a Congress and a president.[7]

It was a powerful and eloquent speech. As he typically pointed out during the speech, Edwards knows both Americas personally, growing up the son of a mill worker and creating his own $30 + million fortune as a trial lawyer fighting the excesses of corporate America. Despite his unquestionably authentic stump speech, Edwards was trounced and dropped out of both races early. Yes, America wanted change, particularly in the 2008 primary election. But the rhetoric of a wealthy elite living dramatically different lives simply didn't resonate with the American public, even though there is considerable objective truth to it. Indeed, today, we even struggle to find the words to articulate anger over income inequality. During the industrial era, words such as *plutomania* (an obsessive lust for wealth), *plutolatry* (the worship of wealth), and *plutocrat* (someone who exercises power by virtue of wealth) were commonly and angrily used. They all derive from the Greek *ploutos*, meaning "wealth," but they are so obscure today that few know their meanings.

America's plutonomy is not on the verge of a revolution, or even a "throw the bums out" vitriol at the ballot box, in part because it culturally "isn't us." But there are other important reasons the resentment about how "the other half lives" (more technically, how the other 5 percent lives) has barely simmered, let alone boiled over. Many aspire to become wealthy themselves, and recognize that inequality is inherently part of the American dream. Perhaps most important, while the lower and middle classes have not benefited tremendously from the wealth boom, they largely have the ability to meet their basic needs. Thanks to the massification of luxury, they even enjoy a handful of products and experiences that would once have been very high end. These luxury items include a sophisticated cell phone; a video game system with more memory and sophistication than the *Apollo* capsules that landed on the moon; reliable and inexpensive cars with a touch of panache; large-screen televisions, typically more than one, with cable service; a $3 cup of regular coffee; and an occasional night out at a nice restaurant (or at least a pizza at the Wolfgang Puck franchise at the mall). Sure, they may struggle with debt and want more money; indeed, surveys show that people in every income bracket want more money, even those in the top 1 percent. But they could meet their basic material and emotional needs in most marketplace contexts, resulting in a relatively stable social environment where the vast majority of the population can meet its basic needs.

As you might expect, revolutions tend not to happen when most of the population lives in relative comfort. Interestingly, however, revolutions don't necessarily happen when there is a large population in poverty. Instead, research has shown that revolutions tend to happen in societies with a large population in poverty that begins to experience upward mobility—when they break through the feeling of learned helplessness and begin to realize that change is possible and that their aspirations are potentially achievable.

Of Plutonomies and Politics

"Democracy . . . is a charming form of government, full of variety and disorder, and dispensing a sort of equality to equals and unequals alike."

—Plato

The American plutonomy is relatively stable, but that doesn't mean that its impact on the political system is minimal, or even necessarily straightforward. In fact, the new generation of American wealth is rewriting the rules of money and politics, but in ways far more subtle and varied than revolution or simple class conflict. Wealth today isn't even as simple as Democrats versus Republicans, as the stereotypical notion of the wealthy Republicans, like so many other stereotypes about the wealthy, has less validity than one might expect.

Forty percent of the wealthy describe themselves as Republicans, a figure that has dropped about ten percentage points from

2005 to 2008, likely reflecting both the changing nature of wealthy individuals and a dissatisfaction with the Bush presidency. About one-third are Democrats, and one in five are self-described Independents. As we saw in Chapter 8, political affiliation differs dramatically across segments, with nearly three-fourths of directors being Republicans, and mavericks skewing toward Democrats.

Certainly the wealthy are highly connected with one another, and with the politically powerful as well, but that doesn't necessarily equate to political interest or an attempt to leverage their connections into personal gain. Half feel they have greater access to, and sway over, politicians and thought leaders than less affluent individuals, but fewer than one in five reports using that access and influence to further his or her business aims. Influence peddling in smoke-filled rooms isn't the style of today's entrepreneurial wealthy. Instead, among the relatively small percentage with a passion for politics, they are more likely to use their wealth to run for office. In this way, they insert themselves directly into the political process, bypassing the traditional methods of spending years as a professional politician climbing the ladder of a political party.

Ross Perot, a classic maverick, paved the way. The son of a cotton picker, Perot attended the U.S. Naval Academy, after which he became a salesman for IBM, and in 1962 founded Electronic Data Systems (EDS). Despite being an elite salesman at IBM, his first eighty-eight sales pitches as CEO of EDS were reportedly unsuccessful, but he persisted and eventually won a string of large government contracts. EDS went public in 1968, giving Perot his first liquidity event and landing him on the cover of *Fortune*. He went on, in 1982, to sell EDS to General Motors for $2.4 billion. At the same time, he became something of a political troubleshooter for then Texas governor Bill Clements, bringing an outsider's mentality and entrepreneurial approach to reworking laws on education and drug use.

Of course, Perot was best known for his 1992 presidential bid, which he approached in true maverick fashion, from running as a third-party candidate, to his unique combination of political stands (pro-choice and pro-environment, but hawkish on the federal deficit and the war on drugs), to truly innovative approaches in political advertising (half-hour infomercial ads), to language that even opponents found candidly refreshing (such as the "giant sucking sound" of jobs he believed would go to Mexico if NAFTA was passed). He was estimated to have spent over $60 million of his own money in the effort.

As wealth exploded in the 1990s, a growing number of successful entrepreneurs used a similar model, reinventing themselves as politicians and using their personal wealth to bypass traditional political stepping-stones. Political aspirants of lesser means typically move up from local office to state office and so on, but wealth offers the opportunity to leap directly into high-profile positions. Jon Corzine went from growing up on the family farm, to becoming Goldman Sachs CEO, to spending $62 million of his own money to become the U.S. Senator from New Jersey, followed four years later by spending over $35 million to become governor of New Jersey.

Michael Bloomberg, the son of a real estate agent, left his job as an equity trader at Salomon Brothers to start the information services firm of Bloomberg L.P., which now accounts for the bulk of his $11+ billion wealth. His first political position was not city councilman, but mayor of New York City.

Self-financing is not a new phenomenon, but it has grown consistently throughout the wealth boom. In 1990, only three congressional candidates spent more than a million dollars on their campaigns; by the mid-1990s and beyond, sixteen to nineteen were doing so in each election.[8] Members of Congress were so concerned about the threat of self-financing to the fabric of democracy, or, more cynically, their own reelections, that they included a "millionaire's amendment" to the Bipartisan Campaign Reform Act of 2002.[9] Once a candidate exceeds a threshold of personal spending ($350,000 in House races; a more complex spending formula is used in Senate races), then his or her opponent is no longer bound by a variety of fundraising restrictions, including how much individuals may contribute and how much the party can spend on their behalf.

To date, self-financing has yet to rewrite the political landscape as some had feared and others had hoped. Although some deep-pocketed self-financers have won high-profile elections, about 80 percent of self-financers lose.[10] There are many theories as to why, all of which probably have some validity, ranging from a lack of political experience, to voter distrust of their motives, to the tendency of self-financers to be challengers rather than incumbents. But that may be about to change, as political victories appear to be less about the amount of money spent and more about the quality of the candidate and the savvy with which money is spent. And the entrepreneurial wealthy are nothing if not savvy. Moreover, they are adept at learning from the successes and failures of others, and at hiring the right consultants for the right jobs. As voters become more familiar with entrepreneurial candidates (and there is a hunger for outsiders that remains largely untapped by politicians), expect that their successes will multiply and that self-financing will reshape both parties.

Author Jonathan Rauch coined the term "Learjet liberal" based on his analysis that self-financed entrepreneurs-turned-politicians who contributed "moderate" amounts ($1 million to $4 million) were predominantly Republicans, whereas those spending more were predominantly Democrats.[11] Although that certainly appears to have been true during the 1990s, we believe that is more of a historical artifact subject to fluctuation rather than a lasting trend based on underlying dynamics of money and political attitudes. Across all of our studies, we see no consistent relationship between party membership or political orientation (e.g., liberal vs. conservative) on the one hand, and net worth or tenure of wealth on the other.

Ex-Massachusetts Governor Mitt Romney is an interesting illustration, not only of a high-spending Republican but also of the changing face of wealth in America.[12] Romney was hardly the result of a modest upbringing. His mother Lenore ran for the Senate in 1970, and his father George was considered by some to be one of the last high-profile champions of the liberal wing of the Republican Party, serving at various times as the governor of Michigan, secretary of Housing and Urban Development, and Richard Nixon's opponent in the 1968 Republican primary election. He was well connected, naming his son Willard Mitt Romney for his close friend and hotelier J. Willard Marriott. But most interesting for the current discussion is the elder Romney's tenure as chairman of American Motors Corporation from 1954 to 1962. He was bold in his decision making, dropping then-classic brands Nash and Hudson in favor of the upstart Rambler; the resulting surge in company performance and tenfold increase in stock price helped land him on the cover of *Time* in 1959.

George Romney's salary of $275,000 made him one of the highest paid people in America, placing him in the top one-hundredth of 1 percent of the income distribution. In other words, he was making more than 99.99 percent of Americans at the time. His salary bordered on embarrassing, and Romney declined a $100,000 bonus in 1960, telling his board that his salary already exceeded what any executive "needs to make." Adjusting for inflation, his salary would equate today to roughly $1.8 million—certainly comfortable, even wealthy, by any standard, but far below the 99.99th percentile. To reach that rarefied air today would require an income of over $10 million.

Romney's son Mitt would pursue a different path to wealth. Rising from a summer internship at Boston Consulting Group to be vice president at consultancy firm Bain & Company in ten years, he left to cofound Bain Capital, a spin-off focused on private equity investments. In other words, he was heading into the heart of the entrepreneurial wealth boom, investing in high-risk, high-reward start-ups, some of which would become household names like Staples. Bain Capital claimed an annual rate of return of 113 percent during Romney's tenure, a stunning figure that catapulted their assets to over $50 billion and Romney's personal wealth to approximately $350 million.

Mitt Romney invested $7 million of his own money into his first campaign, but lost his bid for the U.S. Senate in a battle of new versus old money to Senator Edward (Ted) Kennedy, who outspent Romney with $10 million out of his own pocket. His $6 million investment in his 2002 gubernatorial bid was more successful. The $37 million he invested into his 2008 presidential bid brought him far short of the Republican nomination, but even that dramatic investment still left him with a net worth of over $300 million.

Plutonomy and the Two Economies

"Oh, East is East, and West is West, and never the twain shall meet."

—Rudyard Kipling

While the American plutonomy is slowly reshaping the political landscape, its impact on economic and social institutions has been profound, pervasive, but in many ways surprisingly subtle. Just as John Edwards spoke about the two Americas, there are increasingly two economies—one for the wealthy and one for everyone else. By virtue of their spending levels, this high-end plutonomy economy plays a vital role in the overall health of corporate America, and the national economy as a whole. The diverging nature of these two economies has implications for everything from national spending forecasts to the nature of commerce itself.

For example, when Harrison Group develops its annual holiday retail forecast, we find that making projections by income group is crucial. Simply basing projections on overall responses such as "Americans are planning to spend an average of x percent more this holiday season" essentially weights all respondents equally—fine for counting votes, but very much off target when it comes to spending money. An average spending decrease may reflect significant spending declines among the vast majority of the population, but be offset by small percentage increases in the big holiday budgets of the wealthy.

The plutonomy economy, as one might expect, has thrived with the boom in wealth. In addition to coining the word *plutonomy,* Citigroup's Kapur also created a Plutonomy Index to measure the overall financial performance of companies that serve the very wealthy. This index incorporates reasonably well-known brands and companies highlighted in our previous discussions, including luxury conglomerates LVMH and Richemont, as well as Hermès, Porsche, Four Seasons Hotels, Tiffany, Polo Ralph Lauren, and Sotheby's. It also includes a number of billion-dollar companies that are big players in the plutonomy economy, but that fall into the "if you're not rich, you've probably never heard of them" category: Julius Baer and Von-tobel (private banking), Beneteau and Rodriguez Group (yachts), Shangri-La Asia (hotels), Kuoni (travel), Toll Brothers (homes), and Tod's (leather). Since the Plutonomy Index was introduced in 1985, it has averaged a return of 17.8 percent annually—far better than comparable indices of global stocks. Its performance remains strong even after controlling for sector effects, survivorship, changing membership in the index, and other potentially confounding factors.

Comparable indices reveal the same general trend. *Forbes*'s Cost of Living Extremely Well Index (CLEWI) tracks price changes among forty-one extremely high-end products and services that one might consider hallmarks of "old money," including sable coats, Beluga caviar, Lenox silverware, Harvard tuition, yachts, horses, tennis courts, face-lifts, helicopters, Learjets, and so on. Since 1976, the CLEWI (representing the cost of goods in the plutonomy economy) has risen at twice the rate of the Consumer Price Index (a measure of the cost of goods in the "everybody else" economy).[13] Why did these companies raise prices? For the most part, because they could. The wealth boom has lessened price sensitivity at the high end, and paying twice as much for sublime quality is less of a concern when your net worth has increased tenfold.

With their middle-class backgrounds, the wealthy will often play a key role in the "everyone else" economy; we've seen their enthusiasm for Costco, Target, and other mainstream retail outlets. Indeed, they will often account for the bulk of sales and profits in many of these outlets. But increasingly, there is a separate and decidedly unequal economy that caters specifically to the wealthy, one that the middle and lower classes not only don't participate in, but also are often totally unaware of. We've seen some of the brands and companies known primarily to the wealthy, and the wealthy have long had nearly exclusive access to some sophisticated financial services, from private banks and hedge funds to the inside track on venture capital investments and IPOs. But over the past decade, plutonomy markets and "everybody else" markets have been diverging in new categories and new ways.

Consider health care. The hottest trend among health care for the wealthy is the emergence of "concierge doctors."[14] Membership as a patient in such a practice often starts with an annual fee of up to $20,000. After that, the patient gets, well, pretty much anything he or she wants. Personalized, sophisticated medical care goes without saying, but the difference is in the perks. No waiting. House calls. The doctor's personal cell phone number. Someone who handles all the insurance hassles for you. The growing healthcare option for the "everybody else" economy? The Clinic at Wal-Mart is expected to be in over 400 stores by 2010. Target, CVS, and Walgreens are following suit, with the total number of "convenient care" facilities expected to double nationally to 1,500 by the end of 2008. The notion of a two-tiered medical system based on the ability to pay raises ethical, regulatory, and insurance issues, but it is likely here to stay in one form or another.

Health care isn't the only field in which ethical standards have historically been based largely on egalitarian principles, but that are now being shaken by the two-tiered economy. In principle, fire departments have long been public institutions serving everyone in need equally, making decisions by balancing need and safety concerns. Now, some high-end private insurance companies are also employing private firefighters to protect homes from wildfires.[15] This raises questions about how a variety of decisions might be made, including when to deploy those firefighters, with what equipment, how to prioritize their efforts, and so on. The ability to pay top premiums, and the cost-benefit trade-offs to the insurer, creates potential conflicts of interest.

Not every aspect of the plutonomy economy raises ethical issues, but many do create the image of financial inequality driving people to live parallel lifestyles. Members of the "everybody else" economy fly in and out of New York City via LaGuardia and JFK. Members of the plutonomy economy fly in and out of Teterboro Airport on private aircraft.

Television for Those Who Happen to Be Rich

The financial elite even have their own television stations, and we're not talking about mainstream financial news channels such as CNBC. We're talking about Plum TV, a network whose average viewer has an annual income of $600,000, and one-fourth of whom fly on private jets. Never heard of it? You probably don't vacation in Aspen, Nantucket, the Hamptons, Sun Valley, Miami Beach, Martha's Vineyard, Telluride, or Vail—the only markets in which Plum TV airs. In other words, you're probably not part of the plutonomy economy.

Plum TV is a fascinating story, not just as a TV network that has been remarkably effective at connecting with the financial elite, but also because of the insights into wealth that emerge from the personal story of its founder. In 1976, when he was just nine years old, Tom Scott saw a business opportunity in the cars lined up at gasoline pumps. He and a friend went from car to car selling juice, muffins, and newspapers. Ten years later, he applied the same concept of selling juice and snacks to those who had moored their boats in Nantucket. A few steps later, he and partner Tom First founded Nantucket Nectars, and the business took off slowly. As Tom put it, "We were poor. We remained poor for a quite a while thereafter."[16] By his own admission, he failed accounting in college (as did his co-founder), and couldn't tell you what a profit margin was. But he had a passion for quality and authenticity, and his devotion to those principles guided every step that came thereafter. Similarly, he didn't know much about the juice business, but he did know that most of the juice available was, in his words, "junk."

The business was started simply, by selling lemonade off Tom's boat, but he encountered a series of challenges as he decided to scale up his business and manufacture lemonade on a larger scale. As Tom tells his story today, he asks people what ingredients go into lemonade, and nearly everyone answers water, lemons, and sugar. But he then defies people to walk into any store to find a bottle of lemonade with just those three ingredients. He found out why first-hand as he toured factories. He would say, "I want to put my lemon pulp in there," only to be told, "You can't do that—it will clog my filter tubes." He would explain "I want to use real sugar, not high fructose corn syrup," only to hear, "You can't—it will crystallize and clog the equipment." "I want the caps to be purple" (actually, plum), only to be told, "You can't put purple paint in my cap-painting machine—I'll have to clean it afterwards."

The two Toms persisted, spending more for real ingredients, investing more time to manually clean clogged equipment, spending more for real pasteurization rather than using cost-cutting chemicals. The extra time and costs were a financial nightmare; Scott jokes that if either he or his partner had passed accounting, they may never have started the business. But guided by principles rather than by P&L statements, they persisted and were able to achieve profitability without compromising quality.

They used the same general approach in advertising. They used no script when recording their radio ads, describing the process as, "Let's just talk and tell our story, and we can edit it together afterwards." They started with what would become their iconic phrase— "Hi, I'm Tom and I'm Tom, and we're juice guys"—and like jazz musicians, they ad-libbed and riffed around their two key themes of quality juice and the "evolution solution" of focusing on continual improvements. They went on to win Mercury awards for excellence in radio advertising. The authenticity that came through so clearly in those original radio spots became a mantra that Tom has repeated throughout his marketing messages, telling his advertising and creative teams, "Don't be creative ever again. Don't create anything. Just tell the story. Don't try to be funny. Don't try to be cool. Don't try to be anything. Just understand what it is we do. It's the 'evolution solution'—make juice better every time you can. That's our mission. Then tell the story about that's what we do. Tell the story in a way that's real."

Within a few years, the two Toms were selling 280 million bottles of juice a year. Substantial liquidity came into their lives after a joint venture with Ocean Spray in 1998 and then selling Nantucket Nectars to Cadbury Schweppes PLC in 2002. When asked about his success, Tom half-mockingly suggests that a lot of people tell him, "Yeah, you're geniuses." His response is:

> All I can tell you is, we're not geniuses. We tried to do it all the wrong ways, too. But when you are focused on principles, you can look back and say, "I can see how we connected those dots." But when you are looking forward, there's no

way you can know how you will connect those dots. *We ended up succeeding because of our principles, not our plan.*

Soon after cashing out, Tom Scott found himself looking for new, challenging ventures. A local cable station in Nantucket piqued his interest, so he bought it, renaming it Plum for those initially troublesome purple caps. Again, he started less with a business plan and more with a passion for storytelling, authenticity, and sincere enthusiasm for the Nantucket community. And he used another insight from his days selling juice: the seemingly simple but often overlooked principle of talking to people when they want to be spoken to.

It's an often violated principle of advertising, but one that he experienced personally during efforts to give away free samples of Nantucket Nectars. Instead of giving away juice in the busiest New York City intersections with the highest population density, he gave away juice at Coney Island. There people are relaxed; they want to have fun. They want to stop and talk, and try new experiences. In a sense, they want to be spoken to. That is the same mind-set, he reasoned, that people have on vacations in places like Nantucket. Tapping into that mind-set would be key to launching Plum successfully, and proving that the wealthy people who spend time in these communities are more open to advertising when their relaxed vacationing mind-sets allow them to let their guard down.

Once again, a willingness to ignore conventional wisdom was crucial to success. People told Tom, "Rich people don't watch television. They particularly don't watch television while they're on vacation." Tom's response was, "All I know is people want vacation when they are on vacation. When they are vacationing in Nantucket, they want Nantucket. They want to connect with the local community, and experience the fun and personality that make it unique." At its core, Plum TV is not "television for rich people," as many in the media have labeled it. Instead, it is authentic television, giving the local community the local programming it wants, at a time when people most want to listen. The fact that most people watching are extraordinarily wealthy is obviously nice for advertising sales, but from a content and editorial perspective, it is almost a coincidence.

According to Tom, "Lots of people want to go there—it just happened that the ones with lots of money got the good seats."

The programming on Plum TV is a fascinating mixture of quaint localness and tremendous sophistication. On the *Today*-like morning show, you might see an interview with the local cheese shop owner or the local football coach, followed by an interview with a vacationing John Kerry or Carly Simon or Russell Simmons. That eclectic mix comes across as remarkably authentic and engaging. Tom says, "We would be hated if we were all polished and all external." He calls it one-degree marketing: if you see an ad with Michael Jordan, neither you nor anyone you know has ever met him. But in these communities, everyone knows the cheese shop owner.

At the end of the day, Scott sees very little difference between selling lemonade and marketing the TV network with the highest average-net-worth viewers in the world. In many ways, marketing in the plutonomy economy is quite similar to marketing in the "everybody else" economy. In both cases, it is largely about being guided by authenticity, relevance, and storytelling. In both economies, effective marketing is about meeting people's unmet needs and developing communications that resonate with their attitudes. As we've seen, the attitudes of the wealthy are more likely those of mainstream Americans than one might have anticipated.

Notes

1. Ajay Kapur, Niall Macleod, and Narendra Singh, "Plutonomy: Buying Luxury, Explaining Global Imbalances," research report, Citigroup Global Markets, http://www.billcara.com/archives/Citi%20Oct%2016,%202005%20Plutonomy.pdf (accessed April 14, 2008).
2. Daniel Gross, "Don't Hate Them Because They're Rich: The Trickle-Down Effect of Ridiculous, Ostentatious Wealth," *New York* magazine, April 11, 2005, http://nymag.com/nymetro/news/culture/features/11721 (accessed April 14, 2008).
3. For example, see the Index of Social Health, published by the Institute for Innovation in Social Policy, http://iisp.vassar.edu/index.html (accessed April 14, 2008). See also David Myers,

The American Paradox: Spiritual Hunger in an Age of Plenty (New Haven, Conn.: Yale University Press, 2001).

4. Plato, *The Republic*, trans. Benjamin Jowett (New York: Random House, 1950).

5. Alexis de Tocqueville, *Democracy in America*, trans. Arthur Goldhammer. (New York: Penguin, 2004), p. 57.

6. Kevin Phillips, *Wealth and Democracy* (New York: Broadway Books, 2002), p. xviii.

7. See http://www.iowacaucuses.info/IA_Caucus_Candidates%20-%20John_Edwards.html (accessed April 16, 2008).

8. Jonathan Rauch, "Are You a Learjet Liberal? Take This Simple Test," *National Journal* and *Reason Online*, February 10, 2001, http://www.reason.com/news/show/34571.html

9. Federal Election Commission, http://www.fec.gov/pages/brochures/millionaire.shtml (accessed April 14, 2008).

10. Jennifer Steen, "Maybe You Can Buy an Election, But Not With Your Own Money," *Washington Post*, June 25, 2000, available at http://www.washingtonpost.com/ac2/wp-dyn?pagename = article &node = &content Id; eqA56043-2000Jun24&notFound = true (accessed April 16, 2008). See also Jennifer Steen, *Money Isn't Everything: Self-Financed Candidates in Congressional Elections* (Ann Arbor: University of Michigan Press, forthcoming).

11. Rauch, 2001.

12. The information in the next three paragraphs is synthesized from a variety of sources, including David Leonhardt, "Two Candidates, Two Fortunes, Two Distinct Views of Wealth," *New York Times*, December 23, 2007, http://www.nytimes.com/2007/12/23/business/23wealth.html?pagewanted = 1 (accessed April 14, 2008); Matthew Rees, "Mister PowerPoint Goes to Washington," *The American*, December, 1, 2006, http://www.american.com/archive/2006/december/mitt-romney (accessed April 14, 2008); Bart Barnes, "George W. Romney Dies at Age 88," *Washington Post*, July 27, 1995, http://www.amxfiles.com/amc/romney.html (accessed April 14, 2008).

13. "The Cost of Living Extremely Well Index" is described more fully at the *Forbes* website: http://www.forbes.com/2006/09/

18/cost-of-living-well-index_lists-06rich400_clewi.html (accessed April 16, 2008).

14. Amy Zipkin, "The Concierge Doctor Is Available (at a Price)," *New York Times,* July 31, 2005, http://www.nytimes.com/2005/07/31/business/yourmoney/31doctor.html (accessed April 16, 2008).

15. For example, the "Wildfire Protection Unit" of premium insurer AIG is described at http://www.firebreaksystems.com/insurance info/aig-wildfire-protection-unit (accessed April 14, 2008).

16. Personal communications and Tom Scott's presentation at Harrison Group Invitational, October 17, 2007, New York.

A Final Word

IN THE FINAL ANALYSIS, we have learned that people of wealth today are children of Middle America, and their values reflect the bedrock values of America in the 1950s and '60s. But now they have co-opted those values and made them the values of the New Elite. The wheel of history demonstrates that, at least in part, change is driven by the reaction of underclasses to the preoccupations of the elites. The success of middle class values may turn out to be the worst enemy one could have imagined for the maintenance of those values. The next couple of generations will find out whether the children of the New Elite will corrupt those values, or reinforce and strengthen them. This much wealth combined with these values may be the most potent force for good in the history of the world. Or we may be seeing the last gasp of a brilliant ideal.

Our Methodologies for Studying the Wealthy

WHEN WE ADD up the interviews, questionnaires, focus groups, and people in business whom we have met in the process of building our understanding of America's wealthiest households, we have had the pleasure of speaking with over 6,000 people in the past four years. This appendix briefly describes the methodologies we used in our larger quantitative studies.

Throughout our research, we have been fortunate to have sponsors who devoted their time and thought to helping us refine our research, focus our sampling methodology, and fine-tune the implications for their specific categories. These sponsors include Agency-Sacks, American Honda, Bank of America, Bank of New York, Mellon, Bombardier Flexjet, Cadillac, Cartier, Chanel, Fairmont Hotels & Resorts, Fireman's Fund Insurance, Four Seasons Hotels & Resorts, Gucci, Infiniti, Leading Real Estate Companies of the World, Lexus, Lincoln, Louis Vuitton, Lyle Anderson, Maui Land &

Pineapple Company, Mercedes-Benz, Neuberger Berman, Saks Fifth Avenue, U.S. Trust, and Union Bank of California.

Our Three Surveys

To date we have conducted three large syndicated studies of the affluent and wealthy in America. In each, we have used a variety of methodological techniques to ensure that our samples of individuals are demographically and psychologically representative of today's financial elite.

The 2005 *Worth*-Harrison Taylor Study on the Status of Wealth in America

Our first study was carried out in the spring and summer of 2005, beginning with focus groups in New Mexico, Dallas, and Los Angeles. Based on those initial groups, we assembled the questionnaire and developed a research methodology that required us to visit each of our participants personally. Eleven extraordinary interviewers, plus the first two authors, fanned out across America to conduct nearly half-day sessions with 503 families, sometimes singly, sometimes as couples. We met our successful respondents mostly in their homes, occasionally in their offices, and several times in their clubs. Each person we spoke with gave us at least two hours of his or her time for the interview and then spent another hour filling out a questionnaire that detailed the individual's spending, investing, brand acquisition, and material life.

We were very fortunate to have Curtco Media—publisher of *Worth* magazine and the *Robb Report*—as our partner in this study. Our initial group of participants were selected from names provided by Curtco Media and by study sponsors Lyle Anderson Company, U.S. Trust, and AgencySacks. These recommended names were then distilled into a list of nearly 300 "start points" who were demographically representative of the 750,000 families who make up the top of the American economic pyramid (the top one-half of 1 percent of the total U.S. personal asset pool).

These 300 initial respondents yielded 200 completed interviews.

The interviewees, in turn, referred us to 200 more families to interview. The resulting "snowball sample" of 200 additional families—following the method pioneered by Dr. Alfred Kinsey in his work on human sexuality—gave us a larger sample that continued to reflect, geographically and structurally, the distribution of American wealth.

To assure ourselves that our sample was not significantly skewed by factors related to nonrandomness, we pulled a sample of 100 wealthy households by conventional means. This involved using high-quality "panel providers"—companies that use online and offline methods to recruit diverse and representative groups of individuals for participation in research. By combining these methods, we were able to obtain a final sample of 503 families that was representative of the 750,000 households constituting the top half of 1 percent of the American economy, with a project sampling error of plus or minus 5 percent.

Our criteria for inclusion in the study were simple but stringent. Participants were required to have a minimum of $5 million in liquid net worth, not including their primary residence, collections, or any nonliquid business ownership interests. In addition, they had to reside (at least part-time) in the United States and had to make themselves available to our staff interviewers or ourselves in person.

The modal household in our sample had a net worth of $7.5 million and an annual income of $1.9 million per year, of which they spend nearly $850,000 (the rest goes primarily to taxes and investments). When generalized to the national population of 750,000 households, the study indicates that America's wealthiest 0.5 percent holds at least $8 trillion in liquid assets. Were we to add in real estate, fixed assets, and collectables, this group represents an estimated $21 trillion. As of 2004–2005, this upper echelon had a collective annual income of $1.4 trillion and represented a consumer market of over $650 billion in spending annually.

In summary, the study included:

- 503 households with liquid assets of $5 million +
- 11 interviewers "of the class," and the first two authors
- Over 300 start points

- "Snowball" interview technique pioneered by Alfred Kinsey
- Supplementation by participants from research panels
- Two-hour personal interview; 30–60 minutes for self-adminis-tered questionnaire

See a brief description of the study in Table A-1.

Table A-1 **Worth–Harrison Taylor Study sample and population characteristics of the wealthy**

	Our Sample ($)	Total Population ($)
Net worth	28 million (mode: 7.5M)	~21 trillion
Average annual income	1.9 million	~1.4 trillion
Annual household consumption	850,000	~650 billion

The 2007 Survey of Affluence and Wealth in America, by American Express Publishing and Harrison Group

Following the 2006 American Express Publishing Luxury Summit, the Harrison Group partnered with American Express Publishing, whose titles include *Travel + Leisure, Food & Wine,* and *Departures,* to take an annual look at the attitudes, values, and preferences of today's affluent and wealthy. We designed this study to deepen our understanding of wealth derived from our first study, for which we identified three key goals. First, we wished to conduct a comprehensive study of the top 5 percent of American consumers, as defined by discretionary household income. Second, we wished to examine the different ways these people value their resources, time, and shopping experiences. And third, we set out to examine how brands, the shopping process, the media, and personal experiences affect the way consumers bring quality and value into their lives.

To more fully understand the dynamics of wealth in America, we "cast a broader net" and delved deeper into the income distribution than in our previous study. Instead of looking solely at the financial elite with more than $5 million in liquid assets, we also examined those who were merely "affluent." We also refined our definitions to focus less on net worth and more on discretionary income, arriving at three key income groups for analysis:

- *Affluent:* from $125,000 to $249,999 in annual discretionary household income
- *Super Affluent:* from $250,000 to $499,000 in annual discretionary household income
- *Wealthy:* $500,000 or more in annual discretionary household income

All three groups combined represent approximately 5 percent of the American population. The wealthy group alone represents approximately one half of the top 1 percent of the financial distribution. In addition, we ensured that we had large enough samples to accurately examine those in the top one-tenth of 1 percent—roughly those with $1.5 million in annual discretionary income.

We conducted the study during October and November of 2006, collecting 1,300 interviews via a forty-five-minute Internet-based survey. Once again, we used multiple panels and starting points to ensure proper demographic and psychographic representations within each segment. Overall, our respondents are demographically representative of the 6.1 million households in America with at least $125,000 in annual discretionary income. The average respondent household has discretionary income of $375,000. Our sample averaged approximately $5.2 million in assets—which means that the total assets held by the affluent and wealthy in America are approximately $32 trillion. They also "consumed" $1.3 trillion, or approximately 25 percent of all U.S. personal consumption.

In summary, the study included:

- 1,300 interviews using a forty-five-minute Internet survey
- Multiple panels and starting points to ensure total representation
- Three key segments, based on annual discretionary income —affluent, super-affluent, wealthy

See a brief description of the study in Table A-2.

Table A-2 **The Annual Survey of Affluence and Wealth in America, 2007, sample and population characteristics**

	Total	Affluent	Super-Affluent	Wealthy
Mean income	$430,163	$243,700	$407,800	$1,730,900
Mean discretionary income	$374,152	$198,859	$358,864	$1,583,774
Mean value of household assets	$5.2 million	$1.9 million	$3.6 million	$30.6 million
Number of households (est.)	6.1 million	4.1 million	1.4 million	600,000
Net consumption (est.)	$1.3 trillion	$600 billion	$361 billion	$374 billion

The 2008 Survey of Affluence and Wealth in America, by American Express Publishing and Harrison Group

Our 2008 survey used much the same methodology as our 2007 study, but we expanded the sample size to 1,800. We broadened our scope even further, reaching into the upper middle class—those who fall within the top 10 percent of the economic spectrum, but not the top 5 percent.

Our Approach to Market Segmentation

In Chapter 8, we explored the five lifestyle choices of the wealthy—neighbors, wrestlers, directors, patrons and mavericks—and we provided brief profiles of each. We have conducted literally hundreds of segmentation studies over the past decade, and our methodology combines art, science, and experience to identify segments that are unique in their attitudes, needs, values, and purchasing patterns. Here is a breakdown of the steps involved in this process:

- *Step 1*: A series of factor analyses are performed to group similar questionnaire items into a smaller number of broader themes. The resulting multi-item factors are more meaningful and statistically reliable than individual items. These factor analyses are conducted separately for each major content area addressed in the research (e.g., attitudes toward wealth, motivations driving category purchase behavior, etc.).

• *Step 2:* The most meaningful factors are combined with demographic variables and financial metrics and used as inputs into a series of analyses that identify distinct clusters of individuals. Segmentation analyses performed in this manner produce more distinct segments as the dimensions that work together in the real world to create customer differences (motivations, behaviors, and demographics) also have an opportunity to work together statistically. This approach yields far more stable segmentations than traditional attitudinal-only or demographic-only approaches, allowing for more effective tracking over time, and an enhanced ability to replicate these segments in other research efforts.

• *Step 3:* The initial cluster analyses are examined for their ability to yield interesting, targetable segments that maximize the differences between groups, and minimize the differences within groups (technically speaking, they maximize between-group heterogeneity and within-group homogeneity). This serves to further strengthen the discrimination found between segments, as only the core drivers remain to produce unique segments. Those variables that are not particularly effective at producing unique groups of customers are eliminated from subsequent analyses. The process continues and additional analyses are performed until a final solution has been selected.

• *Step 4:* In addition to the key criteria mentioned above, we consider additional factors in selecting the optimal segmentation, to ensure that each segment: (A) Has face validity—in other words, is intuitively plausible, and one can visualize individuals within the various segments; (B) Is sufficiently large to make targeting efforts worthwhile, with some representing disproportionate "value" relative to their size (for example, a small segment that accounts for a large proportion of the purchases in a given category); and (C) Represents different levels of current and future value for companies in a variety of industries.

- *Step 5:* The final step in the process is to conduct a series of statistical analyses that identify a small number of variables that can reliably classify individuals into the segments. This allows for the creation of short batteries that can be used to identify the segments in future research or marketing efforts.

Using research to understand a phenomenon as complex as wealth in America today requires both science and art. We have explored our scientific methodologies in detail above. But whenever possible throughout this book, we have attempted to supplement our scientific research with quotes from wealthy individuals themselves. These qualitative insights in the words of the wealthy themselves lend a complementary depth and insight to our quantitative studies.

Index

About the Authors

Jim Taylor, Ph.D., is Vice Chairman of the market research consultancy Harrison Group and is among the country's most respected marketing and branding consultants. He was named "Marketer of the Year" by *Brandweek* and cited by the *Wall Street Journal* as one of America's five leading business futurists. He is the author of many articles, and his previous books include *The 500 Year Delta: What Happens After What Comes Next* and *The Visionary's Handbook: Nine Paradoxes That Will Shape the Future of Your Business.*

Jim is an acknowledged expert in the fields of branding, marketing, interactive media, future forecasting, and customer acquisition and retention. He provides advice to the highest levels of some of the world's leading companies and brands, including American Express, General Motors, Lexus, Audi, Bombardier Flexjet, Neiman Marcus, Plum TV, Lehman Brothers, Wachovia Bank, Gucci, Chanel, Mercedes-Benz, the Walt Disney Company, and Louis Vuitton.

Jim is a highly requested speaker at conferences throughout the world (represented by Greater Talent) and has lectured at many leading universities, including Harvard and Stanford. His insights are regularly quoted in the media, particularly on topics related to wealth and luxury marketing.

Prior to joining Harrison Group, Jim served as Chief Executive Officer of Yankelovich, Skelly & White, and later was Executive Vice President and head of Hill and Knowlton's flagship New York office. He was also Chief Marketing Officer of Ernst & Young and held similar positions at Gateway Computer, Iomega Corporation, and The Lyle Anderson Company. Jim is a graduate of the University of California in Rhetoric and received his Masters and Ph.D. in Communication from Michigan State.

Doug Harrison founded Harrison Group in 1996 and has led it to exponential growth over the past decade. He built the company from a single-person operation to one of the leading strategic research companies in the world, with a staff of over thirty professionals and sales of more $12 million annually. The growth of the company has been based on three core principals: first, a commitment to delivering insights to clients that surpass client expectations; second, market research findings anchored in real-world projections relative to the cost to a client's business; and third, a responsibility to deliver clients outstanding results in which they can feel ownership.

Doug is recognized as a leader in the area of volumetric forecasting and specializes in developing sophisticated methodologies to produce actionable market segmentations, brand equity evaluations, new product forecasts, and optimized product designs. He consults for some of the world's greatest companies and brands, including Coca-Cola, Microsoft, Bombardier Flexjet, Fairmont Hotels, Lehman Brothers, Cartier, Lexus, and Neiman Marcus. In addition, Doug helped formulate the groundbreaking studies of the wealthy that form the basis of *The New Elite.*

Prior to founding Harrison Group, Doug ran strategic research and volumetric forecasting at Yankelovich Partners. An honors graduate, Doug earned a BS degree in business and marketing from Cornell University.

Stephen Kraus, Ph.D., is a Vice President with Harrison Group, where he provides senior leadership to the company's wealth consultancy and leads the firm's sales training practice. Steve is the author of *Psychological Foundations of Success: A Harvard-Trained Scientist Separates the Science of Success from Self-Help Snake Oil*. His articles have appeared in *Brandweek, AdWeek,* the *San Francisco Chronicle, Contemporary Psychology,* and a variety of scientific psychology journals.

With more than twenty years of consulting experience, Steve is an acknowledged expert in forecasting lifestyle trends and social changes. His research on the relationship between attitudes and behavior is cited in major psychology textbooks.

Steve is a featured speaker at conferences across the country, where he discusses his insights into human behavior and their marketing implications for fields as diverse as technology, financial services, media, and retail sales. He has also spoken at numerous scientific conferences, including those held by the American Psychological Association and the Society of Consumer Psychology. Steve has been quoted in the *Wall Street Journal, Investor's Business Daily,* and many other national publications. His clients have included Neiman Marcus, McKinsey & Co., the National Football League, IBM, American Express, Staples, and many others.

Prior to joining Harrison Group, Steve was president of the consultancy Next Level Sciences. He also spent six years as a partner with Yankelovich Partners, where he provided senior leadership to the Yankelovich Monitor—the longest continuously running study of consumer attitudes and lifestyles in America. A former psychology professor at the University of Florida, Steve received his Ph.D. in social psychology from Harvard University and twice won Harvard's award for teaching excellence.